# Bad Banks

Alex Brummer is one of the UK's leading financial journalists and commentators. After a long and successful stint at the *Guardian* he moved to be City Editor at the *Daily Mail* in 2000. He has won prizes both as a foreign correspondent and economics writer. Awards received include Business Journalist of the Year 2006, Newspaper Journalist 2002 and Best City Journalist 2000. His books include *The Crunch* (Random House 2008), *The Great Pensions Robbery* (Random House 2010) and *Britain for Sale* (Random House 2012).

## Praise for *Bad Banks*

Grimly fascinating…This is a pacey, accessible and astute summary of what has gone wrong with the banks, and what the banks have done wrong…It is a sobering narrative in which Brummer's judgements are nuanced and reliable.

*The Times*

Like a surgeon at his operating table, Brummer dissects each British, American and European scandal of the last 10 years. He spares nobody, but his demolition job is made all the more powerful by the sparing language he deploys towards his targets. This is controlled menace at its best.

*Observer*

[Brummer] is a doyen of British financial journalism and it shows in the maturity of his judgments and breadth of his knowledge…It is all skilfully woven together by a writer who knows when to fly high and when to swoop lo⸺

An informed, riveting and ultimately disconcerting read.

*Business Life*

Thorough and expansive.

*Management Today*

# Bad Banks

## Greed, Incompetence and the Next Global Crisis

## Alex Brummer

BUSINESS
BOOKS

Published by Random House Business Books 2015

3 5 7 9 10 8 6 4

Random House Business Books
20 Vauxhall Bridge Road
London SW1V 2SA

Random House Business Books is part of the Penguin Random House group of
companies whose addresses can be found at global.penguinrandomhouse.com.

Penguin
Random House
UK

First published by Random House Business Books in 2014

www.randomhouse.co.uk

A CIP catalogue record for this book is available from the British Library.

ISBN 9781847941145

Penguin Random House is committed to a sustainable future for
our business, our readers and our planet. This book is made from
Forest Stewardship Council® certified paper.

Print                                                                    lc

# Contents

# Preface

Since *The Crunch* (one of the early books on the Great Panic and subsequent Great Recession) was published in the summer of 2008, just a few months before the collapse of the American bank Lehman Brothers, there has been a torrent of works and reports released on the events leading to the crisis. There also has been a debate on how to create a less risky, more reliable financial system and more robust global economy. Many of the events surrounding the crisis and the rescue have been well chronicled in books such as *Too Big to Fail* by Andrew Ross Sorkin and *The Big Short* by Michael Lewis.

But it would be a mistake to think that the crisis began and ended in the period 2007–9 when it was at its most acute. Banking and financial stability have come to dominate the global business and economic agenda over the last six years. As efforts to stabilise and reform the banking system in Britain, the United States, Europe and across the world have been relentlessly pursued by policymakers and regulators, past skeletons have tumbled out of the cupboard.

Most people outside banking would, for instance, have looked blankly at the very mention of the London Interbank Offered Rate (Libor), which is responsible for setting the cost of all kinds of borrowing around the world. However, following the eruption of the Libor-rigging scandal in the summer of 2012, when Barclays Bank agreed to a settlement with the authorities, it came to dominate the political and public debate. The very idea that such an important market tool was being manipulated, and that the regulators – who had first been made aware of the problem in 2008 – had done little to address it, was shocking to the public. Regulators sought to re-establish their authority and, some might say, overcorrect for past mistakes. They behaved a little like the football referee who awards a soft penalty because he missed a brutal tackle earlier in the game. Bad behaviour by the banks has been endemic, so there has been no shortage of corrections, and over the period in question the levels of distrust in banking grew to crescendo. Indeed, bankers now top the league of most distrusted professions, along with politicians.

Almost every sector of society was affected by some aspect of the misfiring banking system, whether it be the sale of payment protection policies by Britain's high-street banks to hapless consumers, the reckless gambling in futures markets by the world's most powerful bank, JPMorgan Chase, or the discovery that it was not just Libor that was being rigged but the foreign-exchange markets too. Even those banks that appeared immune to the crisis, such as Britain's Asian-facing institution HSBC, found themselves in trouble over wrongful activity in areas of the world that stretched from Mexico to the Middle East.

The second stage of the crisis, the implosion of euroland, did not make itself apparent until 2009. But when it arrived it did so with a vengeance, sparking widespread violence on the streets of Athens, the collapse of banking systems from Ireland to Spain, and mass unemployment across the region. The rise in popularity of extremist political movements from Golden Dawn in Greece to Jobbik in Hungary and the Front National in France can be directly related to stressful economic dislocation across Europe. Amid the panic and the market disruption, recovery from the Great Recession stalled and political leaders seemed at times to be paralysed by overwhelming market forces.

As the City editor of the *Daily Mail* I have found my life dominated by these developments, not least the more recent dramatic disclosures of turmoil at the Co-operative Bank. The *Daily Mail* never accepted claims by the banks that they have cleaned up their act and we have relentlessly challenged the bonus culture – which incentivised bad practice – and demanded a cleaner, more accountable and more consumer-focused banking system that better serves the public and the economy.

It has been a big agenda and the task goes on today with the support of the paper's editor Paul Dacre and the rest of the senior editorial staff. Being on the wrong side of the banks has been uncomfortable at times but we have relentlessly sought to hold their feet to the fire. This volume is intended to trace the battles since the financial crisis – many of them unfinished – and to remind readers of the depth of depravity that at times gripped the system. I find it personally remarkable, for instance, that some six years after Halifax Bank of Scotland (HBOS) all but collapsed an official forensic report into events still remains unpublished.

In the course of my daily work I have been fortunate enough to spend time with many of the fascinating characters in this narrative, from Bob Diamond to Stephen Hester. They and many others contributed to and at times cooperated with this project. Similarly, through my day job I have had access to the senior regulators and policymakers, including successive Chancellors of the Exchequer Alistair Darling and George Osborne and successive governors of the Bank of England Lord (Mervyn) King and Mark Carney.

In a speech to mark the 125th anniversary of the *Financial Times* in October 2013 Carney was bold enough to paint a picture of the City of London rising phoenix-like from the gloom. 'London acts as Europe's window to global capital; is a centre of emerging market finance; and can play an important role in the financial opening of China. The UK's financial sector can be both a global good and a national asset – if it is resilient.' It was an expression of confidence required after the relentless succession of scandals that at times made it seem as if the Square Mile would never return to its previous glories. All of these individuals, plus many others who made themselves available for informal and formal talks – including several of the bankers featured in the narrative – deserve my gratitude.

As a full-time journalist this book could not have been written without some excellent assistance. I am indebted to my colleague Roger Baird who scoured the official reports, did a great deal of the research and assisted me in constructing a proper narrative. Many of the arguments in the book have been rehearsed in the *Mail* and ushered onto the opinion pages by Leaf Kalfayan and onto the City pages by associate City editor Ruth Sunderland. She has been a constant source of inspiration and support. My other colleagues in the City office, especially current and former banking correspondents Lucy Farndon, Simon Duke and James Salmon and economics correspondent Hugo Duncan, have provided invaluable insights.

On the administrative front, City office assistants Georgie Godsal and Dilin Dixon deserve enormous thanks for their help in arranging interviews and meetings and organising a complex diary. I am grateful to Sue Carpenter for allowing me to use her handsome Dorset country home as a writing retreat. My son Dr Justin Brummer deserves enormous credit for helping me out of countless problems with technology and compiling the bibliography.

Getting serious non-fiction books published these days is not that easy. My agent Jonathan Pegg deserves great credit for seeking out my publishers, Random House Business Books, and his constant messages of encouragement through the process. Special gratitude goes to Nigel Wilcockson, the editor of this volume, as he was of *The Crunch*. Nigel has a great eye for a good story and spent countless hours reading and reshaping the transcript. He rightly saw it as picking up the themes first developed in *The Crunch*, with greed and bonuses still as big an issue for banks and policymakers today as they were in 2007–8. Some things never change – without the banks and their sometimes crass behaviour the book would be much duller.

All of those who have helped me deserve applause but they should in no way be held responsible for the errors that will inevitably have crept into the text. They are mine and mine alone.

I am dedicating this book to my wife Tricia and to my family. It has dominated my life for the last year or so and Tricia has been uncomplaining as vacations, bank holidays and weekends have been occupied with me at the keyboard, surrounded by papers, rather than enjoying ourselves. The rest of the family – daughter Jessica, son-in-law Dan, grandchildren Rafi, Natasha and Benjamin and sons Gabriel and Justin – have cheered me up endlessly.

Alex Brummer.

# 1

# The Crystal Methodist:
# Crisis at the Co-op

On Sunday 17 November 2013 the *Mail on Sunday* published the most arresting front page of that year. It showed a video image of Methodist minister the Rev. Paul Flowers waving around a thick bunch of banknotes as he prepared to spend £300 on cocaine. Flowers, a well-upholstered figure with a ruddy face and white moustache, made no secret of the fact that he was buying the drugs for a homosexual orgy. He also openly boasted about his use of other illegal drugs, including crystal meth and the veterinary drug ketamine.

The very idea of a practising Methodist minister seeking to buy illegal drugs on the streets of Leeds was surprising enough. Even more so was his admission that he intended to use the drugs for illicit sex. It all made for a wonderful newspaper scoop of the old-fashioned style, so rare since the *News of the World* closed in 2011.

But what gave the story a particular twist was that Flowers wasn't just a Methodist minister with unusual extra-curricular interests. Until June 2013 he had been chairman of the ethical Co-operative Bank and vice-chairman of the whole Co-operative Group. And that bank was now in crisis.

On the surface at least, Flowers seemed an unlikely choice

to be chairman of a bank. True, as a young man in the 1960s he had worked for four years as a bank clerk at NatWest, but he had then gone on to take a theology degree at the University of Bristol, before becoming a Methodist minister in Bradford in 1976. Over a decade later he entered local politics, serving as a Labour councillor in Rochdale from 1988 to 1992; he was subsequently elected as a Labour councillor in Bradford in 2002.

Flowers rose to the senior echelons of banking via a long-standing involvement with the Co-operative movement. There he first made a name for himself as an activist, supporting for example the Palestinian boycott campaign, which resulted in the Co-op becoming the first sizeable commercial concern to ban fresh produce from the West Bank and Gaza. Over time he was elected to an area board, and from there he was propelled onto the powerful north-west regional board of the Co-op. This carries almost 30 per cent of the votes at the national level and therefore has a significant voice in selecting people for the national boards, where Flowers was ultimately to find himself.

In 2009 Flowers became a non-executive director of the Co-op Bank. It may seem strange that a man with a political background should assume such an important commercial position, but then the Co-op is no ordinary organisation. In the words of Lord Myners, who was appointed to the Co-op Group as senior non-executive director in the wake of the Flowers affair, the Co-op's arcane three-tier system of governance 'consistently produced governors [directors] without the necessary qualifications and experience for effective board leadership'. Inside the group the practice was that the elected political members were 'on top' and the executives 'on tap'. It's not surprising that Myners should have concluded in his report on the Co-op that the organisation has a 'democratic deficit'.

A year after Flowers' elevation to the Co-op Bank came a further opportunity. In 2010 the Co-op merged with the Britannia Building Society and Flowers skilfully manoeuvred his way into the chair of the enlarged bank. As chairman of the bank and vice-chairman of the group he received the not-ungenerous salary of £132,000. Flowers' political rivals within the movement were reportedly disappointed that the regulator, the Financial Services Authority (FSA), failed to block his passage.

A review by the former Parliamentary Commissioner Sir Christopher Kelly, published on 30 April 2014, noted that Flowers, who refused to take part in the inquiry, was 'not suitably qualified for the role of chairman'. Kelly added: 'It is difficult to avoid the conclusion that, despite their apparent readiness to consider other candidates, the panel [that selected him to the role] placed great weight on the Chair being a champion of the co-operative movement.'

Given the financial turmoil of the previous few years, it was a challenging time to become a senior figure at any bank. It was certainly a demanding time to take on a senior role at the Co-op Bank. Although it had emerged from the banking crisis of 2007 and 2008 with its squeaky-clean image largely intact, like its rivals it had racked up debt from the American sub-prime mortgages on its books. There were other more local issues, too.

As Flowers' path to the top suggests, the command and control and ownership structure of the Co-op was notoriously opaque, and the relationship between the bank and other parts of the Co-operative Financial group, including Co-op Insurance, was correspondingly fuzzy. All the financial services businesses were operated under the umbrella of Co-operative Financial. But they were separate entities with their own boards, each wholly owned by the Co-operative Group. In reality the relationship between the bank and the insurance arms was limited to cross-selling of insurance products through bank branches.

The situation was also complicated by the Co-op's long-standing relationship with the Labour Party. The Co-op was Labour's banker, as well as sponsoring more than 50 Labour MPs including Ed Balls, an influential minister in Gordon Brown's government, who received £50,000 of support a year for his constituency office. Paul Flowers was entertained regularly by the Labour leadership. Such was the close bond between political party and financial institution that as late as April 2013, when the Co-op Bank was in serious trouble, it still committed itself to providing Labour with a £1.6 million loan to be repaid by 2016 – the latest in a series of loans totalling £34 million over a 20-year period, many at rates as low as 2.5 per cent. All this meant that when issues arose that had a political element, party politics would inevitably play a role in decision-making.

The Co-operative Group, however, was in bullish form at the time Flowers assumed his new role. In 2008 it had bought the Somerfield chain of supermarkets for £1.57 billion in what it described as a cash transaction. And in August 2009, after almost a year of talks and in a move that was to take Flowers the next step of the way on his career path, the Co-op Bank and the Britannia Building Society announced that they were to merge to create a 'super-mutual'.

The road to a merger had been cleared after the banking crisis by new laws that allowed different types of mutually owned firms to come together for the first time. The possibility excited the expansion-minded chief executive of the Co-op, Peter Marks. Being part of the bigger Co-operative Group, with its rich set of assets from supermarkets to pharmacies and funeral homes, also suited the Britannia, which was suffering some funding difficulties as a result of its links to two banks that had failed in the previous year.

Neville Richardson, the chief executive of the Britannia, grandiloquently announced that the deal would be the 'next step in the renaissance of the co-operative and mutual sector'. The

Co-operative Bank, for its part, said the merger would create 'a super-mutual as a unique, ethical alternative to shareholder- and Government-owned banks'.

It's not hard to see why many favoured the merger of the Co-op Bank and the Britannia Building Society. Banking, at the time, was scarcely popular with the public. The idea of two mutually owned organisations coming together must have seemed a godsend – not least to the Labour politicians and regulators who blessed the deal. What's more, the merged enterprise would be a major player on the financial stage. The Britannia was, after all, a huge bite for the Co-operative Bank, promising to triple its size from just 90 branches to 300 branches with more than 4 million accounts.

Behind the scenes the regulators, too, were pressing for a deal. In 2008–9 the Britannia had been identified as one of a small group of building societies that might need to be rescued. Without a merger partner the FSA had concluded it would require some sort of 'resolution or remedial measures'.

As would later emerge, such was the eagerness of the politicians, the regulators and the leadership of the two banks to get the deal done that it was agreed without full due diligence. The Co-op's auditors KPMG told the Treasury Select Committee in December 2013 that the diligence was 'thorough'. However, the firm admitted it was unable to examine the building society's loss-making corporate loan book, which was a major factor in the bank's subsequent £1.5 billion shortfall. The flaws in KPMG's due diligence would become the subject of a probe by the Financial Reporting Council (FRC), the watchdog for City and accounting standards.

The April 2014 Kelly review was shocked by the lack of attention paid to the Britannia loan book by KPMG:

The cursory due diligence on Britannia's corporate lending

portfolio is startling in view of how different that lending was to the Co-operative Bank's own business and that of comparable building societies. It is particularly surprising in respect of the commercial real estate lending, with its high concentration risk at a time of a deteriorating macroeconomic environment characterised by collapsing commercial real estate prices.

It was never sufficiently recognised that the Britannia had moved well beyond the traditional retail focus of a building society and had an extensive commercial property loan book – something that came to haunt the organisation during the Great Recession of 2009. Moreover, it had not invested sufficiently in the sort of new systems essential to the smooth running of a modern bank. And, like the Co-op and so many other banks, there were skeletons in the Britannia cupboard. It would emerge in March 2014 that the Co-op and the Britannia were being required to put aside an extra £400 million to cover compensation claims for financial misconduct ranging from selling payment protection insurance (PPI) to lapses in procedures when providing mortgages.

Even the basic mechanics of a merger had been ill considered. The IT implications of creating an organisation with 4 million customers, for example, were not properly addressed. Nor was it properly appreciated that there were covenants in place which limited the ability of the Co-op Group as a whole to finance the bank should the latter ever fall upon bad times. Yet in January 2009, according to the Kelly review, the investment bankers JPMorgan Cazenove advised the Co-operative Bank that it considered the transaction to be 'fair' and described its commercial and strategic logic as 'compelling'. 'The Bank Board minutes', reported Kelly, 'record JPMorgan Cazenove as telling the Board that the due diligence undertaken by KPMG "exceeded that normally undertaken for listed companies"'. Kelly went on to observe: 'It is not easy to understand how JPMorgan Cazenove came to this view about due diligence. It seems that much of the evidence for the assertion came from assurances given by management, rather than any detailed review of the work itself.'

While KPMG and JPMorgan Cazenove did nothing to put impediments in the way of the merger, any objections raised by others were swept aside. I can recall raising concerns about lack of accountability and lines of control within the Co-op Group both to the Britannia chief executive Neville Richardson and the Co-op leader Peter Marks, and being told that I simply didn't understand the robustness of the processes and the essential democracy within the Co-operative movement.

The ever-confident Peter Marks seemed to feel that the company had a monopoly on accountability. 'There is only one democratic retailer and that is us,' Marks confidently claimed. In his devastating interim review, released in March 2014, former City Minister Lord Myners described the Britannia deal together with the takeover of the Somerfield supermarkets – both led by Marks – as 'breathtakingly destructive'.

Scarcely was the Britannia deal done than in July 2011 the Co-op revealed it was interested in acquiring 632 branches of Lloyds Bank, being sold under the codename Project Verde. The background to this opportunity was political rather than commercial. Back in November 2009, after extensive negotiations, and in the wake of the state bailout of Lloyds at the height of the financial crisis, the EU's competition commissioner Neelie Kroes had reached an agreement with Lloyds and the UK government on steps to ensure that Lloyds did not benefit unfairly from the government help it had received. Essentially this involved an undertaking on Lloyds' part that it would sell 632 branches within four years and pay no dividends for two years.

To achieve this, Lloyds created a single entity out of the branches that formerly traded under the Cheltenham & Gloucester and TSB brands. Interest in a deal was expressed by a number of potential buyers, including the Australian bank NAB, the insurance buyout group Resolution, headed by serial entrepreneur Clive Cowdery, and the Nationwide Building Society, all of which requested sales prospectuses. But when the formal bids arrived in July 2011 there were just two parties left in the race: the Co-operative Bank and NBNK, a new banking entity headed by the former chairman of the Lloyd's of London insurance market, Lord Levene.

As was the case with the Britannia–Co-op merger, there was a strong political component to the proposed deal. The new Coalition government had included a commitment to supporting more mutual organisations in its May 2010 pact, and a Project Verde deal with the Co-op, viewed from this vantage point, looked very attractive. The Chancellor George Osborne enthusiastically welcomed the choice of the Co-op as the preferred bidder. It would, he claimed, help to create 'a new banking system for Britain that gives real choice to customers and supports the economy. The sale of hundreds of Lloyds branches to the Co-operative creates a new challenger bank and promotes mutuals.'

Within the Co-op, though, there were dissenting voices. Peter Marks was strongly in favour, but Neville Richardson warned the Co-op Group board of 'disastrous consequences' should it push ahead with the Lloyds transaction. The merger with the Britannia still had a long way to go before it could be claimed that true integration had been achieved. The creaking IT system still needed to be upgraded, and a management restructuring process, known as Project Unity, was still under way.

The projected new deal would add to all these challenges, creating a bank with 1,000 branches and some 11 million customers, responsible for running 7 per cent of the nation's personal bank accounts. And all this against a background of financial turmoil and severe economic recession.

It was becoming clear that the Co-op's ambitions were running ahead of its resources. At a July 2011 meeting the senior regulator Andrew Bailey, on secondment to the FSA from the Bank of England, informed the Co-op Group board over dinner that if the Verde deal were to proceed, then the bank would need more capital. And in the same month the tensions between Richardson and Marks reached breaking point. It was announced that Richardson would walk away from the ethical bank he promoted by 'mutual consent'. He left with a pay-off and package of pension entitlements that amounted to £4.3 million, an astonishing sum for a Co-operative organisation ostensibly different from other banks and operating exclusively in the members' interests.

Richardson left behind a mountain of problems: loans that had gone sour at the Britannia, an IT nightmare, and capital that was viewed by the regulators as being insufficient for the tasks ahead. Further evidence of internal problems inside the Co-op Bank came a few months later. In February 2012 the chief financial officer, James Mack, announced he would be leaving the business after just two years in the job (the Kelly review suggested that the 'limited extent of James Mack's experience made it unlikely that he would have been appointed to this role under other circumstances'). Mack gave no reason for his departure. But losing the finance director in the middle of a potentially transforming transaction was highly unusual.

Richardson's successor was Barry Tootell, the former head of Co-operative Financial Services and a man of whom the Kelly report took a rather dim view. It also emerged that on a Friday afternoon in February 2012, prior to the publication of the bank's 2011 annual report, the bank's finance and risk teams recommended that an extra provision should be charged against the corporate portfolio, but that, according to the Kelly report, on the following Monday morning the additional £20 million provision was reversed. Kelly concluded that 'if it had been left in place the additional provision would have had the knock-on effect of nearly halving the Bank's £40 million bonus pool for its employees and directors.'

Through all these changes in personnel the bank continued its pursuit of the Lloyds' Project Verde deal, and, as the sales process continued, it became apparent that the Co-op was becoming the preferred bidder in what was projected to be a £750 million deal. To deal with some of the basic problems Lloyds proposed to build and take charge of the IT systems on behalf of the Co-op so that the customers in the 632 branches could be assured that services would not be interrupted.

It would also lend money to the Co-op to allow the transaction to be completed. The deal was approved by the Lloyds board of directors, with the support of 41 per cent shareholder UK Financial Investments[1], months before the Portuguese boss of Santander (UK), Antonio Horta-Osorio, was to take the helm at Lloyds from the American Eric Daniels – one of the people widely blamed by investors for Lloyds' disastrous 2008 takeover of HBOS.

Yet worries persisted in some quarters. In a private letter to Paul Flowers on 20 December 2011, the FSA regulator Andrew Bailey (who was later to move back to the Bank of England as a deputy governor and the first head of the Prudential Regulatory Authority) left the Co-op Bank chairman in little doubt of his concerns:

[1] UK Financial Investments (UKFI) was the arm's-length organisation set up by the Labour government to hold the shares in Lloyds, RBS, Northern Rock and other failed banks in the aftermath of the 2008 rescues.

Our current view is that it is not clear that the Co-operative Banking Group has the ability to transform itself successfully and sustainably into an organisation on the scale that would result from acquiring the Verde assets.

Bailey urged Flowers to develop a 'credible liquidity and risk management framework' and urged the Co-op to put together 'a permanent and suitable senior executive management team'. He informed Flowers that he had 'already communicated elements of our concerns to Lloyds Banking Group' ahead of their decision regarding a preferred bidder.

The suggestion of a marriage between Lloyds and the Co-op Bank infuriated Lord (Peter) Levene, the former chairman of Lloyd's of London (the specialist insurance market), who had served as a senior executive at investment bankers Deutsche Bank and in Whitehall, and who was widely regarded as one of the big beasts in the City of London. I recall talking to him at a charity dinner at the Royal Courts of Justice early in 2012, when he set out his views very forcibly. On the one hand, he argued that there was too much politics in what was going on: essentially, the government (and the Lib Dems in particular) were committed to establishing a mutual sector to challenge the quoted banks. On the other hand, he suggested, there really was a viable alternative. Were his consortium NBNK to take over the deal, he said, it would be worth more to Lloyds, there would be fewer attendant risks, and the charge made in some quarters that the Co-op–Lloyds deal was more about political convenience than financial reality would vanish. On the last point, his reservations seemed to be borne out by a seemingly inexplicable decision on the part of the Financial Services Authority in June 2012 to offer the Co-op Group a three-year waiver as a 'mixed financial holding company' – in other words, the pressure was off the Co-op to increase its capital in the short term.

Levene didn't just voice his objections privately. He also took them directly to the Lloyds board, arguing rightly, as it would turn out, that the Co-op deal was 'fraught with risks' and that it lacked the cash to mount a credible bid. (When questioned by the Treasury Select Committee in June 2013 about the Levene letter, City grandee and Lloyds chairman Sir Win Bischoff said he had never seen the document. Even if he had not seen the letter, it is hard to think that Bischoff could have been wholly ignorant of Levene's well-founded objections, which had been widely aired in the media.)

On 21 March 2013 the Co-op Bank revealed a startling loss of £673.7 million against a profit of £54.2 million a year earlier. Much of the shortfall was attributed to bad debts stemming from the Britannia takeover, with £150 million coming from the mis-selling of payment protection insurance. The ethical bank, like its bigger rivals on the high street, had exploited its own loyal customers by pressurising them to buy expensive insurance products they did not need. As for the Britannia, like other troubled building societies it had moved out of its comfort zone, the provision of mortgages, into the provision of commercial property loans, but had discovered to its cost that this move carried a sting in its tail. When the property market collapsed, in the wake of the 2007–9 financial implosion, many of the loans on its books had to be written down in value, or written off altogether.

The Co-op Bank's March 2013 financial results showed that bad debts stemming largely from the Britannia loan book had surged to £14.5 billion. In an effort to start rebuilding its finances the group announced that it planned to sell its life insurance and asset management arm to rival mutual the Royal London and said it was also looking for a buyer for the general insurance arm. This was perhaps an understandable tactical move in the circumstances, but from a strategic point of view some were surprised that the Co-op Group should be so ready to dismantle an insurance arm that had been a core service for its members for decades and paradoxically served many of the same customers as the bank.

Given such disastrous results for 2012–13 it was clear that the Lloyds deal could not possibly go ahead. On 24 April 2013 Peter Marks admitted defeat, blaming a 'worsening economic outlook' for the decision. (As it happens, 2013 saw a sharp fall in unemployment, and economic indicators were starting to point towards recovery.) A couple of months later, on 18 June, in evidence to the Treasury Select Committee, Lloyds' bosses Sir Win Bischoff and Antonio Horta-Osorio stated that they had been aware of the capital shortfall at the Co-op since December 2012 and had been 'sceptical' then that it could be plugged in time to complete the sale of the 632 Verde branches by March. On that basis one wonders whether the proposed deal was ever actually feasible.

The full extent of the problems faced by the Co-op Bank was presented in a devastating paper released by the credit research department of Barclays Bank on 10 May 2013. The report tied the Co-op Bank's trouble to the acquisition of the Britannia 'which tripled the size of the bank and added a meaningful amount of high risk exposures'. Barclays estimated the bank's capital shortfall as £800 million in a base case if conditions in the economy and the real-estate markets remained stable and confidence could be maintained in the bank's management. That figure, though, could potentially rise to £1.8 billion in a stressed case – in other words, if market conditions were to worsen and further doubts arise about the ability of the management team to sort out the bad loans. The paper noted that because the financial assets of the group were ring-fenced from the food, funeral and pharmacy operations the options for closing the capital hole were limited. The Barclays analyst Jonathan Glionna warned clients: 'While the range of potential outcomes for the Co-op is broad, we believe investors should remain cautious on the subordinated securities[2], even after today's [10 May 2013] sharp price decline.' Barclays feared that the Co-op Bank was in grave danger of reneging on its debt.

The Barclays credit report was released to clients on the same day as the Co-op revealed that it had a massive £1.5 billion black hole in its accounts. Previously there had been a determination to put the best complexion on the condition of the bank, the Co-op claiming that 'billions of pounds of cash' could be transferred from the healthy parts of the group to support the bank. That was no longer a tenable position.

In the light of such an admission the position of chief executive Barry Tootell (formerly the finance director) immediately became unsustainable and he resigned. He was temporarily replaced by another Co-op Bank executive, Rod Bulmer.

Two weeks later Bulmer moved and a new chief executive, former HSBC banker Niall Booker, was parachuted into the top job. As an HSBC executive closely involved in that bank's loss of tens of billions of dollars because of poorly secured loans made by HSBC's American sub-prime lending arm Household, Booker was not short of experience in handling mounting rotten debts.

His arrival, however, failed to calm market nerves and on the same day the credit ratings agency Moody's left no doubt about its concerns when it downgraded the bank's credit rating – an assessment of the quality of its debt – by an astonishing six notches to 'junk' status. Anyone holding bonds in the Co-operative Bank had been shown a flashing red light.

[2] Subordinated securities are debts or bonds that in the event of liquidation or bankruptcy are only repaid after others with a higher priority or status have been recompensed.

Desperate times called for desperate measures, and the Co-op's promise to become a challenger bank, willing to serve the needs of small and medium-sized enterprises (SMEs), was abandoned. It announced that it had no choice but to suspend corporate lending as part of its effort to conserve capital and keep the bank from falling over a cliff.

At such a time – with executives going down like ninepins, the bank's credit reputation under enormous pressure, and the regulators demanding that it come up with a plan to fill the nasty chasm in its accounts – the role of chairman is vital. The job is to steady the ship and ensure that executives are making decisions which are in the best interest of the bank and its customers. But in Paul Flowers the bank had a chairman who barely seemed capable of steadying himself, let alone a bank. His job was to be in constant contact with regulators, the Co-op Bank's own lenders and bondholders in an effort to reassure them of the bank's viability. In reality, his background as a political appointee to the post and his deepening personal problems made him unsuitable for such a high-pressure role.

In June 2010 Flowers resigned as chairman of the Bank and deputy chairman of the whole Co-operative Group. At the time it was assumed that his decision to go was connected to the condition of the bank, rather than anything personal. In November, as scrutiny of Flowers' personal life intensified, it was revealed that the colourful banker had been asked to leave his job because his personal expenses had ballooned out of control and bore little relation to his work for the bank.

With no chairman and confidence in the bank draining away, desperate measures were needed if the Co-op Bank was to be saved. On 3 June it announced that it was selling 8 per cent of the Britannia loan book to an undisclosed buyer for £237 million in an effort to raise cash. Perhaps more importantly, Richard Pym, a former chief executive of the Alliance & Leicester, agreed to become chairman. (He, too, would resign in May 2014.)

Pym was no stranger to sorting out failed banks. He has been employed by the Treasury to run the 'bad bank' carved out of the loan books of Northern Rock and the Bradford & Bingley, both of which had failed in the credit crunch of 2007–8. He would be joined by Richard Pennycook, the former finance director of grocer Wm Morrison, who had experience of difficult takeovers from his own role in the supermarket's messy takeover of the Safeway group in 2004.

The perilous finances of the Co-op and the ill-conceived takeover of the Britannia attracted the attention of the Treasury Select Committee, which revealed on 13 June 2013 that it intended to conduct hearings into the Co-op's abandoned bid for 632 branches. It wanted to understand how the bid had been able to proceed in the first place, given the concerns aired by the media and such figures as Lord Levene. It wanted to comprehend how the individuals at the various institutions involved had approached the transaction. And it wanted to get an insight into the stance of the regulators, who had failed so miserably in the build-up to the Great Panic and who had apparently nodded this particular deal through.

On the latter point it soon became clear that the regulators had indeed had serious concerns and had relayed them to Flowers and the Co-op board. Unfortunately, though, because their worries were expressed in technical language and were, arguably, less than direct, the message had not been fully understood.

In his letter of 20 December 2011 to Paul Flowers Andrew Bailey wrote: 'We wanted to be open with you on our thinking so that if your Board chose to pursue its interest in the [Verde] acquisition, it did so with full knowledge of the regulatory risks such a course presented.' Bailey wanted to see a number of issues resolved, including assurances on liquidity and risk management, a suitable management team, effective governance and a sound plan for capital.

In other words, Bailey had concerns about almost every aspect of the Co-op Bank's ability to complete the purchase of the Lloyds branches. Bailey had identified the problems and counted on Flowers and the Co-op Bank board to recognise the severity of the warning and call the deal off. The strictures were, however, put to one side and the pursuit of the Verde branches continued.

A similar situation occurred at Barclays back in April 2012, when the chairman of the FSA, Lord (Adair) Turner, wrote to Marcus Agius, chairman of Barclays, to express a series of concerns about the way the bank was being run. Turner wrote:

I wished to bring to your attention our concerns about the cumulative impression created by a pattern of behaviour over the last few years in which Barclays often seems to be seeking to gain advantage through the use of complex structures or through arguing for regulatory approaches which are at the aggressive end of interpretation of the relevant rules and regulations.

Turner went on with a laundry list of examples of how Barclays, led at the time by chief executive Bob Diamond, was engaged in activities that disturbed regulators. Among the disputed issues were Barclays' attempts to pull the wool over the eyes of regulators during tests on the strength of its balance sheet and the schemes it offered clients to assist them in avoiding UK taxes. Barclays, however, failed to heed the criticism or the warnings, both of which subsequently turned out to be fully justified. (In July 2012 Barclays admitted to rigging the Libor interest-rate market that sets the cost of trillions of dollars of mortgages and commercial loans.)

At both Barclays and the Co-op the thinking appeared to be that actions required by the regulators could be safely delayed and the tension would pass over time. This attitude was a legacy of the 'soft touch' regulation in the run-up to the 2007–9 financial crisis, when City watchdogs had been so ineffectual.

On 14 June 2013, a day after the Treasury Select Committee inquiry into the Co-op was announced, the Prudential Regulatory Authority[3] finally showed its hand. Andrew Bailey, now deputy governor of the Bank of England, revealed that the regulator had assessed the black hole in the bank's balance sheet to be £1.5 billion and ordered it to come up with a credible plan by the end of the day. This confirmed the Co-op's own May estimate, and was arrived at after a careful inspection of the books and an independent assessment of the bank's capital needs, having conducted stress tests. If a plan could not be formulated and agreed, the only other route that could be taken would be to place the Co-op Bank into 'resolution' – the post-crisis process for rescuing and winding down banks that get into difficulty.

Two days later on 17 June, with the agreement of the regulator, the Co-op Group, ultimate owner or shareholder in the bank, announced a plan to save the bank from failure. Most of the burden would fall on the bank's bondholders, who would take on responsibility for some £1 billion and who, at the same time, would see the value of their investment reduced and the bonds turned into ordinary shares of uncertain value and with far lower returns.

[3] The Prudential Regulatory Authority (PRA) was one of an alphabet soup of new regulators that began work in 2013. Under reforms of financial regulation introduced by the Tory-led Coalition government, supervision of banks and big insurers was moved from the ineffectual Financial Services Authority to the Bank of England.

In the parlance of bank rescues it would be a 'bail-in' where the bondholders would bear the burden, as opposed to a bailout where the taxpayer foots the bill.

The Co-op planned to find the rest of the cash required from the sale of its insurance assets and planned to float 25 per cent of the mutual champion on the London Stock Exchange. The reshaped Co-op Bank would be split in two – a good bank and a bad bank. The latter would contain £14.5 billion of toxic mortgages and commercial property loans mainly inherited from its takeover of the Britannia Building Society in 2009, along with large corporate lending business, and would be wound down or sold. The good Co-op bank would concentrate on lending and taking deposits from personal customers and small firms.

The plan was unveiled with a hard sell by the Co-op claiming that without it there would be no choice but to wind it up. New chairman Richard Pym claimed that the measures would 'provide the foundations to support the long-term success of the bank in offering a real alternative to customers'.

Cracks immediately started to appear. I was contacted by veteran City property man and financier Sir John Ritblat, who was among the bondholders and who in early June 2013 saw plans by the Co-op Group to create an £800 million development in the centre of Manchester – in conjunction with his family firm Delancey – abandoned. Ritblat was furious at the structure of a rescue package that potentially would rob up to 7,000 bondholders of a large chunk of their savings.

'It is absolutely outrageous that bondholders are being punished when it is the Co-op [Group] itself that is the equity holder and should take the pain,' Ritblat told me. 'This affair reeks of gross mismanagement. The bondholders are being asked to fund both the takeover of Somerfield and the Britannia merger. And now they are being asked to pick up the bill for management foolishness.'

Ritblat's analysis was sound. In any traditional financial rescue the first line of defence is made up of the share or equity holders, followed by the unsecured lenders (as Barclays had warned a month earlier), and only then by the bondholders. The Co-op Group plan was putting the bondholders first in the line of fire. In the normal run of events, one would have expected that the Co-op Group, made up of its members and a huge range of businesses including supermarkets, funeral parlours and pharmacies, would have been sold before the bondholders were required to contribute. But there was nothing normal about what had happened at the Co-op Group. So deeply was it in debt following its dash for growth that the new management team, headed by former B&Q executive Euan Sutherland, felt it had no alternative but to turn to the bondholders for a last-ditch rescue.

The unrepentant group chief executive Peter Marks finally resigned on 18 June 2013. But the row with the bondholders escalated. Fixed-income activist Mark Taber, who specialised in standing up for the interests of bondholders in times of stress, launched a public campaign against the rescue on behalf of the smaller investors. Bigger institutional holders also questioned the fairness of the proposal. Amid the outcry chief executive Euan Sutherland had little choice but to open negotiations with investors.

Finances at the bank were going from bad to worse. On 29 August 2013 it was revealed that in the first half of the financial year alone the group had reported losses of £709 million, up from £58.6 million in the same period of 2012. Len Wardle, the Co-op group chairman since 2007 and another of the survivors from the *ancien régime*, decided to stand down. Throughout the crisis he had kept out of the limelight, a decision that had earned him the epithet 'Silent Len'.

As the long negotiations with bondholders dragged on it

was disclosed that some 70 per cent of the bonds in the bank, largely held by institutional holders, had been snapped up by two American hedge funds, Aurelius Capital Management and Silver Point Capital. Effectively they were now in the driving seat. Sutherland insisted that this new reality would not alter the core ethical principles of the bank and that the values that the Co-op traditionally espoused would be built into new articles of association that had been drawn up.

But with so much voting power in the hands of little-known overseas investors, not thought to be long-term holders, there was some doubt as to whether it was even legal to call itself a co-operative bank any longer. As for the private bondholders, concessions were made and they were given the choice of continuing to receive interest payments, but risking a loss of value for the bonds when they finally mature in 2025, or taking a reduced interest payment in return for higher capital return.

The shrinkage of the bank sped up. On 4 November the Co-op announced that it would be closing 50 of its 324 branches and dismissing 1,000 of its 9,000 employees by the end of the year to save costs. The scope of its business also narrowed when it suspended services to more than 100 local authorities nationwide – most of them Labour-controlled – so as to concentrate on its retail customers. It was a case of *force majeure* in that many local authorities already had pulled deposits because the bank no longer met the strict conditions for handling public monies.

Approval of the scheme to reshape the ownership structure of the bank required the approval of at least two-thirds of the bondholders. Ahead of this vote on 30 November 2013, which effectively secured the bank's future, the roof fell in and the Co-op saga changed from a story that had struggled to break its way out of the financial pages or onto the broadcast news bulletins into a national scandal. The footage of the Rev. Flowers negotiating drugs deals so as to engage in homosexual orgies turned the Co-op into a source of huge public fascination as every aspect of his troubled life came under scrutiny.

Questions as to how such an unfit person came to hold a senior job at a major financial institution, and one handed so many political favours, proliferated. Flowers was suspended as a minister of the Methodist Church. Len Wardle felt he had no choice but to bring forward his own departure. 'I led the board that appointed Paul Flowers to lead the bank board and under these circumstances I feel that it is right to step down now,' he stated. It was the most that was heard from 'Silent Len' throughout the whole sordid affair. He was replaced by Co-op insider Ursula Lidbetter, who had been with the organisation for many years. Lidbetter was chief executive of the independent Lincolnshire Co-operative, one of the largest employers in the county. Her CV did not include any knowledge of high finance.

The noose was closing ever tighter on Flowers, all those involved in the debacle, and the Co-op movement itself. Flowers' Bradford home was searched by police investigating allegations of drugs misuse. On 20 November, with Tories baying for blood at the sight of the Labour-supporting Co-op movement in full retreat, Prime Minister David Cameron promised the Commons an independent inquiry. 'There are clearly a lot of questions that have to be answered. Why weren't alarm bells rung earlier, particularly by those that knew? Why was the Rev. Flowers judged suitable to be chairman of a bank?' he asked.

The Labour Party found itself on the back foot with Ed Balls, the Shadow Chancellor, insisting that it was a 'lie' to say that the £50,000 donation he had received from the Co-op in 2012 had been authorised by Flowers. He had never met him at a personal meeting, although had been in contact at a group dinner. What seemed to be forgotten in all these heated exchanges was that if Labour had close ties to the Co-op, it was the Coalition government that had been so keen to see the Co-op form a super-mutual. It was neither the Conservatives' nor the Lib Dems' finest moment.

The official inquiry proposed would be in addition to one already set up by the refreshed management of the Co-op, which was being conducted by the former Parliamentary Commissioner of Standards Sir Christopher Kelly. But that was far from the end of it. Flowers' suspension from the Methodist Church was made indefinite. And the Charity Commissioners opened an investigation into allegations (first expressed almost a decade earlier) that Flowers had claimed tens of thousands of pounds of false expenses from the Lifeline Project that works with 'individuals, families and communities both to prevent and reduce harm, to promote recovery, and to challenge the inequalities linked to alcohol and drug misuse'.

Now the Co-op itself turned its guns on Flowers, demanding the return of £31,000 of a £155,000 pay-off that he had received. On 22 November the wretched Flowers was arrested on Merseyside in connection with, in the words of the police, 'a drugs supply investigation'. While all this was going on, any hope that post-Flowers the Co-operative Bank could carry on banking as usual withered on the vine. The Treasury ordered an independent inquiry reaching back to 2008 at least and the Financial Reporting Council, which polices the auditors, revealed it was looking at the Co-op's financial reports with a view to a formal probe.

As if this were not enough, on 12 January 2014 the Rev. Flowers was back on the front page of the *Mail on Sunday*, seeking to buy drugs and in search of sexual adventures. Just a few months earlier he had released a personal statement, seeking to excuse his conduct on the grounds that he had been under enormous pressure:

This year has been an incredibly difficult one with a death in the family [his mother Muriel, a year previously] and the pressure of my role at the Co-operative Bank. At the lowest point in this terrible period, I did things that were stupid and wrong. I am sorry for this, and I am seeking professional help, and apologise to all I have hurt or failed by my actions.

Flowers' admission of culpability did not end the torrent of revelations from the group. On Sunday 10 March 2014 a leak of a Co-operative Group board paper to the *Observer* newspaper revealed that Euan Sutherland, the group chief executive who had led the restructuring of the Co-op Bank, was potentially in line for a pay packet of £3.66 million for the year, made up of £1.5 million base pay, a £1.5 million retention payment, pensions contributions and the cost of buying him out of his previous contract with B&Q owner Kingfisher. His Co-op predecessor Peter Marks, author of the group's foolish expansion policy, had received £1.3 million in the previous year.

The following morning Sutherland resigned, accusing the leakers on the board of undermining him and the executive team. 'The senior democrats talk the talk of reform,' he said, 'but in practice they won't do it.' He declared that the Co-op was ungovernable. Sutherland had come up against the power of the 'political' members of the board and found them an immovable object. 'Who is the Co-op for? Is it for the 600 activists, the 90,000 employees or the millions of members and customers? In my view it is for all of them.'

Finance director Richard Pennycook replaced Sutherland as interim chief executive and the new chair Ursula Lidbetter sought to put the best gloss on events:

Euan and the team saved the Co-operative Bank, without

recourse to the taxpayer, and in doing so rescued the group from the biggest crisis in its 150-year history. They have worked night and day to renew the organisation and give it a sustainable future.

Sutherland's untidy resignation provoked senior independent director Lord Myners, who had played a pivotal role in the rescue of the banking system as City Minister in Gordon Brown's government, to go public with his reservations about the way the group was run. In a conversation with me Myners painted a picture of an organisation at war with itself, where the regional barons held the levers of power.

He confided that when he had taken up his post, with a view to cleaning up the governance, he was approached by a Co-op regional committee member and told there could be no reform without his agreement, as he held a substantial chunk of the votes.

It had become clear to Myners that the regional barons and chairs and officials – all of whom received stipends from the Co-op Group – had a vested interest in hanging onto office. Many received payments that were well above the national average wage.[4] Genuine democracy was not on their agenda and they regarded the paid executives as staff who were required to kowtow to political bosses. The Co-op looked to be more like Tammany Hall, the notorious 19th-century organisation that ran New York City, than the community-friendly organisation that it professed to be.

Myners was devastatingly direct. He found that the three-tier system of elected management – local, regional and national committees – 'consistently produced governors without the necessary qualifications and experience to provide effective board leadership'.

[4] The national average wage in 2013 stood at £29,300 for men and £26,600 for women, according to ONS data.

He added that this 'had massively raised the cost of decision-making and diminished genuine accountability throughout its governance hierarchy'. The organisation might claim to have 'one member, one vote' but under the present constitution, ordinary Co-op members do not have the right to attend annual general meetings or to re-elect group board directors.

His proposal was that board directors should be subject to annual election (as is now the case in public companies), and that vacancies should be openly advertised and candidates appointed on merit – not politics – based around very clearly defined criteria of skills and experience. Myners proposed a new group board made up of an independent chair, with no previous involvement in the movement, six to seven non-executive directors and two executive directors. He derided the existing 20-member board that largely comprised people who were there because they controlled block votes in the Co-operative movement. In the end his reforms would 'lie in the hands of fewer than 50 elected members' who, if they acted in concert, could easily defeat them. He also asserted that no new chief executive should be appointed 'while the governance issues remain unresolved'.

It was not just governance issues that remained unresolved at the Co-op. Losses at the bank continued to mount and on 24 March 2013 it was revealed that a further £400 million black hole had opened up. The finances of the group were so uncertain that publication of the accounts was postponed.

The shareholders would be asked for new funds to fill the void in the bank. Two-thirds of this would come from wealthy hedge funds, now in control of the Co-op Bank, but the rest would have to come from the Co-op Group itself. This would mean the further sale of assets beyond the chain of 750 pharmacies and land holdings already announced and the intention to dispose of 200 grocery supermarkets, most of which were acquired with the disastrous Somerfield takeover. The possibility that the Co-op Bank could destroy a mutual movement with a history dating back 150 years to the idealism of the Rochdale pioneers was very real. The Co-operative movement was facing death by a thousand cuts.

In terms of scale the scandal at the Co-operative Bank has been minor league compared to the bill of £18 billion for wrongful selling of payment protection insurance by all the high-street banks, the money-laundering fiasco at HSBC, and Libor rigging by Barclays. But the elements that make up the scandal are worryingly reminiscent of other banking disasters in recent years, and demonstrate that in this sector at least history had – and still has – a habit of repeating itself.

First there was the tendency of ambitious individuals to leap too boldly. The Co-op Bank, as part of the broader Co-operative movement, might have espoused a culture of community, but that didn't mean that key decisions were made in a considered way by a large panel of experts. Instead, the group's former chief executive Peter Marks and his management team very much held sway within a byzantine ownership structure that contained few checks and balances and that employed such placemen as Len Wardle and Paul Flowers. These individuals allowed Marks and his management team to embark on a helter-skelter expansion programme virtually unchecked.

If there was too little introspection on the inside, there was also too little scrutiny from the outside. Such was the desire of successive governments to see a problem 'fixed' or an opportunity 'taken' that decisions were all too often made swiftly and unquestioningly. In such an environment, the regulators proved insufficiently strong to call a halt at pivotal moments.

And then there was the worrying lack of expertise among key players in the drama, Flowers being the prime example. His colourful personal life was of questionable relevance here. Clive Anderson, the senior official at the FSA, who gave testimony before the Treasury Select Committee in 2014, reasonably claimed that a spent conviction for performing a sex act in a public toilet was rightly overlooked when it came to considering Flowers' fitness for his financial role.

'We regarded it,' he said, 'but it was from 1981 and we didn't think the nature of the conviction was directly relevant to his ability to do his job. We had to be very careful not to draw inferences from people's private lives into their professional lives.' Anderson also said he was not aware of a later court conviction in 1990 for driving while drunk, and neither the Co-op Bank nor the regulator appear to have inquired into the circumstances that led Flowers to resign his seat on Bradford Council in September 2011 after pornographic material was allegedly found on his computer terminal. Whether one could argue that there was any cumulative force to Flowers' various misjudgements is a matter of opinion.

But Flowers' lack of banking knowledge was a matter of fact. Anderson denied that his approval of the choice had been negligent, saying: 'I don't think it was a mistake in terms of the decision I had made at the time with the information I had.' Yet when the Treasury Select Committee (TSC) heard initial evidence from Flowers in November 2013 they swiftly discovered that he had failed to master his brief. Asked to disclose the assets of the Co-op Bank, he estimated them at £3 billion. In fact they are £49 billion. Andrew Tyrie MP, chair of the TSC, told Anderson (who now works for the Financial Conduct Authority): 'One of your solutions to taming an unruly board was putting a financial illiterate in charge.' (In fairness, when he worked at NatWest as a school leaver, Flowers had passed

Part 1 of the Institute of Bankers examination and had completed half of Part 2.)

His approval by the panjandrums in the Co-operative movement may only have been a formality, given his background in the church and on the political left. But his approval by the City regulator, the now defunct Financial Services Authority[5], is more surprising. After all, by 2010 all appointments to the banking sector had become highly sensitive and successive reports, by the Treasury Select Committee and others, had underlined the need for future bank chairmen to be more steeped in finance and the ways of the City. The parliamentarians wanted more robust and able chairmen and independent directors capable of questioning and checking decisions taken by powerful chief executives, such as Fred Goodwin and Bob Diamond, who were adept at getting their chairmen and boards onside. In the midst of the post-crisis reforms to the regulatory structure Flowers slipped through the regulatory net. His advance was eased by the perceived democracy of the Co-operative movement, which would later be shown to be a chimera.

To add insult to injury, those senior figures who passed through the revolving doors of the Co-op Bank were often in line for huge payouts when they left. Former Britannia boss Neville Richardson, for example, departed with a pay and pensions package worth £4.6 million. His golden goodbye had included a £1.39 million payment for loss of office, £738,000 in pay and bonuses and a £2.1 million retirement fund built up in service at the Britannia. In evidence to Andrew Tyrie's Select Committee Richardson would claim in 2013 that the crisis at the Co-op came from mismanagement after he had left. The Prudential Regulatory Authority publicly disagreed. As chief executive first of the Britannia, in the period leading up to the

[5] Known to its critics as the 'Fundamentally Supine Authority' because of its weak record in policing the City.

merger with the Co-op, and then of the merged bank, Richardson had direct responsibility for the health of both institutions. The weaknesses in the Britannia's commercial lending book, the IT shortcomings and some of the ill-treatment of consumers – such as the sales of payment protection insurance – took place on his watch. Sir Christopher Kelly in his April 2014 report noted of Richardson: 'In two years running the Bank he had done little to deal with the Bank's developing capital problems, its inadequate risk management framework or the escalating costs of its IT replatforming project.'

If all this seems familiar, it's because there are so many parallels between the story of the Co-op's fall from grace and that of other financial institutions. Time and time again, a similar story has played out with similar actors. The forcefully ambitious Peter Marks at the Co-op was not unique. At Barclays, for example, there was Bob Diamond, whose ruthless approach was tolerated by such veteran figures as Barclays chairman Marcus Agius because he delivered profits and protected the bank from government control in the financial crisis of 2008. At JPMorgan Chase, America's most blue-blooded bank, there was the all-powerful chairman and chief executive Jamie Dimon, who was given a free hand by his board and shareholders because he also delivered record earnings. Fred Goodwin, the former chief executive of the Royal Bank of Scotland, was lauded when RBS appeared to be roaring ahead but was, behind the scenes, an egomaniac who would brook no criticism.

The Co-op Bank's opaque ownership and control structure made it easy for powerful executives to exert extraordinary influence. But the same was also true of more conventional ownership structures, not just at Barclays and JPMorgan Chase in New York but at banks across the European Union. All were and continue to be ineffective when it comes to curbing untrammelled ambition and dangerous risk-taking.

Regulatory efforts to stem the ambition of the Co-op Bank proved to be ineffectual. But then that has regularly proved to be the case. What Lord Mervyn King, former governor of the Bank of England, has dubbed the 'nice' decade from 1997–2007 gave rise to relaxed, soft-touch regulation. Provided the results looked good, no one looked too closely at how they were achieved. It might have been thought that after the crisis and the Great Recession of 2008–10 the banks would have learned greater self-control and the regulators would have become more questioning, but old habits die hard. At Barclays, for example, directors simply chose to ignore the warnings of the Financial Services Authority about some activities, such as organising tax avoidance for clients, because they were so profitable. No one stepped in until too late.

There was certainly no shortage of action when things did go wrong. On 26 October 2013 the Bank of England revealed that it would be launching its own inquiry into the Co-op's affairs. Details of the probe by the Prudential Regulatory Authority and the Financial Conduct Authority – the consumer regulator – were unveiled in January 2014. Both regulators planned to examine the events leading up to the revelation of the debilitating £1.5 billion black hole and whether there was wrongdoing in relation to the bank's capital and liquidity positions. Both the disastrous Britannia merger and the over-ambitious effort to win control of the Lloyds branches would be looked at. There was also a suggestion that some of those in positions of authority at the time potentially faced bans from working in the City again and worse. But, of course, this was all after the event.

The reality is that more than a decade of free-wheeling banking cannot easily be corralled. One might have thought that the banking sector would have put its house in order in the aftermath of the meltdown of 2007 and 2008, but recent years have seen scandals

# 2

# The Long Shadow of 9/11: Global Banking's Slide to Disaster

Stephen Hester was 'merrily enjoying' himself as chief executive of British Land when 'out of the blue' late on a Friday night in October 2008 he received a call from Sir Tom McKillop, who chaired the Royal Bank of Scotland. 'We need a chief executive in short order and we'd very much like you to do it,' McKillop insisted.

McKillop had been authorised to call Hester by Labour's City Minister Paul Myners, the experienced City hand brought into the Treasury to help it reshape the banks amid the unprecedented turmoil in global banking that followed the collapse of the American investment bank Lehman Brothers on 15 September 2008. Myners knew of Hester's work at the retail bank Abbey National, where he had reshaped the business in 2004 before selling it on to Spanish bank Santander, and was impressed by him. And he knew that RBS urgently needed a new strong and confident hand at the tiller. The bank was in serious trouble.

While the earthquake that brought Stephen Hester to RBS and shook British, European and global banking to its very foundations in the autumn of 2008 seemed to be of recent origin, the roots of what became known as the Great Panic can actually be traced back to developments over several years and to one world-changing event in particular: the al-Qaeda outrages of 9/11. In immediate terms, the wanton attack on the Pentagon and the destruction of the twin towers of the World Trade Center in September 2001 was seen as a military-style assault on the US and so became the trigger point for the War on Terror that followed. But the 9/11 attacks also had profound economic consequences. To many, the selection of the twin towers as a target, peopled as they were with thousands who worked in finance and business, seemed a calculated hit on American capitalism. In the uncertainty of the days that followed, markets went into freefall and the New York Stock Exchange was closed for an unprecedented six days.

As the global economy shut down, the emergency phone and communications links that connect the central banks of the world's seven most advanced economies – the US, Japan, Germany, Britain, France, Italy and Canada – went into overdrive. In the words of the late Eddie George, then governor of the Bank of England, the pipes of the world's payments systems had become hopelessly clogged and there was a realisation that drastic measures were required to unblock them. Moreover, the world's financial policymakers were determined to demonstrate that the free-market, capitalist system was durable and could resist an attack on its Wall Street heartland.

Dr Alan Greenspan, the renowned chairman of America's central bank, the Federal Reserve, had a clear sense of what needed to be done. US interest rates had to be cut to free up money around the world and flush it through the pipes of the financial system. That way a potentially devastating world recession could be staved off and confidence restored. The Fed had gone into 2001 with a target interest rate of 6.5 per cent with the aim of cooling a mini-boom in credit and housing. Following the attacks, and at Greenspan's instigation, it immediately lowered its target, making four cuts in rapid succession and ending the year with rates at just 1.75 per cent. Other central banks followed and by the end of 2003 key US interest rates had been brought down to just 1 per cent, the lowest level in 50 years.

These drastic interest-rate cuts came at a critical moment in the evolution of the financial world of New York and London. Up until the late 1980s and early 1990s, fairly tight regulation had been the order of the day, but as the millennium drew near the rules were loosened. In the US, President Bill Clinton's administration of 1992–2000 brought in various measures to free up the financial sector. The Glass–Steagall Act, the Great Depression-era measure that kept retail banking separate from investment or casino banking, was allowed to lapse.* A new breed of universal banks, such as Citigroup and JPMorgan Chase, which provided every kind of financial service from mortgages for ordinary consumers to sophisticated derivatives deals for companies, was encouraged to emerge. Banks became brasher and more gung-ho. Their leaders encouraged them to be more entrepreneurial and hungrier for growth. In the United Kingdom, similarly, the New Labour government that came to power in 1997 adopted what became known as light-touch regulation. Recognising that the British banking system and the City of London could be a cash cow that provided the tax income necessary to fund improvements in public services, the government was anxious to ensure that it did not stand in the way of new enterprises and the expansion of financial services.

The combination of light-touch regulation and low interest rates proved a heady mix. Over the next decade share prices soared on both sides of the Atlantic. The Dow Jones Industrial Average, which closed at 9,605.51 on 10 September 2001, had soared to an all-time high of 14,000 by October 2007 amid a tide of rising optimism about economic prospects. The good times were most visible in the

No, it was dismembered over 35 many years. Clinton put the nail in the coffin. Destruction of Glass Steagall enabled greedy bankers to gamble with depositors money

US housing market. Fuelled by low interest rates and lax lending rules, and encouraged by the Clinton administration's policy of making mortgages more readily available to the less well off via the partly government-controlled mortgage intermediaries Fannie Mae and Freddie Mac, housing prices rose at an annual rate of 8.26 per cent in the period 2001–5. This was twice the rate of growth that had been seen the previous decade. The leap in median prices from $166,600 in 2001 to $221,900 in 2006 sparked a nationwide spurt in house-building.

In the three years leading up to 9/11 and after 26 years of deficits that had flooded the world economy with dollars, the United States under Bill Clinton actually managed to produce surpluses. President George W. Bush's sweeping tax cuts in June 2001, in the wake of the dot-com collapse of the year before and the recession, changed all of that. A combination of the tax cuts and the wars in Afghanistan and Iraq saw the deficit zoom up to $1 trillion with big surplus countries like China and Japan soaking up the excess dollars. The dollar is the world's reserve currency; as a result, when the US runs a budget deficit there is no shortage of other nations, banks and financial institutions (such as pension funds) willing to buy US Treasury securities, denominated in dollars, and hold them as capital or make them work by lending them on. The recycling of these huge dollar reserves through the global banking system left the world awash with cheap credit. It also created global imbalances with big exporting nations like China, Japan and Germany in surplus, because of domestic restraint on consumption, at a time when the US continued to create dollars.

Cheap credit, light regulation and a housing boom that extended to less well off members of society offered a new and potentially very profitable avenue for Wall Street to explore. Millions of mortgages were dished out, many catering to high-risk borrowers with sketchy credit histories. There were loans that required low documentation ('low doc') and some that needed no proof of income or credit history ('liar loans'). Other types of mortgage included 'jumbos' which, as their name suggests, were large loans, disproportionate to a borrower's income and house value. For the banks, all these mortgages involved fees, commissions and bonuses. Moreover they could then be packaged up into bundles and converted into securities.

Rubber-stamped by the credit agencies Standard & Poor's and Moody's, these securities were sold on to banks, insurers and pension funds around the world as suitable assets to be held on the balance sheet. Paradoxically, the shakier the basis of a security, the more attractive it looked: house buyers who were regarded as more likely to default on repayments were invariably signed up to mortgages that involved higher than usual interest rates. This false equation was accompanied by two other fundamental misconceptions. One was that most payments would be kept up, even though millions of the loans made were to inner-city and 'trailer-park' borrowers who lacked the means to keep up with instalments once the incentives of cheap borrowing costs for the first year or so had fallen away. The other was that property would continue to rise in value so that in those cases where people did default on debt their repayment shortfall would be met from the sale of the house they were forced to forfeit.

Another mistaken assumption was made by many of the experts watching the markets – including Alan Greenspan. They believed that because mortgage securities were so widely spread through the banking system the risk was evenly distributed, and that if the credit and housing bubble were to burst then the capacity of the system to absorb the impact would be far greater than had been the case in the past.

In reality, of course, this huge financial edifice of rotten mortgages, packaged mortgage-backed securities and insurance products – so-called credit default swaps – had been constructed on quicksand. Consequently when the losses on bad mortgages started to mount in 2007, they did so at an alarming rate and the markets froze over. In Britain Northern Rock, a retail bank that adopted an investment-banking culture by turning its mortgages on the homes of ordinary people into securities sold in America, suddenly found that it could no longer obtain loans in the money market. As its travails became apparent in late August there was a full run on the bank, followed by a rescue by the Bank of England and the government and eventual nationalisation.

There was scarcely a bank in the Western world that wasn't in some way exposed. From Citigroup in the US to Bankia in Spain, major institutions found themselves holding assets on their balance sheets that were all but worthless. To make a bad situation worse, when the US authorities decided to teach the dangerously overstretched Lehman Brothers a lesson in 2007 and allow it to go into Chapter 11 bankruptcy, a chain reaction of collapses was sparked that brought the global financial and economic system to a shuddering halt.

Banks are the lifeblood of the economy, acting as circulation systems for the cash pumped into the money markets by other financial players and governments. The collapse of Lehman led to mutual suspicion among banks and other financial players who now refused to lend to each other. The result was a catastrophic shortage of credit and a plunge in confidence that affected the whole global economy. Mortgage finance that had been so plentiful in the go-go years was all but non-existent as banks drew in their horns and refused to lend. Businesses stopped borrowing and investing and many small and medium-sized enterprises were plunged into despair and collapse as the banks stopped lending. Credit used to buy everything from fashion items to cars dried up, destroying activity across the economy. In Britain the onset of recession in the spring of 2009 saw output plunge by an astonishing 7.4 per cent from its peak. The Great Panic had transmogrified into the Great Recession.

If there was one bank that exemplified both many of the causes and most of the consequences of the recession, it was the Royal Bank of Scotland. Over three decades, the City of London and the financial services industry ballooned until the size of its assets reached 400 per cent of the UK's gross domestic product (GDP). Over the same period RBS grew from a provincial Edinburgh bank to being – briefly – the largest bank in the world with a balance sheet in 2007 worth £2 trillion. At this point in its history it employed more than a million people in the UK and around the world and contributed 13.9 per cent of all tax revenues, helping to pay for the new schools and hospitals in which the Labour government was investing so heavily.

RBS was led by the obsessive and fiercely bright Fred Goodwin who, up until 2007 at least, had enjoyed a glittering career. The first member of his family to go to college, he graduated from Glasgow University with a law degree, then went on to qualify as an accountant at Touche Ross. He achieved his first great success before he turned 30 – leading the administration of the collapsed Bank of Credit and Commerce International (regarded as one of the most complicated bank frauds in financial history) so successfully that he managed to restore close to 100p in the pound for creditors. It was an extraordinary achievement.

In 1995 he joined the small Scottish lender Clydesdale Bank as deputy chief executive, and soon earned the nickname Fred the Shred, as he cut back numbers in order to boost profits. Years later the FSA would describe him as a 'somewhat cold, analytical and unsympathetic figure'. Colleagues portrayed him far more harshly. One called him a 'sociopath'. Another said: 'Fred was your classic bully.' My own experience of him was of someone so confident in his own abilities he was deluded into thinking that everything he touched would turn to gold.

Those who had reservations about him early in his career, however, expressed them privately. At this point he was generally regarded as an outstanding leader, and few were surprised when in 1998 he was recruited by RBS chief executive Sir George Mathewson to be deputy chief executive. Within two years he had pulled off an impressively ambitious deal, triumphing over Edinburgh rival the Bank of Scotland in 2000 by buying NatWest for £21 billion. It was Britain's largest banking merger at the time.

In 2001 Mathewson became chairman, and at the age of 42 Goodwin took over as chief executive. Twelve months later Forbes voted him businessman of the year. But there were aspects of his leadership even then that were questionable. When he moved the bank from its old headquarters in the centre of historic Edinburgh to a new £350 million mini-village set in 100 acres of woodland on the site of a former psychiatric institution on the outskirts of the city in 2005, he secured for himself an office the size of a football field (after his departure it housed not just his successor Stephen Hester but also the bank's new chairman Sir Philip Hampton, along with their staff – and there was still plenty of room to spare). He also personally oversaw the location of the directors' kitchen to ensure that scallops, a great culinary favourite of his, could be delivered to his desk with precision timing that would prevent them spoiling.

There were other signs of hubris, too. Under his stewardship the bank ran 12 chauffeur-driven Mercedes S-class cars, which Goodwin ordered to be spray-painted Pantone 281 so that they would precisely match the RBS corporate blue. Their beige leather interiors were selected to match exactly the colour of the carpets in the management offices in the new headquarters. The vehicles were stamped throughout – down to the gear lever knobs – with the RBS logo, making the fleet virtually unsellable, except for oddball souvenir hunters, when Stephen Hester took over the controls in late 2008. And then there was the bank's £18 million Falcon 900EX jet – registration G-RBSG. Insiders joked that the letters stood for Royal Bank of Scotland Goodwin.

The chief executive proved a freakish stickler for details that other senior executives found baffling. He hated mess of any kind. Noticing that staff often piled papers on the flat tops of filing cabinets in RBS offices, he ordered thousands of filing cabinets with rounded tops to discourage the practice. He disliked the use of Sellotape in public areas of the bank and banned it. On the surface everything was shiny and new. Underneath there was a lack of substance. It was perhaps more than a little symbolic that the sparkling new headquarters should have been sited rather close to the local pig farms. From certain directions the wind around the offices carried more than a hint of manure.

My own impression of him, garnered over a lunch at RBS's Bishopsgate headquarters in the City in the summer of 2008, was not a favourable one. He was all too eager to tell me all about his hotel suite at the Savoy and the efficient valet service that cleaned and pressed his clothes. When it came to business matters, he airily swept aside any views that ran counter to his own. I found such confidence disconcerting.

Others, though, were wooed by it. Above all, many bought Goodwin's claim that he had smoothly managed to integrate the bank's IT and other systems. In reality, it seems that Goodwin was more interested in the hygiene of branches than with modern IT data management. The result of his neglect of the backbone of well-run banking enterprises was the meltdown of RBS's IT systems a decade later, in July 2012, leaving millions of customers unable to access their own money.

Goodwin bragged to journalists and analysts that he was not interested in 'mercy killings' of Britain's weak mutual financial sector. Instead, RBS started to look across the Atlantic, buying US bank Charter One for £5.9 billion in 2004 and adding it to the Citizens network being built by Goodwin's American counterpart, the ambitious Larry Fish. In a few short years he completed 25 takeovers on both sides of the Atlantic.

His rationale was a simple one: his bank had to be a player in the global banking premier league, a league that included New York's Citigroup and JPMorgan Chase, Spain's Santander and Britain's HSBC (the dominant bank in Hong Kong and across the Pacific region). And to be a player, not only did it need to be big, but it also needed to be a universal bank. That early takeover of NatWest had given Goodwin a huge retail franchise in the United Kingdom. The bank's control of Greenwich Capital based in Stamford, Connecticut, took it into the investment arena. It built up a US retail business and also bought into insurance, commodity trading and leasing activities. In Britain the deals occurred at a similarly frantic speed. Goodwin took full control, for example, of general insurers Direct Line and Churchill, founded by the insurance genius Peter Wood, and invested heavily in railway rolling-stock leasing firms.

On the surface, all seemed to be well, so it did not come as much of a surprise to most people when in 2004 Goodwin was knighted for services to banking (this was in no small measure due to his good relationship with Chancellor Gordon Brown). True, even when the going was good, occasional concerns were aired. Dresdner Kleinwort Wasserstein analyst James Eden, for example, voiced some investors' worries directly to Goodwin at a presentation in August 2005, telling the seemingly invulnerable chief executive: 'I think there's a perception among some investors that Fred Goodwin is a megalomaniac who pursues size over shareholder value.' But while Goodwin, having initially brushed such criticisms away, did then promise to slow down, ultimately nothing changed. He had never seen a deal he did not like and could not bear the prospect of letting one of his rivals' banks steal a perceived prize from under his nose. The Bank of Scotland's offer for NatWest had led him to outbid his own bank's ancient Edinburgh rival in 2000, and he was similarly determined to prevent Barclays, with its strong overseas experience and fast-growing investment bank Barclays Capital (BarCap), from becoming ever more powerful. The macho competitive instinct kicked in and he was back in the race again.

In 2007 Barclays' patrician chief executive John Varley and the brash American president of the bank, Bob Diamond, had set their cap at buying the underperforming Dutch bank ABN Amro. Barclays was even ready to abandon its Canary Wharf headquarters for Amsterdam and discard its famed Germanic-style eagle logo to satisfy the sensibilities of its Dutch counterparts.

At first it appeared that Goodwin was nothing more than an interested spectator. The deal-maker in him, however, viewed ABN Amro as offering a huge potential leap forward that would expand RBS investment-banking activity and take it into the fast-growing Asian markets for the first time. Soon his powerful communications chief and fixer Howard Moody was softening up the media and analytical community with hints that the RBS boss was ready to pull off the deal of a lifetime. Meanwhile, in the background, Goodwin lined up a consortium made up of RBS, Spain's Santander and Dutch–Belgian Fortis. Then, together, they lodged a £55 billion bid for ABN Amro. It was a price that friendly bidder Barclays could not

43

match, and with regrets and some recriminations Barclays retreated.

The deal could not have been more badly timed or ill-designed for RBS investors and the safety of the bank. By the autumn of 2007 Northern Rock had gone to the wall. In the US the first reverberations of the sub-prime crisis were being felt as HSBC, owner of trailer-park lender Household, set aside £1.75 billion against future losses. The credit markets were beginning to tighten. Yet, remarkably, the RBS takeover of ABN Amro was nodded through by Britain's regulator, the Financial Services Authority, and was duly completed in October. Former FSA chief executive Hector Sants felt that there was considerable political enthusiasm for the deal. 'The various correspondence between Downing Street and the chair of the FSA shows that the FSA was under pressure not to take a more proactive approach,' he later recalled.

By the spring of 2008, however, the FSA had recognised that if banking tragedy was to be averted it needed to be much more aggressive. Sants instructed a listing RBS and a weak HBOS 'to raise as much capital as they could'. Fred Goodwin's RBS went cap in hand to investors to raise £12 billion to plug holes in its balance sheet. It was the largest rights issue in UK corporate history at that time. Goodwin had to swallow his pride and personally call on critical investors like the Prudential, asking them to subscribe to the rights issue. He was as persuasive as ever and investors felt they had little option but to respond positively.

Even with this £12 billion in its back pocket the bank's capital was too thin, its cash resources pitiful and the ratio of lending to deposits and reserves off the scale. As shock waves from Lehman Brothers' collapse reverberated around the world in September 2008 and the credit markets froze, RBS found it could no longer fund its most basic day-to-day operations. In an emergency measure, designed to prevent the hole-in-the-wall cash machines from seizing up, Bank of England governor Mervyn King ordered a secret injection of £61.6 billion into RBS and HBOS to keep the two banks in business. The emergency loans bought time for the government as it pieced together a £46 billion capital injection at RBS that would leave taxpayers owning 82 per cent of the struggling institution. Even so, the situation at the end of 2008 was grim. The bank posted an operational loss of £40.7 billion, the largest ever recorded by a UK enterprise, and recorded hits on a range of assets including its US sub-prime housing loans; in some cases, it was noted, these were virtually worthless.

At the time those keen to defend the bank were at pains to point out that many of its woes were due to global circumstances beyond its control; indeed, the credit crunch had taken the whole financial sector by surprise. The findings of an FSA investigation into the failure of RBS published in December 2011, though, were clear about the extent to which blame attached to the bank.

The report kept personal criticism of Fred Goodwin and his fellow executives to a minimum, after challenges by the former chief executive's high powered City legal team, but pointed out that RBS's capital base had been too low when the crisis hit – by some £166 billion. It also found that RBS was desperately reliant on short-term funding obtained in the money markets as opposed to the safer funds it acquired from depositors. RBS, through its investment bank, had dealt heavily in sub-prime debt, something of which other financial institutions had been aware at the time. Goldman Sachs had even gone so far as to target it as a customer for a package of toxic debt created for another client, the US hedge-fund trader John Paulson. The so-called 'Abacus' deal led to Goldman being fined $550 million in September 2009 by its own regulator, the Securities and Exchange Commission (SEC).

But it was the ABN Amro deal, above all, that had pushed RBS over the brink; it soon became apparent that, as later with the Co-op Bank and its dashes for growth, RBS had been both overconfident and insufficiently rigorous. The FSA report found that because Barclays had withdrawn from the ABN Amro deal the transaction had ceased to be considered a contested takeover and that, consequently, the Dutch bank had not had to open its books to the RBS-led consortium. Indeed, according to the FSA, all that RBS had in its possession on ABN were 'two lever arch files and information contained on a CD'. RBS did in fact do its own research and sent senior staff to Amsterdam to find out more, but, given the size of the transaction, it has to be said that this was 'due diligence' at its most cursory. Consequently it was only when the deal was actually done that the vast problems, many of them concerned with ABN Amro's own US sub-prime mortgage investments, were revealed.

Goodwin and the board were used to takeovers and confident that they could work on limited due diligence. Johnny Cameron, head of RBS's investment-banking arm Global Banking Markets, a trusted right-hand man of Goodwin's and widely seen as his successor, later said of the ABN Amro deal:

> One of the things that went wrong for RBS was that, and I say this to many people, we bought NatWest as a hostile acquisition. We did no due diligence. We couldn't because it was hostile. After we bought NatWest, we had lots of surprises, but almost all of them were pleasant. I think that lulled us into a sense of complacency around that. The fact is that the acquisition of ABN was also hostile. There's this issue of did we do sufficient due diligence? Absolutely not.

To make matters worse, RBS was the lead partner in the consortium even though it was responsible for buying only 38.5

per cent of ABN Amro. This meant that it had to hold the whole of the deal on a balance sheet that was already stretched thin for several months during the crisis until the Dutch bank was broken up among its partners. Its debt problems were thus considerable when credit began to tighten. And ABN Amro was bought with debt rather than with shares, which further increased RBS's already heavy reliance on the short-term funding markets. 'Even without ABN Amro, RBS would have had significant problems; but ABN Amro made the situation much worse,' the FSA concluded in its detailed 452-page report.

It was a view shared by Sir Philip Hampton, the astringent former finance director of Lloyds TSB, who succeeded Sir Tom McKillop as chairman of RBS in February 2009. Hampton told the FSA: 'I don't think there can be any doubt that the key decision that led RBS to its difficulties was the acquisition of ABN Amro. That is the painful reality that we can now do nothing to change. With the benefit of hindsight it can now be seen as the wrong price, the wrong way to pay, at the wrong time and the wrong deal.'

RBS's strategic failings over ABN Amro were made possible – and made worse – by management failings. The FSA found that the board, chaired at the time of its collapse by Tom McKillop, the former chief executive of drug company AstraZeneca, had little banking experience. They had not committed any offences, but their 'poor decisions' had caused the bank to end up being severely undercapitalised.

Above all, their lack of experience meant that they never formed an adequate counterweight to the ambitious Goodwin. In the process of its inquiry the FSA interviewed a number of non-executive directors who acknowledged that Goodwin had rarely been challenged in his decision-making. 'Given the CEO's excellent grasp of detail and skill in forensic analysis, it was sometimes difficult to raise more general questions or concerns that were not readily supported by detailed, objective facts and evidence,' they told the regulator. Questionable business opportunities resting on questionable foundations thus had a habit of becoming realities. And because a culture of bullishness existed, it tended to spread to all corners of the bank. The decision to buy ABN Amro was passed by 94.5 per cent of voting shareholders.

Goodwin's ultimate fall from grace is well documented. When RBS was rescued by the taxpayer and he was forced out, he walked away from RBS with a £16 million pension pot that paid £700,000 a year. In the heat of the crisis the City Minister Lord (Paul) Myners had neglected to check Goodwin's pension arrangements and the RBS board, headed by McKillop, placed no financial obstacles in his way. Myners subsequently sought to persuade Goodwin to forgo some of his pension out of a sense of propriety. The RBS banker refused, insisting on his full contractual rights. It was only after a public outcry and protracted negotiations with his lawyers that he agreed to cut his pension in half (after first taking out a £2.7 million lump sum). Goodwin offered a muted public apology, but reasoned that like many banks around the world, RBS was the victim of unforeseen events.

Goodwin's private life became public property. His 23-year marriage to Joyce, with whom he has two children, came under pressure in 2011 after an earlier affair with a senior member of staff looked set to be exposed in the press. His efforts to keep the affair secret, via a super-injunction, failed after an MP revealed her name in Parliament.

But the Goodwin case ultimately demonstrates how difficult it was – and remains – to bring erring bankers to book. Several investor groups have mounted court cases against Goodwin and the bank because they claim they were misled about RBS's finances. A class action brought by US investors was, however, thrown out by a New York judge in 2012. In April 2013 an RBS Shareholders Action Group brought a case in London similarly claiming that there had been misinformation about the 2008 rights issue of £12 billion and demanding £4.5 billion in damages. Manchester Business School senior lecturer Ismail Erturk is sceptical about their claims:

> This is an opportunistic move by a coalition of shareholders that belatedly tries to shift the blame for the RBS failure to everyone but themselves. I do not think anyone but lawyers will benefit from this and shareholders should have done their jobs to a higher standard before RBS collapsed.

In January 2010, on his return to Edinburgh after a spell at his villa in the south of France, Goodwin landed a job as a globetrotting consultant to the architecture and engineering practice RMJM. He was subsequently quietly dropped. He now lives alone in Edinburgh, occupying himself with shooting and playing golf. Ultimately, the worst to happen to him came in January 2012, when the *London Gazette* announced that because he had brought the honours system into disrepute he would forfeit his knighthood.

Of all those involved in the RBS debacle only Johnny Cameron, Goodwin's loyal lieutenant, really had to face the music. As head of the group's investment bank he oversaw £10.5 billion of losses in 2008 alone, a quarter of the group's losses that year. He left RBS in January 2009 and then made a number of attempts to return to work. The FSA, however, blocked talks when he sought to take up an advisory role with Greenhill, a boutique bank in London.

In September 2009 he took up a role at headhunter Odgers Berndtson, only to resign days later when UK Financial Investments, the government body that manages the taxpayer's stake in the country's banks (including RBS), citing its majority stake in Cameron's former employer as a conflict, withdrew its business from Odgers. In 2010 he joined Gleacher Shacklock, a privately owned investment bank in London, as a consultant; the post was approved by the FSA, with whom he struck a deal in May of that year never to work in the regulated financial sector again.

The Royal Bank of Scotland is far from being the only British bank where management ambitions of greatness have overwhelmed the ultimate interests of investors, consumers and the majority of the workforce. HBOS, the bank carved out of the £30 billion merger of the former Halifax Building Society and the Bank of Scotland in 2001, offers another forceful case of hubris getting the better of prudence. Indeed, in some respects, its fall from grace is even more shocking in terms of the circumstances and decisions that finally led to disaster.

When the Bank of Scotland proved to be the underbidder to RBS for control of NatWest in 2000, the bank's chief executive Sir Peter Burt, a financier who exuded traditional banking values, but who also believed that the larger the bank the better, was drawn into a friendly deal with the Halifax. Under the merged group's first chief executive Sir James Crosby, a trained actuary who had led the Halifax, the bank set its sights on rapid growth. Over time Burt faded into the background as deputy chairman of HBOS and governor of the Bank of Scotland. Crosby, for his part, was succeeded as chief executive in 2006 by his hand-picked choice for the role, former Asda executive Andy Hornby, aged just 38 years.

Hornby, an Oxford English graduate with an MBA from Harvard, began his business career at the cement maker Blue Circle. He then switched to the supermarket Asda, which at that time boasted an impressive roster of managers mentored by chief executive Allan

Leighton. In 1999 he joined the Halifax, candidly admitting: 'I don't pretend to know about pricing products.' Over the next seven years he worked his way up the corporate ladder, before taking on the top job within the merged business.

The novice banker continued the group's high-growth strategy of lending at the risky end of the market, winning praise from the City as he did so. In 2006 analysts at Dresdner Kleinwort Wasserstein went so far as to say to investors: 'Andy Hornby is a superstar', adding: 'And he's good-looking.'

Guided first by Crosby and then by Hornby the bank embarked on a madcap dash for growth, snapping up wealth managers such as St James's Place, insurers Clerical Medical and leasing groups including Godfrey Davis and Lex Vehicle Hire. It was so desperate to expand that it even paid £83 million for 55 showrooms of the Irish Electricity Supply Board in 2005, believing it could convert them into suitable HBOS branches. Crosby and Hornby were ambitious to turn HBOS into a fifth force in British banking (along with RBS, Barclays, Lloyds and HSBC) and they appeared to countenance no limits to its expansion.

The bank increasingly came to rely on the short-term lending markets rather than on cash from depositors. In 2001 it borrowed £61 billion directly from the credit markets. By the end of 2008 this figure had leapt to £212.9 billion. When the money markets began to tighten in the summer of 2007, the writing was on the wall for a modest bank like HBOS and, in particular, for the Bank of Scotland, effectively the corporate banking arm of the larger organisation.

The Bank of Scotland had, to put it mildly, been expansive in its lending, opening its wallet to virtually every entrepreneur who walked through its doors. Some, like Sir Philip Green, the retail genius who turned Topshop owner Arcadia into a high-street success story, paid the bank back handsomely. But others were less grounded and cash poured out of the Bank of Scotland into reckless top-of-the-market property and care home deals that went horribly wrong. Even so, Peter Cummings, who headed the corporate lending arm under the Bank of Scotland rubric, remained confident until the last minute. As the financial system began to crack in 2007 under the weight of sub-prime and undisciplined lending he noted: 'Some people look as if they are losing their nerve, beginning to panic even in today's testing property market; not us.'

Just how appalling the state of the HBOS loan book had become when the credit crunch bit did not fully emerge until the Parliamentary Commission on Banking Standards reported in April 2013. Its study, the first serious analysis of the events leading to HBOS's implosion, concluded that the quality of the loans HBOS made were so bad it probably would have failed even without the financial crisis. To that extent therefore it 'was an accident waiting to happen'.

The Parliamentary Commission estimated losses on business loans that originated at HBOS as £25 billion, or 20 per cent of the bank's total loans in 2008. Losses in Ireland over the same period hit £10.9 billion, or 36 per cent of its loan book. The bank's treasury unit, traditionally a place for safe investments, lost £7.2 billion over this period.

Even at the time it was clear that HBOS was in such a parlous state, with its shares plunging so alarmingly towards zero, that it needed to seek a merger partner. Accordingly, in the autumn of 2008 Lloyds came into the frame, competition clearance for a deal having been arranged by Prime Minister Gordon Brown in a series of private conversations with Lloyds chairman Sir Victor Blank. It's a matter of speculation whether, had either the Prime Minister or his Chancellor Alistair Darling known the full extent of HBOS's travails, they would have been so keen to broker the deal. As it was, HBOS's toxic legacy infected its new partner to the extent that it threatened the very stability of Lloyds, arguably Britain's safest and best-capitalised bank.

The Parliamentary Commission was absolutely clear as to who was to blame for what went wrong at HBOS:

> It is right and proper that the primary responsibility for the downfall of HBOS should rest with Sir James Crosby, architect of the strategy that set the course for the disaster, with Andy Hornby, who proved unable or unwilling to change course, and Lord Stevenson, who presided over the bank's board from its birth to its death.

Sir James Crosby responded almost immediately to the Parliamentary Commission's excoriating findings. He returned his knighthood, pledged to forgo 30 per cent of his £580,000 HBOS pension and gave up his position as a non-executive at food-service group Compass. 'I have never sought to disassociate myself from what happened. I am deeply sorry for what happened at HBOS and the ensuing consequences.'

Hornby wanted to work on. Indeed, he had hoped to become deputy chief executive of the merged bank, a dream that was speedily dashed despite initial support from his new boss, the American Eric Daniels. There was an element of self-pity to the public statements he made: he pointed out, for example, that he had almost been wiped out by the collapse because so much of his income derived from HBOS shares.

Lord Stevenson, a left-leaning peer, was similarly unrepentant, keen at first to defend the actions of the bank. I still recall an angry confrontation with him in 2008 at a social event at the Tate Modern gallery in London after I had posed questions in my *Daily Mail* column about the high cost the bank was paying to raise funds on the global markets. Then he protested that the bank was entirely safe. Later he argued that the bank was a victim of circumstances outside its control.

'This was not an organisation that was obsessed by growth or had a culture of optimism,' he told the Parliamentary Commission. 'You can go through the history of any organisation and find decisions that look overambitious. If you go through HBOS, you will find quite a lot of decisions that were quite conservative.' Ultimately he paid a price for his time at HBOS. Previously he had served on the boards of many high-profile firms including broadcaster BSkyB and banker Lazard Brothers. He retained a directorship at bookseller Waterstones.

As at RBS, one senior member of staff was held more severely to task, and at HBOS that person was Peter Cummings, head of the group's corporate unit. In September 2012 he was fined £500,000 by the FSA and banned from working in financial services for life for his role in the collapse. His division had racked up £25 billion of losses at the bank between 2008 and 2011. Instead of exercising caution going into the crisis he accelerated lending. In 2007, the year Northern Rock imploded, he grew the corporate loan book by 22 per cent; in 2008 it expanded by 12 per cent. It was this unchecked recklessness that attracted the opprobrium of the regulators.

'Despite being aware of the weaknesses in his division and growing problems in the economy,' said Tracey McDermott, director of enforcement and financial crime at the FSA, 'Cummings presided over a culture of aggressive growth without the controls in place to manage the risks associated with that strategy. Instead of reacting to the worsening environment, he raised his targets as other banks pulled out of the same markets.'

Cummings accused the FSA – not without some justice – of targeting him to mask its own failings in regulating UK banks during the crisis. 'We are not the only failed bank,' he pointed out.

'There are at least four or five of them, and I find it curious that I was singled out. So someone, somewhere decided that was the appropriate action. I think it is sinister and curious.'

Britain's banking system in 2008 and 2009 resembled a battlefield littered with the wounded and fallen. RBS and HBOS were the most notable victims. But along the way a number of smaller institutions, including buy-to-let lender Bradford & Bingley, Alliance & Leicester and the Dunfermline Building Society, all but vanished from the nation's high streets. No bank was spared. Barclays would turn to the Middle East for a bailout, a choice that would leave a stain on its reputation. HSBC would be scarred for years by its investment in trailer-park lender Household, which would gobble up billions of pounds of shareholders' funds.

Ironically, one of the cures proffered for the catastrophe of 2007–9 was more of the medicine that had helped to cause it. Interest rates were again cut to the quick, this time to the lowest level in history – zero to 0.25 per cent in the US and 0.5 per cent in Britain – and these super-low interest-rate regimes were accompanied by large-scale quantitative easing to free up the market and get money flowing again.[1] Such was the scale of the meltdown, however, that the two measures in themselves proved insufficient to fix the problem. Large-scale intervention by governments, central banks and regulators therefore became a regular and necessary event. And it was the complex interplay between bankers and the authorities over the next few years that was to shape the developing economic landscape, and the next phase of the banking crisis.

[1] Quantitative easing is a process by which central banks buy in government-issued debt and other assets, such as mortgage securities, in exchange for cash. The cash manufactured is then washed back into banking system to keep financial institutions afloat and to provide funds for companies and individuals seeking to rebuild their balance sheets.

# 3

# International Rescue: The Anglo-Saxon Response

Such was the magnitude of the banking crisis of 2007 and 2008, and such was the rapidity with which it spread from one institution to another, that central banks were taken largely by surprise. Initial official responses were therefore often uncertain and sometimes unhelpful. In the early days, for example, Mervyn King, governor of the Bank of England, decided to play hardball. The Bank, he said, would offer help only to institutions that ran short of cash overnight – and it would punish their recklessness by charging them a penal rate of interest. It soon became evident, however, that such a tough stance threatened to be counterproductive. It increased jittery nerves rather than calming them. When in the summer of 2007 Barclays, one of Britain's best-capitalised and strongest banks, asked the Bank of England for a £1.6 billion overnight loan – a demand that, normally, would have gone unquestioned – it found itself interrogated about its long-term stability. This was the very opposite of what the situation required.

Gradually, though, a way forward was found, and to a large extent it was one that was pioneered by the British government and the Bank of England. Essentially it involved restoring confidence in the markets at virtually any cost, amid concerns that failure to act could have grave repercussions for the future of the City as a financial centre and the value of sterling on international currency markets. In 2007 Mervyn King contemplated letting Northern Rock go to the wall. In 2008, following the collapse of Lehman Brothers and the turmoil that ensued as banks around the world discovered that short-term funds were being withdrawn by other banks, King ordered that some £61.6 billion of covert cash be pumped into two of Britain's biggest lenders, the Royal Bank of Scotland and HBOS (Halifax Bank of Scotland), whose automated teller machines (ATMs) had come within hours of freezing up. This time there was no hesitation. The Old Lady of Threadneedle Street was doing what central banks need to do in times of crisis: it was acting as 'lender of the last resort'.

The subsequent fate of HBOS illustrates the determination of the authorities to keep individual banks going at all costs. In the autumn of 2008, following a series of private and informal conversations between Prime Minister Gordon Brown and the chairman of Lloyds TSB, City veteran Sir Victor Blank, the way was opened for Britain's safest bank, Lloyds, to take over the beleaguered bank. Coming just four days after the Lehman receivership, the news of the £12.2 billion rescue plan was an enormous relief to many. Not that the deal was without controversy. Strictly speaking, Brown and Blank's private conversation should never have taken place, given that what they proposed would give Lloyds such a dominant position in the mortgage and current account markets. Unsurprisingly, perhaps, the chairman of the Competition Commission[1], Peter Freeman, was privately indignant that tough new competition laws, inaugurated by none other than Brown himself, were bulldozed aside. Immediate political expediency had arguably overridden banking common sense in this instance.

[1] Superseded in 2013 by the Competition and Markets Authority.

In several conversations with me, Blank made it clear that, at the Lloyds end of the transaction, the HBOS merger had not been his idea alone; indeed, there is a trail of documents within the bank showing that the American chief executive of Lloyds, Eric Daniels, had long been in favour of such an alliance. At the time the merger was done it was 'the only option' for HBOS and eventually the taxpayer would make 'many billions of pounds' when the 41 per cent government stake was sold down.

It was left to Daniels to sort out the poisonous HBOS legacy. He set about his task firmly, reshaping the IT system, shedding staff and branches and simplifying the business. But the smooth, very formal American, with a penchant for handmade coloured shirts with white collars and cuffs, was never a favourite among his new Treasury masters. His smooth manner earned him the nickname of 'the salamander' among officials who were aching to see the back of him. In September 2010 Daniels, under some pressure, announced his departure. He would be replaced by Portuguese-born Santander executive Antonio Horta-Osorio.

Ultimately the HBOS deal was a rather mend-and-make-do affair, but it did also signal indications of a more joined-up approach. On the day it was announced I happened to be having a sandwich lunch with Alistair Darling at the Treasury, and while I could see that the Chancellor and his advisers were relieved that HBOS was not going to end up in administration, I could also sense that they knew that this piecemeal approach was a short-term fix. The problems of Northern Rock, Alliance & Leicester and HBOS had been sorted out in immediate terms, but it was apparent that a radical restructuring would be necessary to restore confidence in the high-street banks and stabilise the markets. One senior official confided that he feared for the value of sterling on the foreign-currency markets unless decisive, holistic action to prop up the whole system was taken.

Mervyn King was determined that the Bank of England would be fully armed should a further crisis occur. In the summer of 2008 he and his team at the Bank therefore discussed best strategies and likely outcomes exhaustively with Prime Minister Gordon Brown at Number 10. Brown, like King, wanted to take a conceptual approach to the growing crisis in financial markets amid realisation that much of the sub-prime debt and other credit held by banks and other institutions was not worth the paper it was written on.

It was King's view that the biggest problem the banks faced was one of solvency, and that to resolve this they needed new capital. The team in the financial stability arm of the Bank of England therefore set about producing numbers to estimate the capital shortage of the banking system. This required looking at the assets on each bank's balance sheets – such as housing loans – and estimating the amount of losses likely to be caused by a fall in house prices.

In effect the Bank of England was engaging in the first set of stress tests of the banking system; at the end of the process King and his officials at the Bank sent memos and papers to Number 10 setting out what they thought to be the scale of the problem. The figures were eye-watering. The Bank's estimate of the requirement was almost twice the figure of £50 billion announced by Chancellor Alistair Darling on 8 October 2008 and far bigger than those being discussed in preliminary talks between the banks and the Treasury. The Bank also proposed to make £200 billion available in short-term loans via the special liquidity scheme, under which the Bank took mortgages as security for cash injections. It also made a temporary offer of guarantees of up to £250 billion to British banks lending to each other. The guarantee was intended to restart lending in the money markets where banks provide short-term facilities to each other. Shadow Chancellor George Osborne described it as 'the final chapter in the age of irresponsibility'. Darling, on the other hand, told the House of Commons that the UK plan 'led the way' for other nations.

When Darling, King and other senior officials arrived in Washington a few days later for the annual meeting of the International Monetary Fund, the Americans showed extraordinary interest in the British approach to the crisis. King found himself giving unrehearsed explanations to key US officials at the Treasury and the Federal Reserve, America's central bank.

Speaking privately to a group of British financial journalists in Washington, King let slip that in his view the bailout plan might not have been adequate and the UK government might eventually have to take several of the banks fully into public ownership. Under the Darling–Brown rescue the government had acquired a 43.3 per cent stake in Lloyds and an 84 per cent holding in the badly holed Royal Bank of Scotland. So excited was the reporter from *The Times* at this piece of intelligence that the information temporarily leaked onto the paper's website, causing a short period of new havoc on the financial markets, before the report was taken down after urgent requests from Bank of England officials.

Despite this hiccup the UK approach did seem to the US authorities to present a feasible way forward, for they, like their British counterparts, were rather feeling their way through the crisis. Initially, in early August 2007, Ben Bernanke, chairman of the Federal Reserve, had sought to calm the markets by offering exceptional funds to banks that were hurting. Then, in the middle of that month, he had given in to market pressure and, in a dramatic act seen by his critics as a policy switch, had cut the 'discount rate' (at which banks can borrow directly from the Fed) by half a point to 5.75 per cent. It was the first time since 9/11 that the American central bank had acted to cut either of its key interest rates between scheduled meetings.

A year later, with no end in sight to the financial crisis, the US Treasury Secretary Hank Paulson, a no-nonsense former chairman of investment bankers Goldman Sachs, took action. He unveiled details on 19 September of a $700 billion facility to rescue America's financial system. President George W. Bush declared it was a 'pivotal moment' for the United States. 'America's economy is facing unprecedented challenges, and we are responding with unprecedented action,' Bush declared at the White House.

By the terms of the initial Bush–Paulson blueprint, known as the Troubled Asset Relief Program (TARP), the Federal Reserve would assist in removing rotten sub-prime mortgage assets from the balance sheets of American financial companies in exchange for cash. The bad assets would be held by a new independent financial organisation, allowing credit markets to return to normal. The shape of the scheme was modelled on one deployed by President Bush senior in the 1980s when he launched a bailout for an overextended Savings & Loans industry.

At the same time the US authorities offered a $50 billion insurance guarantee to money-market based mutual funds, the equivalent of the UK's unit trusts and ISAs, which had suffered a catastrophic haemorrhaging of funds. TARP was intended to stand alongside the $200 billion that the US government had already made available to the mortgage intermediaries Fannie Mae and Freddie Mac. Earlier in the month it had injected $80 billion of cash into the credit insurer AIG (American International Group).

Announcing the TARP plan was simple enough, but persuading a reluctant Congress to translate it into legislation and getting the banks to use it would prove far more difficult. Hank Paulson's sketchy presentation to the House of Representatives on how the plan would work failed to impress. On 29 September 2008 the House rejected Bush's bailout package amid carnage on the financial markets. The

Dow Jones Industrial Average suffered its worst loss in history, with $1.2 trillion of values wiped off American stock markets and the Dow closing 7 per cent down on the day. For a few brief hours it looked as if capitalism – or at least capitalism as the West knew it – was coming to an abrupt end.

The markets had spoken. Congress capitulated after Paulson and Fed chairman Ben Bernanke returned to Capitol Hill with a more detailed plan and dire warning of the consequences of a further rejection. And a few days later, on 3 October 2008, the Emergency Economic Stabilization bill, which established TARP, was finally passed. However, Wall Street remained unconvinced that the rescue plan was either adequate or practicable and the Dow Jones weakened by a further 1.5 per cent. The condition of credit markets was precarious, and when Citigroup found it lacked the wherewithal to rescue North Carolina-based Wachovia Bank on 9 October 2008, causing the Dow to lurch down a further 7.8 per cent, US officials decided they needed more radical solutions if the banking system was to be stabilised.

This was the state of affairs when Paulson and Bernanke first heard from Alistair Darling and Mervyn King about the recapitalisation approach taken in Britain, at the fringes of the International Monetary Fund's annual meeting. They seized on the idea and on 13 October, just ten days after the original TARP bill had been passed, the federal authorities announced that they were changing direction. President Bush and his Treasury Secretary Paulson declared that the US government would be buying stakes, in the form of preferred stock and warrants (a right to buy ordinary shares), in all the major Wall Street houses.

The approach adopted by the American authorities was a firm and undeviating one. Simply put, they decided to force-feed the banks with capital. By so doing they would both underpin their safety, in the eyes of the financial markets, and seek to ensure that normal service – in terms of lending – would be restored for homeowners amid record levels of foreclosures. Nine banks were essentially bullied into taking cash from Uncle Sam in exchange for preferred stock, a form of equity. Bank of America Merrill Lynch, JPMorgan Chase, Citigroup and San Francisco-based Wells Fargo, a bank with few problems, were each required to accept a $25 billion injection of capital.

Goldman Sachs, which had already negotiated a $10 billion influx of capital from the legendary investor Warren Buffett, was now required to accept the government as a shareholder as well, taking a further $10 billion in capital. New York rival Morgan Stanley also received $10 billion, while a smaller sum of $3 billion was injected into Bank of New York Mellon and a further $2 billion into State Street. Having secured the stability of the biggest commercial and investment banks Paulson made it clear that there were further sums available, should they be required, to keep smaller institutions afloat.

By insisting that the American banks take government funds the US Treasury made sure that side deals by the banks with foreign governments and banks would be curtailed. Morgan Stanley, for instance, had sought an investment from China Investment Corporation, Beijing's sovereign wealth fund, before securing funds from Bank of Tokyo-Mitsubishi. In the battle to survive the New York banks had been searching far and wide in the Middle East and Asia for new investors.

The US administration also gave itself a voice in the way banks behaved. It's interesting to note that when push came to shove the capitalist US government, red in tooth and claw, was fully prepared to take enterprises into part-public ownership. After all, it had already acquired full ownership of Fannie Mae and Freddie Mac and the majority of shares in AIG, propped up nine Wall Street banks and guaranteed tens of billions of money-market funds.

On top of all this, the Federal Reserve provided direct financial assistance to one of America's biggest corporations, General Electric, which has a large financial arm. As the recession deepened in the spring of 2009 the new administration of Barack Obama nationalised General Motors, the manufacturing group that perhaps most symbolised American power (a former chief executive, Charlie Wilson, who went on to become US Defence Secretary, had famously told Congress in 1953: 'What is good for the country is good for General Motors and vice versa'). In the Great Panic of 2008 and the slump that followed the US came to regard public ownership and part-public ownership as comparable to the intensive-care unit in a hospital. As one senior central banker would comment, the Americans were 'on the front foot on recapitalisation'. Moreover, they swiftly moved to follow up the rescue with stress tests designed to see if the banks had enough capital to be fit for purpose or would need to return to the governments or markets for more.

The radical Bush–Paulson recapitalisation plan did the job of restoring stability to the financial system. It also encouraged the US banks to recognise fully their bad loans in super-quick time, restore their balance sheets and resume lending – and so get the government off their backs. They were helped by the fact that the politics were very simple. Neither the Republicans who rescued the banks nor the Democrats who took control of the White House in 2009 felt it was a good idea for the government to be running Wall Street: if the banks didn't want central government to be there any longer than was needed, the feeling was reciprocal. The economics were also relatively straightforward, certainly in comparison with the UK. While the financial sector in Britain was worth an eye-watering 400 per cent of gross domestic product (GDP), the value of the US banking system was a rather healthier 80 per cent. Replacing government capital with private capital over time in the US was therefore a rather easier proposition than it was to be in the UK.

It became a badge of honour for banks to repay the government debt as quickly as possible, and simultaneously show they could obtain capital in the markets and operate without the government looking over their shoulder. Goldman Sachs was among the first to slip back fully into the private sector, repaying the $10 billion of government equity in April 2009 when the world was still deeply in recession. JPMorgan Chase restored $13 billion to the government in November 2009. Citigroup, one of the banks most weighed down by bad debts as a result of the sub-prime mortgage crisis, paid back its $20 billion of federal capital in December of 2009.

Even more remarkably, the US government began the process of returning American International Group, the biggest firm nationalised during the Great Panic, to the public markets in May 2011. In its determination to restore a degree of normality the Treasury's stake was cut from 92 per cent to 77 per cent, with the government initially taking a loss. It regarded it as more important to re-establish a market in the shares of the big insurer, the largest creator of the credit default swaps at the heart of the financial crisis, than to court public-relations success. By March 2012 the free-float price of AIG shares had risen to above the price at which the group had been taken into public ownership and the US stake had been brought down from 77 per cent to 70 per cent.

The decision to take a loss on the early share sale paid off handsomely. In December 2012, four years after the taxpayer bailout, AIG had been restored to health and the remaining 234 million shares were sold back to the market at a price of $32.50, raising $7 billion. Instead of being out of pocket the taxpayer had actually made a gain on its AIG stake of $22.7 billion. The policy of starting the share sales at a loss but continuing to sell at ever higher prices was a triumph. The profit made amounted to more than the whole budget of the US Department of Agriculture and was ten times the annual cost of the Food & Drug Administration.

Even General Motors was able to begin its return to the public markets in November 2010; with shares going to an immediate premium, President Barack Obama, who had taken the company into state control, was able to claim that American taxpayers were now in a position to recover more than his administration had invested in GM. As for the two mortgage intermediaries Fannie May and Freddie Mac, which had been at the centre of the sub-prime crisis and which had been taken into 'conservatorship' by the Bush administration in September 2008 at a cost of $187.5 billion: they were able in March 2014 to pay back every cent to the US government. Both outfits were now in profit, their shares soaring 24 times to yield a potential profit in the billions of dollars for hedge fund Perry Capital, headed by Todd Westhaus, which bought preferred shares when they were just 2 cents apiece.

The coup was likened by the financial news service Bloomberg to the profits made by George Soros on the devaluation of the pound sterling in 1992 and the wager that hedge-fund manager John Paulson made on sub-prime debt in the heat of the financial crisis, which yielded him profits estimated at $15 billion. Remarkably, Fannie and Freddie had been brought back from the dead and the near-worthless preferred shares, remaining in private ownership, rose 1,800 per cent in the period from February 2013 to March 2014. Legislation to reshape Fannie and Freddie, and to decide whether the semi-government agencies should be fully in the private sector, is not seen as likely to happen until 2017.

There's no doubt that the restoration of the financial sector in the US was made a good deal easier by the fundamental resilience of the economy. For the majority of Americans the worst of the recession may have been sharp but it was also relatively short-lived. Massive infusions of cash into the financial system by the Federal Reserve ensured that in the course of 2010 signs of recovery started to appear. The UK, by contrast, had to wait until 2013 for growth in the economy to manifest itself, and even then output lagged behind its pre-recession peak. Over-reliance on the financial sector, and the impact of the eurozone crisis of 2011–12 on Britain's trade with its biggest partner, cast a long shadow.

The American approach to the financial crisis was also permeated by a single-minded can-do spirit that helped to sweep the country back to relative economic health. While other countries dithered – or, in the case of the UK, held endless inquiries – the US authorities just got on with it. They knew that restoring the health of the financial system and of manufacturing was the number one priority, and if that meant stretching the federal balance sheet for a while, then so be it.

It was only when the banks were fully restored to the public markets after 2012 that the US authorities began the process of punishing the banks and financial institutions for their mistakes. In January 2013, for example, Bank of America Merrill Lynch agreed to pay the government $11.6 billion in penalties relating to mortgage transactions it had conducted with intermediary Fannie Mae. Withholding punishment until such time as the banks were strong enough to take the pain was a shrewd move. Retribution may have come too slowly for some critics, but it did come eventually, nevertheless, and at a time when offenders could afford to pay.

Although the US approach was inspired in part by what the UK had been doing, the two countries did not always work as one on the crisis. There was, for example, a very bad-tempered spat over the fate of Lehman Brothers. On a bright September afternoon in 2008 the US Treasury Secretary Hank Paulson put through a call to his opposite number in London, Alistair Darling, and requested that Barclays Bank, with its ambition to become a global leader in investment banking, be allowed to rescue Lehman. Darling consulted with colleagues at the Financial Services Authority and Bank of England who concurred with his view that it would be madness for a UK bank to rescue an American-based broker-dealer when no New York bank was willing to do so. Paulson seemed to think that permission from the British authorities was routine and responded with some industrial language when told of the decision, telling colleagues that he had been 'grin-fucked'. 'The British screwed us,' he would recall in his memoir *On the Brink*.

More importantly, from the point of view of the future well-being of the banking sector in the UK, the British authorities did not ultimately grasp the nettle in the way that their American counterparts did. The arch-capitalists of the US were prepared to countenance close intervention on the part of the state when it was deemed necessary. The more politically nervous British adopted a far more ad hoc approach. On the one hand, the government was prepared to pour money into the system to unfreeze the markets (almost a trillion pounds in all); on the other, it was reluctant to strong-arm individual banks. Gordon Brown had found it hard enough to take Northern Rock into public ownership, fearing that it would identify his party with a new era of nationalisation. As other crises arose, the government sought to find immediate, local solutions to them rather than build them into some overarching strategy, as the Americans were doing. It was a policy that Mervyn King felt was misguided: in his view the Chancellor Alistair Darling and his City Minister Lord Paul Myners were allowing the process to become one of negotiation between the authorities and the individual banks rather than regulation.

The result was that what in the US turned out to be a thoroughgoing recapitalisation scheme was never more than a partial one in the UK. Over at the Bank of England Mervyn King argued for an approach adopted by the Swedes in the 1990s whereby an independent group of experts, who actually had direct control over the banks, forced them to sort out their balance sheets and then brought the financial firms back into the private sector as quickly as possible. In an effort to weaken Gordon Brown's reliance on investment banks for advice King even invited a leading Swedish banking expert to London to speak to the Prime Minister. The conversation took place but it led nowhere.

In the case of the Royal Bank of Scotland, government unwillingness to get its hands too dirty meant that it dithered. Part of it wanted to believe the new chief executive Stephen Hester's initial assessment that RBS could trade its way out of difficulty. Another part felt that that was too good to be true. Hester thus found himself trying to drive a broken-down car while having to take account of nervous back-seat driving on the part of UK Financial Investments and the Treasury.

Hester is an interesting figure. Superficially, he looks like a hale and hearty country landowner, full of confidence in his own ability and with the accent of a public schoolboy. In fact he was actually educated at Easingwold School, a North Yorkshire comprehensive, before going on to take a first-class honours degree at Oxford. And while he may seem very confident, he is also sensitive to criticism. He felt wounded by 'fat cat' jibes made at bankers (though perhaps he was unwise, in late 2011, to conduct his negotiation with the government about the size of his bonus at the handsome ski chalet he owns at Verbier in Switzerland), and he heartily disliked a repeatedly used newspaper photograph of him on horseback in full hunting gear.

In his new role at RBS Hester's aim was a simple one: to achieve a 'standalone, AA[2] category risk profile and balance sheet'. He set it out in a private aide-memoire (provided to the author) and written, on a single sheet of paper on his arrival at the bank. Hester stated that a key to achieving this goal would be the 'creation and run-down of the non-core division'. This shrinkage, Hester argued, would 'narrow the stretch and scope of our core business'. A vital part of the plan was to be part of the government's 'Asset Protection Scheme' – its second bailout plan for injured banks – 'to give it the stability in the early years . . . to keep our capital ratios strong and to fund the Bank', the aide-memoire stated. If he could turn the ambitions, set out in his note, into reality it should allow 'the government to sell its shares at a profit'.

The remarkable thing about the Hester plan is that it recognised at the start of 2009 what a government review would recommend almost four years later, in November 2013, when it called for the creation of a 'bad bank' within RBS. Hester had essentially already created this with the non-core division, which was ruthless at jettisoning rotten assets. The job of sorting out the non-core and rotten assets was largely carried out by the bank's Global Restructuring Group headed by Derek Sach. His task was to try to recover whatever value he could for the bank. This sometimes meant forcing firms into administration or bankruptcy and where possible securing assets, such as property, for RBS. On other occasions big portfolios of loans were sold on to willing buyers at knock-down prices. The buyers

---

[2] The best financial institutions in the world (of which there are very few left) are 'AAA' rated. 'AA' at RBS would signal that its balance sheet was strong enough for the bank to return to the public markets and be of real interest to external investors, other than government.

believed that as the economy recovered so would some of these loan portfolios jettisoned by the taxpayer-owned bank. The GRG was regarded with such trepidation and suspicion by some of the firms put out of business that in November 2013 its activities would become the subject of probes by both the Serious Fraud Office and City regulators.

Hester also recognised from the start the underinvestment in technology that would so badly let him down in his mission to reconnect with RBS's traditional consumer, small business and corporate customers. The hopelessness of the bank's IT would be horribly exposed in June 2012 when payment systems at RBS and its NatWest and Ulster Bank offshoots packed up, leaving 12 million customers without access to their own money.

When Hester arrived at RBS it had one of the most bloated balance sheets in global banking, having expanded from £400 billion in 2001 to £2.2 trillion at its peak in 2008. The new chief executive set about cutting it with ruthless efficiency, reducing its size by £900 billion by the time he left office in 2013, and sacrificing 36,000 jobs along the way. He disposed of a series of enterprises including WorldPay, the bank's global payments system; RBS Aviation, its aircraft leasing unit; Sempra, its global commodities trading venture; Hoare Govett, the historic British stockbroker; and Direct Line, the general insurer. He showed prodigious energy in the way he tackled the task. But the problems kept on arriving: from Libor to PPI, from foreign-exchange trading to interest-rate swaps to small businesses. Worse of all, the bank's Irish subsidiary Ulster Bank posted a loss of £1.5 billion in 2013. The progress made by Hester in the limited time ultimately made available to him could not erase the mistakes of the past and the bank found itself running on the spot. In such circumstances it would have taken enormous political courage and willpower to sell down the enormous 84 per cent government stake in RBS and risk suffering a taxpayer loss.

If RBS operated with government injections of cash, other banks – notably Britain's two global banks HSBC and Standard Chartered – sought to keep their independence. Barclays was similarly desperate to remain free from government interference or control. Having successfully dodged a bullet in October 2007 when the bank had abandoned its pursuit of a £40 billion bid for ABN Amro, its chief executive John Varley together with his investment-banking chief Bob Diamond moved to secure the bank's financial health and independence by looking elsewhere for support.

Varley's motivation arose in part from a sense of family honour. The Oxford-educated lawyer is married to Carolyn Pease, a direct descendant of one of the Quaker founders of Barclays, and felt an obligation to preserve its heritage. Diamond had ambitions of a different order. He was determined that the hard work he had undertaken at BarCap, making it one of the most successful global investment banks, would not be wrenched away from him by the government.

The result was that rather than selling shares to the UK authorities, Barclays negotiated a £12 billion funding agreement with Middle East investors in Qatar and Abu Dhabi. The deals were brokered with the assistance of former Barclays investment banker and tax expert Roger Jenkins. The other high-profile go-between was the model-turned-financier Amanda Staveley, once an escort of Prince Andrew, the Duke of York.

Staveley's company PCP Capital Partners acted for Barclays in negotiating the £3.5 billion investment by Abu Dhabi's ruler HH Sheikh Mansour bin Zayed Al Nahyan, for which she earned a commission estimated at £40 million. Jenkins, for his part, was responsible for opening Qatar's national wallet, initially raising £4.5 billion. He also put together a further investment of £4 billion in the bank's shares. The commission fees for the October/November fundraisings amounted to £300 million. The first round of transactions, in the autumn of 2008, raised the ire of Barclays' major institutional shareholders – the fund managers and insurers – who found themselves bypassed. They felt that they had sacrificed the 'pre-emption' rights that would have allowed them to be offered shares at the same price. Worse was to come when in July 2012 it was revealed that both the Financial Services Authority and the Serious Fraud Office had opened probes into the circumstances surrounding the Qatari investments. In the US an investigation was launched by the US Justice Department and Securities and Exchange Commission into whether the group's relationships with third parties that assisted Barclays in winning and retaining business were compliant with the US Foreign Corrupt Practices Act.

Barclays had moved mountains to avoid being in the clutches of the UK government. The result was that it had far greater freedom to manoeuvre. It was able, for instance, to buy the US investment-banking business of Lehman Brothers, thus enabling it to compete globally with the likes of Morgan Stanley and Goldman Sachs. Time was to show that not everything in the garden was as rosy as Barclays' executives hoped or claimed. In immediate terms, though, the steps Barclays took during the financial crisis show just how unwilling and unable the authorities were to impose a single, thoroughgoing solution to Britain's banking woes.

Another indication of the UK's less than uniform approach to a recapitalisation plan was that while it set up an immensely complicated Asset Protection Scheme in November 2009 to assist banks still in danger of collapse, only one bank – RBS – ever availed itself of it. Arguably, the scheme helped RBS, which was able to emerge from it in October 2012 having shrunk its bad assets from £282 billion to a less eye-watering £100 billion. But as Mervyn

King pointed out, creating such a piece of machinery for just one institution was madness.

It could be argued, too, that the formation of a separate organisation, UK Financial Investments (UKFI), to hold the stakes in the nationalised and semi-nationalised banks was a further miscalculation. UKFI was designed to protect government officials from having to make the big decisions about how government ownership of the banks was exercised. But if the intention was to inoculate the politicians against making difficult calls – on sensitive policy issues and matters such as bankers' pay and bonuses – it would prove a failure. Because the calls were so politically sensitive, it was ultimately and inevitably the Treasury and the Chancellor of the Exchequer that ended up making them. The principle that created UKFI proved self-defeating.

Ultimately, the task of returning the publicly controlled banks proved to be drearily slow. The 'good' part of Northern Rock, the solid, unencumbered mortgage bank with 75 branches and a £14 billion mortgage book, was sold to Virgin Money for £747 million in November 2011. The public would have to wait until September 2013 to sell down the first 6 per cent of its stake in Lloyds Banking Group. In March 2014 the government sold a further 7.8 per cent stake in Lloyds directly to City institutions, raising £4.2 billion for the taxpayer and reducing the state share in the bank to 25 per cent. A public offer of the rest of the stake, estimated to be worth in the order of £14 billion, was scheduled for sale in the autumn of 2014.

Arguably, the loose, often cautious approach adopted by New Labour and continued by the Coalition government after 2010 had a long-term impact on national economic recovery. Injured and nervous banks remained reluctant to lend. It required the transition of banking regulation from the sub-octane Financial Services Authority to the Bank of England's new arm, the Prudential

Regulatory Authority, before the tough decisions still needed on capital and structures could take place. In the event it wasn't until the second quarter of 2013 that Britain showed signs of moving out of recession and into a period of growth.

The varied approaches across the Western world to the crisis largely reflected different cultures. In the United States, after some initial fumbling, a can-do attitude was adopted by the federal government. Its North American neighbour, Canada, with a less buccaneering culture, was one of the few Western countries to avoid the banking implosion. Its record of stability in the eye of the financial storm was a key factor in propelling the governor of the Bank of Canada, Mark Carney, to the Bank of England in 2013. As for Britain, muddling through ultimately proved the chosen path, as the various authorities and individuals responsible for putting things right mixed firm action with deeply hedged compromises, second-guessing and much fruitless hand-wringing.

Europe, meanwhile, took its own, very individual path, and in so doing was to find the going very bumpy indeed.

# 4

# International Rescue: The European Response

When the crisis of 2007 hit it was not Ben Bernanke in the United States or Mervyn King in Britain but Jean-Claude Trichet, president of the European Central Bank (ECB), who proved to be the man of the moment. Confronted with the news on 8 August that France's largest bank BNP Paribas had suspended some mortgage-backed securities funds, creating enormous market uncertainty, he moved quickly and decisively to intervene in the markets, pumping liquidity to the tune of €95 billion overnight. The *Financial Times* looked on approvingly, noting of his performance: 'Trichet is one of the few to emerge from the turmoil with his reputation enhanced.'

Some five tumultuous years later, in late July 2012, Trichet's Italian successor Mario Draghi gave a key speech that seemed to embody this can-do attitude. The London setting for it could not have been more quixotic. Lancaster House, built in 1825 by the 'Grand Old' Duke of York, with its Louis XIV interior, is a symbol of past glories. Located within a short distance of Buckingham Palace, it reminds visitors of Britain's island independence. The occasion was the first of two weeks of eve-of-Olympics Global Investment Conferences, chaired by the Trade Minister Lord Stephen Green and the brainchild of 10 Downing Street.

It was a tough time for Britain. The economy was struggling to regain the ground lost during the Great Recession of 2009 and was recovering more slowly than any of the other Group of Seven[1] rich nations, with the possible exception of Italy. The objective of the conference was to put the 'Great' back into Britain and re-establish the nation as a terrific place to invest. There seemed to be no better way to begin than with an Olympics that had been brought in on time and within budget – admittedly an extensively revised one. Just a stone's throw from where the economic and commercial elite were meeting, one of the most alluring of Olympic sports, beach volleyball, would be taking place on Horse Guards Parade in plain sight of HM Treasury.

On the platform on 27 July was the governor of the Bank of England, Sir Mervyn King, who opened proceedings by taking a sideswipe at the 'bad behaviour' of banks before blaming the financial failure on the lack of international cooperation on global imbalances. King's role was to introduce the president of the European Central Bank, Mario Draghi.

A wily Italian with a PhD from the Massachusetts Institute of Technology, a powerhouse of economic thought, Draghi also had a deep understanding of markets. A stint as the international chairman of investment bankers Goldman Sachs from 2002 to 2005 had given him clear insight into the thinking of the hedge funds and investment bankers that had laid siege to the euro since a meltdown in the Greek economy had thrown the 17-nation eurozone into paroxysm in early 2010. The crisis had already demanded dramatic steps to rescue much of Europe's periphery, including Portugal and Ireland; more recently it was the far more significant economies of Spain and Italy that had attracted the attention of speculators,

---

[1] The Group of Seven (G7) club of rich nations consists of the United States, Japan, Germany, France, Britain, Italy and Canada.

the result being that the interest-rate yield on their bonds soared into the danger zone on the markets. The big question was whether euroland, with its many voices and conflicting political goals, could pull through.

Draghi's main objective was to show that the ECB could be as focused on sound money as its intellectual paymasters at the German Bundesbank. He had demonstrated a radical streak on taking office in November 2011, by cutting euro interest rates and launching a mechanism that allowed the ECB to buy sovereign bonds and other assets from weak banks, in exchange for 'three year' cash. Now he was going to go even further. His remarks at Lancaster House proved to be a watershed. They were all the more remarkable in that he chose to make them in London, the hotbed of Euroscepticism and the distrusted home of the very free markets and speculative activity that were blamed across much of the Continent for the euro's ills.

Draghi began calmly enough, if a little mystically. In prepared remarks he said:

> The euro is like a bumblebee. This is a mystery of nature because it shouldn't fly but instead it does. So the euro was a bumblebee that flew very well for several years. And now – and I think people ask 'how come?' – probably there was something in the atmosphere, in the air, that made the bumblebee fly. Now something must have changed in the air, and we know what after the financial crisis. The bumblebee would have to graduate to a real bee.

It was in the question-and-answer session that followed that the ECB president stunned the markets. 'Within our mandate,' he said, 'the ECB is ready to do whatever it takes to preserve the euro. And believe me, it will be enough.'

Draghi's words swept through markets like wildfire. Here was a major European figure making a clear and unequivocal guarantee. Not surprisingly, the price of the sovereign bonds of Europe's weakling economies soared in response, bringing the yields down from dangerous levels.[2] What made his words even more remarkable was that at that precise moment Draghi had no policies to back them up. As the shrewd chronicler of the euro David Marsh would write, he was engaging in a 'masterly bluff'. The markets assumed that the ECB had secured the agreement of the Bundesbank and the German government for a programme to buy high-yielding bonds issued by the weakest nations in the eurozone. The reality was that Germany and, significantly, Draghi's colleagues back at ECB headquarters in Frankfurt were almost as surprised as the markets.

The technicians at the ECB set to work immediately to come up with a plan that matched Draghi's rhetoric. Promising, however, proved harder than delivering. The ECB, in contrast to its counterparts at the Federal Reserve and the Bank of England, does not have the political authority to intervene to save any one country. Nor can it make bold moves – which always have the potential to undermine the principles of sound money – without carrying Germany with it.

Nevertheless, within three months of Draghi's announcement the ECB unveiled its latest plan to bring calm to the euro. In keeping with its liking for an alphabet of acronyms the latest scheme was called Outright Monetary Transactions (OMT).

The ECB stood ready, Draghi would claim, to buy the sovereign bonds of euroland countries in unlimited quantities. In other words, the ECB was pledging to share the financial burden more widely by offering to buy in bonds of the weaker eurozone nations. Germany,

[2] Sovereign bonds are issued by governments to fund borrowing. The better the quality of the borrower, the lower the interest-rate yield and the higher the price of the bond. When bond prices fall the yield rises and when yields climb prices fall in a see-saw effect.

the largest economy in the region, would in effect be standing behind the weaker nations in the single-currency region. It was bold talk.

In cold reality, though, the plan lacked the support of the one institution that really mattered: the German central bank, the Bundesbank. It responded by leaking a 19-page document showing that the bond-buying scheme could technically be illegal. Indeed, so outraged was the ECB's German chief economist Jürgen Stark at the proposals that he resigned in high dudgeon in September 2011. If OMT was to fly it would have to go to the German constitutional court. The emperor may have fooled the markets into admiring his new clothes, but the Germans were less than convinced.

The lack of substance to Draghi's plan symbolised a fundamental problem at the heart of euroland: so complicated are its central institutions and so diverse the political and economic outlooks of its various members that it is very difficult to bang heads together and agree on decisive action. Moreover, all too often, economic realities are papered over by political wishful thinking. A classic example of this occurred in 2011. By this time the euro was in crisis, and a new London-based European Banking Authority was therefore given the task of undertaking stress tests similar to those used by UK regulators and the Federal Reserve in the US to assess the strength of the key banks.

It reported in July 2011 with the comforting news that just 8 banks, out of 90 tested, had failed the examination, while a further 16 were deemed to be in the danger zone. The banks concerned, it was explained, had been tested on how well equipped they might be to withstand a sharp downward movement in house prices or a recession.

To the amazement of analysts and others, however, one key measure had been left out of the equation: no test was conducted for the impact of a calamitous decline in the price of sovereign debt.

And yet this was an absolutely fundamental issue. As everyone knew, Europe's banks held on their books large quantities of bonds issued by the peripheral nations. Because of the 'sovereign' guarantee these bonds were valued fully at 100 cents to the euro. But the market reality was that they were trading at a much lower price. In the case of Greece, for instance, the valuation at the time was up to 50 per cent lower than the face value. In other words, the balance sheets of the banks holding these bonds were in effect a fiction. It was all part of the smoke and mirrors that so characterised the eurozone and made it so vulnerable.

Arguably, the eurozone had always been fragile. Back in 1992 the Maastricht Treaty, which paved the way for monetary union, had outlined a range of economic criteria each country had to meet if they wanted to become part of a future currency union. These included two essential fiscal rules: annual budget deficits – the difference between what a nation raises in taxation and what it spends – had to be less than 3 per cent of GDP; and national debt – the accumulated annual deficits down the years – should not rise above 60 per cent of GDP. In reality, though, so anxious were France and Germany that the currency union should have buy-in from the larger Continental economies that the rules were constantly being bent. In 1992 Italy's debt level, for example, stood at 105 per cent of output. To become part of the union it was asked not actually to achieve the treaty requirement but merely to demonstrate that it had plans to cut debt to 60 per cent of GDP.

For a decade or so inherent weaknesses were masked. At the time the euro was launched amid great fanfare on 1 January 1999 and euro notes and coins entered circulation in 2002 the world was in the middle of a 30-year period of sustained growth. Debt was cheap. Germany, the anchor country of the new currency bloc, was in a period of transition, investing in the former East Germany to the tune of €1.3 trillion by 2009 and submitting itself to a tough programme of social welfare cuts and pay restraint to fund it all. By 2006, Germany's growth had again outstripped the eurozone average. In contrast, the peripheral nations in Europe saw monetary policy loosened rather than tightened. The money markets assumed that the eurozone as a whole stood behind debt issued by individual nations, which sent interest rates on bonds tumbling.

The Italian government paid a 13 per cent interest rate to borrow for ten years in 1995; by the year the euro launched in 1999 this had fallen to just 4 per cent. Over the same period Germany's rates for debt fell from 7 per cent to just under 4 per cent. Similar declines in the cost of government debt were seen in Greece, Ireland, Spain and countries right across the eurozone. Cheap money and a belief in the robustness of the euro on the part of speculators led to rises in spending in the private and public sectors. Cash from surplus nations like Germany poured into the periphery, fuelling a credit bubble and what would prove to be a boom in property prices.

Germany itself proved fiscally prudent, holding a tight control on pay despite the good times. In fact, between 1999 and 2008 German unit labour costs – the amount firms pay workers for a specified quantity of output – actually fell 3 per cent. Other countries were less cautious. In Ireland unit labour costs jumped an extraordinary 50 per cent between 1999 and 2008. In Spain unit labour costs went up 35 per cent, while in Portugal, Italy and Greece and France these costs rose between 20 per cent and 30 per cent.

The euro might have been a shared currency, but there was no doubt which nation was in the driving seat. As the world's fourth largest manufacturer and third biggest exporter, Germany was in a strong position to sell its goods more cheaply than its competitors across the eurozone. In 2012 the UK exported 31 per cent of its goods and services to the rest of the world. In the same year France exported 25 per cent and the figure for Germany stood at 45 per cent. France had hoped a single currency would contain German power. Berlin had wanted the eurozone as a bastion against charges that it was seeking a new hegemony or, as the political columnist Simon Heffer would describe it, a 'Fourth Reich'. Instead its economic clout increased. It became just what it had tried to avoid – the leader of Europe, albeit a reluctant one.

Efforts to contain the boom came to nothing. The Growth and Stability Pact of 2003, which was intended to punish countries that strayed outside the core Maastricht fiscal rules, was allowed to slide after the two biggest players, France and Germany, failed to hold their annual budget deficits within the 3 per cent of GDP limit. The former French ECB president Jean-Claude Trichet would reflect in the heat of the euro crisis almost a decade later: 'It was a big moment. Had the major countries continued to say it was essential we would probably be in a much stronger position when the crisis came.'

When the bubble burst in 2007 it seemed initially that the eurozone was going to escape relatively unscathed. The focus of attention was on the disasters at such UK institutions as Northern Rock, the Royal Bank of Scotland, Lloyds and HBOS, and on the failings of American banks Bear Stearns, Merrill Lynch and Citigroup and the fractures at Goldman Sachs and Morgan Stanley. But if some hoped that this represented a triumph of more tightly regulated European finance over the laissez-faire Anglo-Saxon model practised in the UK and the US, they were to be disappointed.

In Germany it soon became apparent that parts of its banking system were loaded up with toxic sub-prime assets. Düsseldorf-based IKB Deutsche Industriebank was the first German bank to be hit by the sub-prime crisis and had to be given €10 billion of state aid. Sachsen Bank, formerly known as Sachsen LB, was forced into a €300 million merger with regional rival Baden-Württemberg Bank in 2007 after injecting €250 million into its rival's balance sheet. Other regional banks including Bayerische Landesbank and WestLB also reported losses during the first wave of the financial crisis.

Some of the problems stemmed from the American sub-prime market, reflecting the interconnectedness and global nature of the world economy. But there was a home-grown aspect to it all, too. The European credit boom had inflated real-estate bubbles in countries as far apart as Ireland and Spain that would prove as devastating as those in Britain and the US, if not more so. In Ireland politicians, bankers and the business community were enmeshed in a web of relationships that were exposed when the real-estate bubble burst. In Spain the regional savings banks, known as Cajas, lent unwisely to real-estate projects for which there were no buyers. When the credit crunch arrived in 2007–8 the country was littered with 'ghost' housing developments with no buyers or tenants.

The first country actually to go bust was Greece. In December 2009 it found itself having to admit that its national debt had reached €300 billion, a sum that amounted to 113 per cent of GDP – almost double the 60 per cent mandated by Maastricht. Rating agencies, caught on the back foot by the American sub-prime crisis, reacted quickly. Greek bank and government debts were swiftly downgraded.

A few weeks later an EU report seeking to get to the bottom of Greece's woes highlighted 'severe irregularities' in its public accounts. Aided by its adviser, the US investment bank Goldman Sachs, some critics argued it had used derivatives to shift debt obligations off its balance sheet and disguise the terrible underlying state of its finances. Or, as former British Chancellor Lord Lawson put it brutally in an interview with the BBC business editor Robert Peston for his 2012 documentary *The Great Euro Crash*, 'Greece with the assistance of Goldman Sachs cooked the books totally.'

Soon Athens found that it had no choice but to seek a rescue and the European Commission and ECB sought the assistance of the International Monetary Fund as an enforcer. It was the first time that the IMF had been invited onto European soil since the 1976 sterling crisis in Britain. In March 2010 a €22 billion emergency loan was agreed and in May the eurozone and the IMF agreed a €110 billion bailout package for Greece. The appalling social – and dangerous political – consequences of the Greek collapse continue to be played out.

For Ireland, next in the row of European dominoes, the crisis might not have provoked the street demonstrations to be seen in Greece, or the rise of sinister extremist political parties, but it did reveal just how deeply implicated so many banks were in the economic meltdown. Ironically, until the credit crunch hit in 2007– 8, Ireland – the Celtic Tiger – was seen as euroland's miracle economy. Reports from London's stockbrokers endlessly extolled the merits of investing there. Benefiting from the low interest rates that prevailed across the euro-currency area, high productivity and extraordinarily low corporation tax levels, its economy took off like a rocket. Dockland areas throughout Ireland sprouted Manhattan-like towers. Flood plains and fields that had once grazed livestock were turned into shiny new housing estates for Ireland's rapidly expanding aspirant classes. In one glorious year, 2006, some 93,419 houses were built, more than three times the number a decade earlier. Lenders had embarked on an ambitious, uncontrolled and too often fraudulent spree of real-estate financing, much of which had no prospect of ever being paid back.

Irish banks such as Anglo Irish Bank and the Bank of Ireland were involved in this spate of free-and-easy lending. Derek Quinlan, a former tax inspector from Dublin, was able to borrow enough to outbid one of the richest men in the world, Prince Alwaleed bin Talal of Saudi Arabia, for control of three of London's fanciest hotels, Claridge's, the Connaught and the Berkeley.

When it all came crashing down after the collapse of Lehman Brothers in September 2008 the true weakness of euroland decision-making was revealed. Far from a centrally organised response to the crisis from the European Commission in Brussels or the European Central Bank in Frankfurt, it was left to the Irish government to come up with its own solutions. And what the government did was rash in the extreme. Quite simply, it guaranteed all deposits in the banking system. In so doing it sent the dangerous message that however badly the banks had behaved, whatever toxic loans they may have on their books, they would be saved for the sake of national stability. In Britain and the US there were mechanisms in place to force the management of the banks to admit the true extent of their problems and to deal with them. Regulators in Ireland had little experience of dealing with a banking crisis; the central bank was powerless and the government shell-shocked at the dramatic turn of events.

Over the next two years, it emerged that the Republic's banks had made such catastrophic loans that the creditworthiness of the entire country had been placed at risk. Instead of imposing tough conditions on the banks, though, the depleted Irish exchequer, brought low by the global recession, continued to drip-feed them rather than sort them out or let them fail. They soon found out, however, that were pumping money into a black hole. In December 2008 the Dublin government bought a 75 per cent stake in Anglo Irish Bank at a cost of €1.5 billion. As the condition of the bank deteriorated a further €4 billion was provided to this single institution between June and September 2009. Over the next two years €20 billion more of assistance, in one form or another, would be required. In 2010 Anglo Irish Bank, which had advanced loans to almost every dodgy borrower on the Irish scene and even backed a speculative project to build the Chicago Spire, billed as America's tallest building, asked for a further €10 billion to keep it afloat.

In an effort to clean up the mess, the late Finance Minister Brian Lenihan put together a plan that he hoped would bring an end to constant calls for bank rescue funds. He formed the National Asset Management Agency, which was given the task of buying the bad loans of ailing banks at a big discount to their face value. The plan was that some €77 billion of outstanding loans would be absorbed by the government, which would pay the banks €54 billion for them – a 30 per cent discount on their original value.

Lenihan declared he had devised 'the cheapest bailout in the world'. The reality was rather different. When the agency actually came to examine the loans, it found that fewer than half of them were ever likely to be repaid. In other words, they weren't even worth 50 per cent of their face value. A culture of misinformation pervaded. Politicians misled the public, Anglo Irish misled the regulators, failing to tell them they had made secret loans of €255 million to directors and connected persons in the 2009 accounts. And, in the biggest deception of all, the bank pretended that the collateral — the security against which loans were made – was good, when in many cases it was near worthless. As the markets learned of the can of worms that the government had opened, they panicked.

Ireland's efforts to control spending in its grotesquely bloated public sector, of which the banks were now a part, lost all credibility. The value of Irish government bonds – a symbol of confidence in the economy – plunged on the markets. The reverberations of Ireland's banking crisis were felt across Europe, but nowhere more acutely than in London where official figures show that British banks are exposed to Irish loans of £140 billion.

It was only at this point, saddled with an incompetent government, a banking system in turmoil, a civil service which repeatedly misled taxpayers as to the extent of the catastrophe, and a public sector whose senior staff lined their pockets with gold-plated pension deals while refusing to accept the pay cuts visited upon those further down the food chain, that the whistle was finally blown. At last the financial police from the IMF, the European Central Bank and the EU – the Troika – were brought in to curb the madness.

In November 2010 the Troika agreed an €85 billion bailout package for Ireland. The UK also independently contributed £7 billion to Ireland, because of economic links between the two countries. Ireland, after all, accounts for 5 per cent of the UK's exports. The two nations also have closely linked banking systems. Two of the four largest high-street banks in Northern Ireland are Irish-owned, and Irish banks also issue sterling.

Over the next two years the Irish government had to bring large swathes of the country's banking system under state control. Anglo Irish Bank was nationalised in January 2009 at a cost of around €34 billion. The faith investors lost in the bank was shown in its share price, which crashed from €17 in May 2007 to 12 cents in December 2009. The state later assumed control of Allied Irish Bank, Irish Nationwide Building Society, EBS Building Society, and Irish Life and Permanent while taking a significant stake in the Bank of Ireland. To prevent these banks from toppling over (although Anglo Irish Bank and Irish Nationwide were wound down) the Irish central bank and the ECB lent them a further €188 billion on top of Ireland's bailout.

The medicine doled out was strong and hard to swallow. Public-sector employees had to accept real wage cuts of up to 40 per cent. Pensions and workplace benefits were cut. Unit labour costs in the country were brought down sharply. By 2013, though, these tough measures were having an effect. Thanks in part to its new, more competitive labour costs, and its low corporate tax rate, the country's appeal as a hub for manufacturing and services was enhanced. It even looked set to become the first of the eurozone weaklings to leave the programme imposed by the Troika without any further assistance. The Irish economy, buoyed by reforms, was starting to bounce back – it was even projected to grow by 2 per cent in 2014. That said, public debt, which had amounted to only 25 per cent of Ireland's GDP in 2007, soared to a peak of 123 per cent in 2013.

Out-of-control banks were not at the root of every struggling national economy. Portugal, for example, which became in May 2011 the third eurozone government after Greece and Ireland to require rescue, was brought down by an economy that had become uncompetitive. Wages had risen inexorably and there had been a number of expensive public projects (especially ones involving transport infrastructure). Moreover, tariffs on cheap exports from Asia into Europe had been reduced, leading to a flood of imports into the domestic Portuguese market that had to be paid for via higher levels of borrowing. When the financial crisis hit in 2008 Portugal had a great deal of debt, which quickly became too costly to fund.

In early 2009 the credit ratings agencies started on a series of downgrades of Portugal's sovereign debt, which in November 2011 was assigned high-risk 'junk' status. The downgrades led to the price of Portuguese bonds climbing to unsustainable levels, and a rescue plan amounting to €78 billion became necessary, put together with the ECB, the European Commission and the IMF. In return for the loan Portugal had to agree to reform its health-care system, pursue a major privatisation programme and reduce its budget deficit from 9.1 per cent of GDP in 2010 to 3 per cent of GDP by 2013. (In March 2013 Portugal's deficit stood at 6.4 per cent, according to the Lisbon-based National Statistics Institute, and unemployment had rocketed to a record 17.6 per cent).

Portugal was something of a special case in that the banks were not at the core of the problem. Elsewhere banks were heavily implicated in the woes that successive members of the eurozone underwent. Nor were these banking problems confined to 'peripheral' nations, as is sometimes popularly assumed.

In the years following the financial crisis of 2007–8 the Dutch banking system was all but wiped out. Some of Europe's oldest banks in Italy and Switzerland came to grief. Spain's banking system demonstrably proved a basket case. The same reckless, greedy and bonus-obsessed culture that placed bankers in the rogues' gallery on the high streets of Britain and the main streets of the US had spread far and wide.

The Netherlands' fall from grace was particularly steep. It had been among the first Continental nations to develop a mature banking system from the late 1580s onwards to finance trade and war with its major rivals, the fading Spanish empire and Britain's emergence as a great mercantile and trading nation. By modern times Holland had built one of the world's leading financial sectors and, despite the country's small size, its top banks and insurers enjoyed an international profile. But in the aftermath of the crash in 2008, the Dutch government had to commit almost €65 billion to rescue its finance sector, injecting capital into insurers ING and Aegon and nationalising what remained of ABN Amro (after its disastrous merger with the Royal Bank of Scotland) and SNS Reaal. The country was left with a banking sector that was a mere shadow of its former self.

As for the cross-border Dutch–Belgian bank Fortis, some €16.8 billion had to be injected in October 2008 as it struggled to integrate the Dutch assets of ABN Amro it had bought from RBS. This was just the start. As the eurozone crisis deepened, Fortis – once portrayed as the model of the future because of its cross-border status and seen as a partner for Britain's Lloyds – soaked up ever more government cash with the costs doubling to about €30 billion.

The pain in the Netherlands was not over. In February 2013 banking and insurance group SNS Reaal found itself on the verge of collapse after making bad property loans. Once again the Dutch government was forced to intervene, heading a €14 billion rescue consortium. The country's fourth largest bank had suffered recurring losses in recent years linked to its Property Finance subsidiary, bought from ABN Amro in 2006. The circumstances leading to the collapse are the subject of an official probe launched in March 2013. Arguably the crisis in the Netherlands – measured purely as a financial crisis – was more devastating than that in any other eurozone country.

Catastrophic though the Dutch banking disaster has been, the Dutch economy has proved sufficiently strong to weather the storm. The fact is that the Netherlands went into the crisis in better shape than several of the eurozone nations that came unstuck. Until the financial crisis hit in 2008 the national budget was close to surplus and overall public debt stood at 64.8 per cent of national output in 2008, not far from the 60 per cent of GDP officially required for eurozone membership. Relatively healthy public finances enabled the country to absorb the big losses in the banking system.

Spain's banking crisis, however, like Ireland's, has had a profound and disruptive impact on its population. And, as with Ireland, the banking meltdown stemmed to a large extent from an explosion in house-building.

During the ten years to 2007 the Spanish built 5 million homes, boosting the country's housing stock by 25 per cent. It was an uncontrolled boom fuelled by cronyism, low interest rates and irresponsible lending. When borrowing costs surged the tide went out and all that was left behind were large unfinished ghost suburbs outside the major cities. To make matters worse, Spain's financial sector, driven by cheap credit and tax rules that encouraged takeovers, had also provided the cash for a stream of debt-fuelled foreign takeovers: Ferrovial bought BAA, owner of Britain's key airports; Telefonica bought British mobile franchise O2; Iberdrola purchased Scottish Power and the banking group Santander bought Abbey and then added Alliance & Leicester and Bradford & Bingley, creating a new high-street force in British banking. It's scarcely surprising that Spain's crisis, as much as any other in euroland, would have an impact on the UK.

As bad news piled on bad news, Spain initially reckoned – as the proud fourth-largest nation in the single currency – that it could solve its own problems. Self-imposed austerity, however, sent the unemployment rate soaring, reaching 27.2 per cent among adults and 55 per cent among 16–18-year-olds by early 2013. At the end of 2012 the bad debts still remaining on the balance sheets of the banks, even after a clean-up, stood at a massive €182 billion.

At the core of Spain's banking disaster stands Bankia. The bank based in Valencia, but with a significant presence in Madrid, was formed in 2010 from the merger of seven regional savings banks or Cajas. A huge organisation, it boasted 12 million customers and assets of €328 billion, and its first chairman was no less a figure than Rodrigo Rato, a former managing director at the IMF.

Unfortunately the timing was bad. The Cajas that came together to make up the core of the business had engaged in wild speculative lending, much of it in real estate and much of it badly contaminated, and the deal was done just as eurozone tensions were spreading through the financial markets.

More than 10 per cent of Bankia's loan book was thus exposed to rotten property lending. Rato, a somewhat enigmatic figure who had left the IMF in unexplained circumstances in 2007, recognised that the bank could not survive without a capital injection and sought €19 billion from the government. As Bankia's problems deepened, the yield on Spanish bonds soared on global markets above the 8 per cent rate at which the country could afford to fund its national debt.

In May 2012 Rato departed after the bank reported a €3 billion-plus loss. An experienced replacement, José Ignacio Goirigolzarri (the former general manager of one of Spain's strongest banks, BBVA), was parachuted in. In March 2013 an independent review of the bank's finances exposed its problems in all their stark horror: underlying losses had spiralled and now stood at €19 billion. It was by far the biggest loss ever recorded by any commercial organisation in Spain and made those of some of the worst-run banks in Europe – such as Britain's Royal Bank of Scotland – look almost moderate by comparison.

Ultimately Spain had no choice but to approach the Troika for help. The first of the eurozone countries to seek assistance specially for the purpose of recapitalising its banks, it needed an estimated €100 billion, to be drawn from the newly established €700 billion European Stability Mechanism, the bailout fund set up the height of the crisis in July 2012.

Inevitably there was a heavy price to pay. Bankia was ordered to cut the size of liabilities by 60 per cent over the next five years, close branches and shed thousands of staff. It duly announced that it would lay off 6,000 staff – 28 per cent of its workforce – and shut 39 per cent of its branches. It also agreed to shrink itself by €50 billion by selling assets to Sareb, a bad bank set up by Spain to house underperforming assets. Bankia was also required to sell off investments in Spanish industry, including a 12 per cent stake in International Airlines Group, the owner of Spanish national airline Iberia and British Airways.

The shock treatment worked. In February 2014 the Spanish government felt confident enough to divest itself of 7.5 per cent of its 68 per cent stake in Bankia, recovering the first €1.3 billion of taxpayer funds pumped into the bank. There was only a small gain for the exchequer but the move was hailed as 'really one of the signs that there has been a change in perception and the reality of the financial system', by Spanish Economy Minister Luis de Guindos.

Bankia was not Spain's only problematic bank. Banco de Valencia was deemed to be in such bad shape that it was forced into a sale with the stronger privately owned Caixa Bank. Among the restrictions placed on these crisis-filled institutions was a ban on new lending to property developers. Instead they were told to focus loans on Spanish households and small to medium-sized businesses. And in 2012 bondholders – many of whom were ordinary, older Spaniards who had been sold preferred shares (a high-risk form of bank debt) by their lenders as a savings product – were made to fork out €10 billion as part of the rescue. It was a highly controversial move, but one that would later have parallels among the depositors in Cyprus and the bondholders at the relatively tiny Co-operative Bank in Britain.

The country's two most significant banks, Banco Santander and BBVA, were able to skirt around the crisis. Santander was a big winner from the break-up of ABN Amro since it had picked up its Latin American assets in the transaction. These proved highly profitable and it was able to sell down its Brazilian holdings to boost capital. Santander and BBVA were nevertheless ordered by the European Banking Authority in December 2011 to raise almost €22 billion between them to adequately fund their operations.

Events at Santander in Spain were closely monitored by the Bank of England. Even though it was set up as a separate subsidiary, with thick Chinese walls, former deputy governor of the Bank of England Paul Tucker feared that if parent Santander were sucked into the inferno it might be impossible to protect Santander's British bank. There was also serious concern about Barclays' exposure through its Spanish offshoot, the former Banco Zaragozano, bought for €1.14 billion in 2003. The risk for the UK was that Spain's banking meltdown, like that in Ireland, could become very expensive for British taxpayers.

By the end of 2012 it must have been hoped that the worst of the crises in the eurozone were, if not over, at least being addressed. Ireland had accepted the harsh terms of the IMF-led bailout and the shock treatment was starting to work. Spain's reorganisation of its banking system was starting to show some signs of success. But just a few months later, in March 2013, a new storm appeared on the horizon – and from a country that had not previously appeared on commentators' radar. Now it was Cyprus's turn to go into meltdown.

Cyprus's place in global banking is an unusual one. It is a eurozone minnow with a national output that represented just over 1 per cent of that of the whole bloc. But it has a banking sector that allowed it to punch above its weight. When the island joined the euro in 2008 its economy was growing at a healthy rate of 4 per cent on the back of property, tourism and financial services. Cypriot banks fuelled by such large inflows of cash began to lend heavily, particularly to Greece, the country's cultural and geographic neighbour. By 2011 banks in Cyprus, led by its two largest institutions, Laiki and the Bank of Cyprus, had become eight times the size of the overall economy. This was a far higher ratio than prevailed in Iceland or Ireland, both countries that were also brought down by their banks. In fact Cypriot financial services accounted for half of GDP, compared with 10 per cent in the UK.

When Greece became the first country in the eurozone to go bust in 2010, Cyprus was immediately drawn into the crisis. The island had bought more than €4 billion of Greek debt and the banks had lent Greek companies €22 billion, more than the entire Cypriot €18 billion GDP. In the first bailout in 2010 the Troika protected holders of Greek bonds. But as Greece came back for more, owners of Greek bonds were required to take a massive loss on their investments of up to 60 per cent.

On 16 March 2013 the Cypriot President Nicos Anastasiades announced a deal with the Troika involving a €10 billion rescue package. The sting in the tail was that Anastasiades had agreed that Cyprus would play its part by finding €5.8 billion on its own.

What this meant in practical terms was a 9.9 per cent levy on all bank accounts containing over €100,000 and 6.75 per cent on all accounts which held less than this figure. The idea that the government could reach into the accounts of ordinary bank depositors and impose a levy was deeply disturbing. Up until then, depositors in debt-stricken euroland countries had not been required to 'bail in'. For Cypriots it all looked a bit like double standards: large countries like Spain were not being asked to demand such sacrifices on the part of their citizens, but Cyprus was small enough to be bullied.

'I wish I was not the minister to do this,' said Cypriot Finance Minister Michael Sarris, but he nevertheless defended the move. 'Much more money could have been lost in a bankruptcy of the banking system or indeed of the country,' he said.

From the day of the public announcement of the rescue terms on 23 March 2013 it was decided that all the island's banks would remain closed until further notice. Cypriots were shocked. Europe was shocked. This was an unexpected break with the past. In the days after queues formed at failed bank Northern Rock in the UK in September 2007, Britain had increased the amount it would guarantee in depositors' bank accounts from £35,000 in stages to £85,000. The EU followed suit in 2009, guaranteeing accounts in the eurozone up to €100,000, which covers the vast majority of ordinary savers. There had never been a hint that depositors might be expected to pay for the calamities brought about by others. And the implications were profound. If Cypriot depositors could be penalised, could those in other countries be next in the firing line? Might it not be sensible to move their cash to safer countries like Germany or Austria? A new danger, that billions of euros of savings might be shifted from southern Europe to northern Europe, further weakening already wobbling banks, had been exposed.

Cyprus reverted to a cash economy within hours of the announcement. Shops would not take cheques or credit cards. Cash was king, if you could get it. The British government found itself having to organise an airlift of €1 million in notes from the Royal Air Force base in Brize Norton to RAF Akrotiri on the south coast of the island to ensure that no service personnel would be caught with empty pockets.

Cypriots took to the streets against the deal the President had struck. Britain's expatriates had their five minutes of fame as 24-hour rolling news crews arrived from all over Europe (along with crusty newspaper reporters) and Cypriot MPs – almost to a person – voted down the agreement.

It was a moment of ghastly truth for the Anastasiades government. It scurried to find a new deal for the country, which was by now days away from bankruptcy. Government workers including teachers and nurses would not be paid, pensions would not be met and the brittle peace of the island threatened to be shattered.

The authorities desperately turned to others for help. David Cameron offered technical assistance in the form of Treasury mandarin Sir Tom Scholar, a veteran of Britain's own banking crisis a couple of years earlier. The Troika, however, backed by Germany, played hardball. Cyprus might have joined the EU back in 2004 (and the euro four years later), but it had a tax agreement with Russia dating back to 1998 that allowed Russian citizens to pay little or no tax on dividends and capital gains made on the island. The credit ratings agency Moody's had estimated that Russian companies and individuals, benefiting from interest rates up to 2 per cent above what was typically available in the rest of Europe, had invested almost €30 billion in Cyprus. The German authorities had a strong suspicion that a fair proportion of this was tainted by money laundering or tax dodging and felt that, in the circumstances, the least the Russians could do was to help bail out what had been a very lucrative bolt-hole for them.

As a result, instead of heading off to Brussels or Berlin, the Cypriot Finance Minister Sarris flew to Russia with a begging bowl. But it proved to be an unproductive mission. President Putin's government was unmoved by Sarris's pleas, despite a pledge to sell the rights to valuable gas fields off the island's southern coast that were due to come on stream in 2020.

With the Troika left as the only game in town, Cyprus prepared to take its medicine. Under a revised rescue plan unveiled on 25 March a higher 20 per cent levy was imposed on those depositors with over €100,000 in their accounts. Nicosia also was obliged to sell off a range of assets, including around €400 million of its gold reserves. Laiki was to be wound up with its bad debts and all savings over

€100,000 dumped into a 'bad bank', run by a special administrator appointed by the Cyprus central bank. Savings under €100,000 and its remaining assets would be transferred to the Bank of Cyprus. A Rubicon had been crossed with large depositors, many of them offshore, paying a heavy price. It was a message that reverberated across the eurozone.

Russians seeking to leave the country with their aluminium suitcases filled with cash and locals seeking to move their money to safer locations found themselves out of luck under the revised rescue plan. Some money already had escaped but the combination of temporary bank closures and new capital controls made it far more difficult to extract funds. People with deposits in their current or savings accounts were forbidden to take cash out of the country. It was a harking back to a previous era when capital controls were common among Western nations. The fear was that otherwise, when the banks reopened, people would rush to take their money and deposit it in safer countries like Switzerland, the UK or Germany. (So out of step were capital controls with the spirit of freedom of movement of capital and labour enshrined in Article 63 of the Single European Act of 1986[3] that when, during the Icelandic banking crisis of 2008, Gordon Brown's government sought to freeze the bank deposits held at Icelandic banks in London, he had to resort to a legal ruling that designated Iceland as a national security risk. The measures are still in place. If the Icelandic example provides any guidance then the 'temporary' capital controls in Cyprus could remain in place for some time.)

The appalling mess in Cypriot banking was revealed in graphic detail in July 2013 in an official report commissioned by the Central Bank of Cyprus and chaired by banking expert David Lascelles,

---

[3] The 'Single Market' which resulted from the Act was implemented in 1993.

associate director of the City of London think tank the Centre for the Study of Financial Innovation (CSFI). Its overall assessment was a stark and simple one: Cyprus suffered its banking crisis because it had no coherent national policy to handle its booming banking sector and failed to restrain the banks as they seemed to be 'doing a good job'. The report recommended a 'comprehensive banking policy which takes account of the risks as well as the rewards of running a big banking sector, and ensures that the country has effective mechanisms to deal with them'. It noted that even though Cyprus banks were shrinking, the country as a whole will continue to be heavily dependent on them because there are few financing alternatives. It also drew attention to the 'taint of politics and cronyism' in the Cypriot banking system, and urged the authorities to bring in 'fresh people and ideas'.

The Cyprus crisis, like those in Greece, Portugal and Ireland, demonstrated that policymakers do not treat all euro countries as the same. The necessity for capital controls provided an illustration of a two-tier ranking in the eurozone between those economies and banking systems that are trusted and those which are not. At the time of the first Greek crisis there was even a suggestion that euro notes coded for Greece (each country has a separate letter denoting where they originated) might be worth less if Greece was to leave the single currency and devalue. Some Greeks went so far as to take their stacks of 'Greek' euros overseas and swap them for the more trustworthy euros from other countries.

But this two-tier thinking does not mean that the problems of Europe's banks were – or are now – confined to 'peripheral' economies. Right across the eurozone, nations and their banks became locked in a drunken embrace (or what economists call a 'doom loop'). In just five countries – Greece, Ireland, Portugal, and most importantly Spain and Italy – banks hold an estimated €3 trillion of their government's sovereign debt. It's a house of cards that only the slightest of breezes could bring down.

To that extent the fact that by the spring of 2013 the markets seemed calmer, thanks in part to Draghi's rhetoric about the euro, was something of an illusion. True, countless EU summits had led to the creation of a permanent bailout fund, the European Stability Mechanism (ESM) – even if no one dared use it because of the onerous conditions attached. True, the European Central Bank, under the leadership of Mario Draghi, had cut interest rates and launched a huge three-year €1 trillion loan programme to stabilise over 1,300 debt-ridden banks in the region. True, the long-term refinancing operations (LTROs) bought time for banks and troubled nations to begin to restructure the debts built up over the last 30 years. But this was all just using lengths of sticking plaster to cover up some very deep wounds. Little was done to resolve the underlying problems of a banking system too weak to support any kind of economic recovery or the underlying imbalances between the wealthy nations of the north and the poorer countries bordering the Mediterranean.

The black hole in the accounts of major banks across Europe keeps investors outside the region on their toes. Roughly half the cash trusted to big American money-market funds is lent on to European banks as short-term wholesale funding, according to credit ratings agency Fitch. But this money is skittish and can be withdrawn at short notice. A huge and present danger to Europe's banking system is that many institutions have yet to acknowledge the bad loans and debts sitting on their balance sheets or to tackle big shortfalls of capital.

The International Monetary Fund has estimated that the potential bad debts of the European banks stand at close to £300 billion.

Making matters worse is the fact that the worth of the government debt that they hold has plummeted in value. Unable to borrow from commercial sources, European banks have been forced to borrow from their central banks. These banks are then expected to buy the national bonds from their country of origin. The downward spiral is exacerbated by a vicious eurozone recession that makes banks reluctant or unable to lend to the wider economy. In other words, what is keeping the eurozone afloat is as much wishful thinking as economic reality.

If one country can be said to embody both the wishful thinking and the huge problems still lurking in Europe it is Italy. As the third largest economy in the eurozone, Italy is seen as critical to the survival of the single currency in its present form. But with debts of €2 trillion, or 120 per cent of GDP, together with a succession of banking problems, it has at times appeared to be hanging on by a gossamer thread. It is hard to forget that at the time of the Exchange Rate Mechanism (ERM) – the precursor to the euro – Italy, like Britain, found it impossible to keep its currency aligned with the Deutsche Mark. In August and September 1992 the speculative pressure against the British pound and Italian lira became too strong and both were ejected from the ERM. The events of that year provided a clear insight into the very different economic performances and strengths of Italy and Germany.

Italy's debts have not suddenly ballooned. They have built up over several decades (Italy's eurozone partners chose to ignore them when the single currency was launched). On the surface things seem manageable. Like Japan (another G7 nation), the country has managed to finance its debts over the years because of a large domestic appetite for Italian government bonds and a lively secondary market. Italy also has one of the strongest manufacturing bases in the whole of Europe. But over the last 15 years, the nation has only managed an average growth rate of 0.83 per cent. And it has been in recession since the middle of 2011.

Debt payments are large. In 2012 the country was required to borrow €450 billion, almost 29 per cent of its GDP, according to the IMF, to keep funding its debt levels. Fears of an Italian default in 2011 pushed up the cost of its 10-year bonds from around 5 per cent to over 7 per cent. If bond interest rates had remained elevated Italy would have struggled to remain solvent and honour its debt obligations. However, as concerns about the euro crisis retreated in 2014 the yield on 10-year Italian bonds tumbled to below 4 per cent and the danger of default disappeared over the horizon. Even so, as the holder of large volumes of Italian bonds the Italian banking system finds itself firmly in the 'doom loop' that ties the fate of the country's financial system to that of its sovereign debt.

Italy's banking system, like that of many eurozone countries, is under severe strain. The failure of the European Banking Authority and Brussels to tackle the fundamental problems has left it struggling. Total gross bad loans stood at €125 billion in Italy at the end of 2012, up 16.6 per cent from a year earlier, according to data from Italian banking association ABI. This compares to bad loans of €78 billion two years previously when Europe's crisis was beginning to become apparent.

UniCredit, Italy's biggest bank by assets, has been forced into a series of emergency fundraising operations to head off market concerns of failure. In January 2012 it raised €7.5 billion, after raising €7 billion in 2008 and 2009. The most emotive struggle for Italy has been the battle to save Banca Monte dei Paschi di Siena. Founded in 1472, the Tuscan-based bank is regarded as the world's oldest and failure would be seen as a deadly blow to the nation's prestige. Despite its distinguished history the bank has been brought low by the cultural corruption that affected bankers across the piece. It is being probed over the alleged concealment of loss-making risky investments. The inquiry is looking into a deal to hedge the risks of buying long-term Italian government bonds. It could lead to another €720 million of losses for the bank.

A series of fundraisings in 2012–14 saw the position of the traditional, secretive foundations – which dominate the share registers of Italian banks – weakened. By the spring of 2014 effective control of the Siena bank had passed from the foundations to outside investors such as the American fund manager Black Rock with a 5.7 per cent stake.

Italy's number four lender, the co-operative bank Banco Popolare, reported a doubling in its full-year net loss in March 2013 to €627 million as it made provisions to cover the poor quality of assets on its balance sheet. Long delays in producing annual results led to the suspicion that a number of other Italian banks sit on the edge of a precipice.

The stop-go approach to repairing the Italian banking system can partly be blamed on the country's broken political system. In November 2011 Prime Minister Silvio Berlusconi was replaced without an election by former EU commissioner Mario Monti, largely at the behest of the euro area's leaders. Monti forced through reforms designed to control the country's spending by cutting pensions, imposing property taxes, chasing tax avoiders and ending some of the nation's restrictive work practices. But Italian voters were less than enthralled with the austerity diet and Monti was thrown out in February 2013. A measure of the Italian population's disgust with its own leaders and its distrust of Brussels is that an Italian former comic, Beppe Grillo, who leads the anti-establishment Five Star Movement, has been able to make his party the second largest in the country. He has vowed to give Italians a referendum on leaving the euro and is also in favour of Italy repurchasing its government bonds and renegotiating the interest rates. 'In reality Italy has long been lost,' he argues. 'In one year we won't have enough money left to pay the pensions and wages of those working in the public sector. There's not much left to rescue.'

Monti has warned his European colleagues of the disenchantment many feel with what they perceive to be the failings of the EU during the banking collapse and the economic crisis that followed. 'Public support for the reforms, and worse, for the European Union, is dramatically declining,' he said at his final EU summit in Brussels in March 2013, 'following a trend which is also visible in many other countries across the union. To revive growth and fight long-term and youth unemployment would be the best message to counter the mounting wave of populism and disaffection with the European Union, showing that Europe is listening to people's concerns.'

By the end of 2013 the eurozone seemed to have weathered the worst of its storms. But there was still cause for concern. Many problems had simply been parked. As for economic policy, this seemed to be based as much on a general hope that the eurozone could trade its way out of deficit as on any kind of strategic thinking. The overall impression was that what politicians, officials and bankers were hoping for was a scenario reminiscent of Latin America in the 1980s, when defaults were placed on hold for a decade until the Western banking system had accumulated enough capital to absorb the losses. In other words, the eurozone was both burying its head in the sand and indulging in some very wishful thinking.

The problem with such an approach is that an unwillingness to fix the balance sheets and the capital requirements of Europe's banks is proving a huge barrier to recovery. In France, the Netherlands and elsewhere national governments were still struggling in 2014 to reach first base on restoring the banking system (though the

Dutch government did state that it aimed to recoup some of the €30 billion it had expended on the rescue of ABM Amro by the end of 2014). Paradoxically it is only in countries such as Spain where the issues have been forced by catastrophic meltdown that recovery has actually begun. In Spain, for example, the bank at the centre of all its troubles – Bankia, an institution carved out of the damaged Cajas – started on the road back to public markets in the spring of 2014.

In April 2014 the Paris-based Organisation for Economic Cooperation and Development (OECD), which monitors the health of the world's larger economies, warned that the bad loans festering on euroland balance sheets were still a key risk to economic recovery. The European Central Bank was urged to act decisively in reviewing the shape of bank balance sheets and making recommendations for repair. Effectively, it needed to face up to the fact that not all the sovereign bonds of euroland nations held on bank balance sheets were of equal value – that Greek bonds, for example, should not be rated in the same way as German ones.

Now a new threat made itself apparent: deflation. The tight squeeze on the economies of weaker nations – from Cyprus to Greece and Spain – where labour costs have been shredded meant that prices across the eurozone scarcely rose in the first half of 2014. With that came the spectre of a damaging spiral of falling prices, wages and asset values and ever more expensive debt (inflation erodes the face value of debt; deflation has the opposite effect). It's worth bearing in mind that in the case of Japan it took nearly a decade and the most radical of policies – including huge money printing – to emerge from a deflationary spiral.

So, despite endless EU summits and various reforms (see Chapter 9), a range of challenges remain for the citizens of the eurozone. Germany has an innate fear of printing new money and sharing risk through Eurobonds. The collective memory of the out-of-control inflation of the Weimar Republic in the late 1920s and early 1930s looms large. Yet the OECD and IMF both fear that failure to lower interest rates further, create new money through quantitative easing and issue Eurobonds could tip the region further into deflation and back into crisis. In such a fragile environment the slightest ripple can cause waves. The 2014 crisis in Ukraine, for example, may well prove to cause not just a geopolitical but an economic crisis. Germany, after all, buys almost half its energy supplies from Russia and can ill afford an all-out economic dispute. This would be a concern even in times of strong economic growth. With the eurozone still weak, such shocks can all too easily prove seismic ones.

# 5

# An Unchanging Culture: Banking after the Crash

If the global economic landscape was transformed by the fallout from the banking crisis of 2007–8, the nature of the banks themselves showed remarkable resilience. Some banks might have crashed. Some might have had to make heavy cuts to expenditure and staffing levels. Some might have had to accept greater outside involvement, particularly from governments. Individual bank bosses might have been fired or replaced. But more striking than these changes was the remarkable continuity of the pre-crash banking culture.

This can readily be seen in the sorts of people called upon to turn around crisis-hit institutions. That they were all very experienced bankers is hardly surprising. But they were also bankers of a consistent and very particular type: investment bankers. In Britain, for example, when Gordon Brown's Labour government needed someone to deal with the disaster that was the Royal Bank of Scotland, they turned to investment banker Stephen Hester. Given his background it's not surprising that Hester believed that he could trade RBS out of trouble using its investment-banking arm. When he joined journalists for festive drinks in late 2009, high up in RBS's headquarters at Bishopsgate in the City of London, he enthusiastically described how in the post-crisis marketplace –

108

thinned out by the collapse of Lehman Brothers and the problems of other free-standing investment banks – it was RBS's markets division that was doing surprisingly well.

At Barclays, similarly, it was decided that the man who should replace chief executive John Varley after he stepped down in September 2010 should be Bob Diamond, the head of Barclays' investment-banking arm BarCap. His chairman Marcus Agius, who first resigned in the summer of 2012 to try and keep Bob Diamond in his post, was also an investment banker, having previously headed dealmakers Lazard in London. When Diamond was eventually persuaded to leave at the behest of the authorities in July 2012, Agius agreed to stay on as chairman to steady the Barclays ship.

At the Lloyds Banking Group in September 2008 it was initially believed that Andy Hornby, who had played such a significant role in the disasters at HBOS, should be kept on as deputy chief executive. Lloyds' American chief executive Eric Daniels did actually succeed in hanging on to the top job until February 2011. The new chairman of the bank, brought in to replace the architect of the ill-fated merger, was Sir Win Bischoff. Bischoff has spent his entire career in investment banking at Schroders and latterly Citigroup.

It has to be said that the relationship between investment banking and retail banking has not been an entirely happy one, and the relationship between investment banking and banking disasters has been a worryingly close one in recent years. Yet the belief that investment bankers were the people to sort out the problems they had helped to create ran deep. One senior Bank of England official I spoke to remarked just how much the Treasury relied on such people during the crisis: 'They thought policy should be driven by investment banks.' The official then went on to expound on the risks that such a policy entailed. 'It's completely mad because investment banks are very good at telling you how to do a transaction, once you know what the transaction is that you want to do. What they are not good at and have no comparative advantage in at all, is thinking about a policy question, it's not what they do.'

For many, the problems with investment bankers went beyond their perceived lack of policy skill. Investment banking involves a very particular mindset. It requires people with a gambling edge, prepared to take high risks for potentially high rewards. This in turn creates an aggressively buccaneering culture. The risk-taking, trading nature of investment banking is very different from the steady skills required in retail banks, which take in deposits from customers and make cautious loans after a careful assessment of the risks. The two can sit uncomfortably side by side. That is why the report of the UK's Independent Banking Commission (IBC) headed by Sir John Vickers and published in September 2011 recommended the 'ring-fencing' of investment-banking activities from retail banking.

One other aspect of investment banking that came to be a hugely controversial issue in the aftermath of the crisis of 2007–8 was the often enormous annual bonuses paid to key players. Even when the financial crisis and recession were at their deepest, in the period 2008–10, and thousands of bankers and City workers lost their jobs, bonuses were the cash machine that never stopped paying out. Indeed, when regulators across the globe sought to curb the sense of entitlement among the bankers, the banks simply found ways to circumvent rules and guidelines. The contrast between the fat rewards in the finance industry and the misery of austerity and lost jobs for the majority of the population was the trigger for the Occupy Wall Street demonstrations that sprang up spontaneously in New York City's Zuccotti Park in September 2011 and with the help of social media spread to the steps of St Paul's Cathedral, in the City of London, and the rest of the world.

It was the moment when anger about the behaviour and bonus

culture of people in banking, which provoked misery for so many people, boiled over into hostile, though mostly peaceful protests. The battle cry of the protesters was 'We are the 99 per cent.' It was based on the findings of a report by the US Congressional Budget Office showing that the wealth of the top 1 per cent income earners in society had increased by three times more than that of the other 99 per cent of society.

In New York Goldman Sachs bankers, crossing Zuccotti Park on their way to the investment bank's luxury tower on the southern Manhattan waterfront, were harried and hassled by the protesters. A lengthy article in 2009 by Matt Taibbi of *Rolling Stone* magazine cast Goldman Sachs as a great vampire squid that had grown rich by wrapping itself around the financial world and squeezing its lifeblood through a long history of sleazy dealmaking.[1]

In London the tent city that sprang up at St Paul's forced the closure of the cathedral at the heart of the financial community. The presence of the occupiers and their cause bitterly divided the clergy, culminating in the resignation of the Rev. Dr Giles Fraser after he opposed efforts to clear the protesters. Andy Haldane, the Bank of England's executive director for financial stability, weighed into the debate arguing that the protesters were right to criticise the bankers and encouraging those bankers to behave 'in a more moral way'.

As part of its effort to deal with the public-relations disaster that was the bonus question Labour commissioned City grandee Sir David Walker, a former deputy governor of the Bank of England, to investigate bankers' pay. His report, released in November 2009, estimated that post-crisis there were still more than 1,000 bankers earning over £1 million a year. His review proposed much greater

---

[1] The *Rolling Stone* article harked back to 1894 and a notorious anti-Semitic tract by 'Coin' Harvey that showed the House of Rothschild as a giant octopus wrapping itself around the world: 'It Feeds on Nothing but Gold.'

disclosure of pay to bankers in their annual reports in bands of those earning between £1 million and £2.5 million, £2.5 million to £5 million and over £5 million. He argued that the revelations would enable shareholders to directly question why remuneration was so high. Initially Sir David favoured the idea that individual recipients of bonuses below main board level be named. But after an open consultation this idea was dropped.

Under the Walker proposals the onus on enforcement would be shifted back to shareholders. Individual directors, not just the chairman, would be subject to re-election annually and a new Stewardship Code, aimed at reinforcing engagement between boards and the owners of the business – the shareholders – would be developed. In parallel with the Walker proposal global regulators, working through the Financial Stability Board under the chairmanship of Mark Carney (at the time governor of the Bank of Canada), developed rules aimed at aligning the interests of bankers more closely with those of shareholders. Bonuses, it was proposed, would mainly be paid in shares, rather than cash, and the ability to cash them in would be postponed for at least three years. But all this is rather easier said than done.

Given what bankers had done to the economy it's scarcely surprising that there should have been public indignation and official investigations. There was also clearly a moral issue here. But there were practical questions to be asked, too. Were the sums paid out each year taking up too great a proportion of banking profits? And could it be argued that it was the lure of bonuses and the casino culture they encouraged that had brought the banking sector down in the first place?

If recent history at Barclays is anything to go by, the answer to the first question appears to be yes. In August 2012, 72-year-old Sir David Walker was propelled into the chairman's seat after the departures of Bob Diamond and Marcus Agius following the disclosure of the rigging of the Libor interest-rate market. Among his first actions was to commission a report by senior City lawyer Anthony Salz into Barclays' business practices.

The review reached the conclusion that bonuses at Barclays were, essentially, too easily achieved and that in future they should only be paid in the case of 'strong performance' across all dimensions of the business. They should also, the report argued, be long-term, simple and transparent. Yet when in early 2014 the bank announced its profits for the previous year, revealing that they were down £1.8 billion at £5.2 billion, it also stated that £2.4 billion would be set aside for bonuses. That figure was up 10 per cent on the previous year and far outstripped the £860 million dividend payout to share-holders. True, chief executive Antony Jenkins waived his personal bonus entitlement but he still picked up a £3.8 million pay packet, based on bonuses from previous years, as part of a £32 million cash bonanza for Barclays' top brass. At a stroke Barclays had created 431 millionaires.

Barclays apologists would no doubt point out that a bonus pot of £2.4 billion is statistically insignificant in an institution that had an income more than ten times that figure: £28.4 billion in 2013. But that £2.4 billion should really be compared with the £2.9 billion that formed the bank's operating profits that year. To award bonuses that are not that far off profit could be hard enough to justify when things are going well. Justification becomes a lot harder when things are going badly. And yet here was a massive bonus being announced just seven months after the Bank of England had effectively ordered Barclays to raise new capital to strengthen its balance sheet and make it more robust. The bankers were getting £2.4 billion. Ordinary shareholders were being asked to stump up £5.8 billion in new capital.

Barclays is not the only bank to pay large bonuses. At the Royal Bank of Scotland Stephen Hester's bonus levels caused enormous embarrassment to the Coalition government and played a part in the political pressure that ultimately led to his departure in 2013. At Lloyds Banking Group the chief executive Antonio Horta-Osorio picked up a £1.7 million bonus despite his bank having to pay out billions of pounds in compensation for mis-selling of payment protection insurance (PPI) and poor sales practices.

Nor is the issue a peculiarly British one. In Germany the bosses of the country's biggest financial group, Deutsche Bank, including co-chief executives Jürgen Fitschen and Anshu Jain, were rewarded with 38 per cent increases in pay and bonuses for 2013. Jain's total pay including pension arrangements soared to €9 million, making him better paid than most of the UK's wealthier bankers. The generous remuneration packages came after a period in which the bank paid out no less than €2.5 billion in regulatory fines. In 2013 profit plunged to €681 billion from €1.1 billion the year before. It remained under the shadow of a global probe into alleged manipulation of the foreign-exchange markets.

In addition to looking at the level of bonuses at Barclays, Anthony Salz also explored the deeper question of whether the bonus culture in itself encouraged unnecessary levels of risk-taking. His view was that it did; indeed, he went so far as to say that 'bank pay helped drive the financial crisis'. In support of this, Salz cited surveys that showed that 80 per cent of market participants believed there to be a link between the bonus culture and dangerous banking practice. While it's hard to dress such an assumption with hard facts, it is certainly the case that in almost every instance of excessive risk-taking it later emerged that those involved were in line for high bonus payouts if their gambles paid off. And while cause and effect are sometimes tricky to prove absolutely, it's hard not to believe that people gambling with money that is not their own are more likely to be relaxed – cavalier, even – about betting it when they know that losses will be borne by the investor and gains will massively swell their own earnings.

Those who defend such high levels of remuneration point out that banking is a global business and retaining the most skilled bankers and their teams requires high pay and bonuses. For individual investment banks to remain competitive and not lose out to their rivals, or to prevent teams setting up on their own as hedge funds or in private equity, it is necessary to pay supercharged rates. Senior bankers and traders have transferable skills, after all, and can easily move from London to New York and from Switzerland to Singapore. Antony Jenkins of Barclays, seeking to justify bonuses in 2014, spoke of a 'death spiral' if key traders were not looked after and well paid. That helps to explain the current situation. Whether it justifies it is another question.

The evidence for an unhealthy relationship between the bonus culture at investment banks and dangerous levels of risk-taking, then, is anecdotal rather than statistical, but the anecdotes are nevertheless powerfully persuasive. And none more so than the sequence of events at JPMorgan Chase that came to be known as the 'London Whale' scandal. It's a debacle that raises profound questions about risk-taking among highly paid individuals, and it also raises broader questions about the extent to which the culture of banking has changed since the chastening aftermath of the bubble years.

JPMorgan Chase is a patrician bank with an enviable record, and few bankers have been more revered than its chairman and chief executive, Jamie Dimon. The silver-fox boss of America's most blue-blooded bank is credited with having steered the group through the Great Panic better than anyone else, picking up two valuable acquisitions – broker Bear Stearns and Washington Mutual – at knock-down prices along the way. In the wake of the crisis, while other banks struggled, JPMorgan produced three years of stunning record-breaking profits.

For most of Barack Obama's first term he was described as the President's favourite banker, visiting the White House 16 times and enjoying three private sessions in the Oval Office. Dimon's frequent appearances on Wall Street's favourite cable station CNBC were treated like a visit from royalty and its most famous presenter Maria Bartiromo, the 'Money Honey', was rolled out to provide the suitably unchallenging questions. In public Dimon has always been a charmer. Those who have worked closely with him inevitably see a slightly different man: a ruthless cost-cutter who comes down hard on what he regards as wasteful spending.

His career has been an impressively successful one. The grandson of a Greek immigrant who rose from being a bank clerk to become a stockbroker, Dimon grew up in the New York borough of Queens. His father, Theodore, was also a broker, eventually working for the Wall Street firm of Salomon Brothers. The young Jamie attended a smart New York prep school, and read psychology and economics at Tufts University before completing an MBA at Harvard. In 1982 at the age of 26 he was offered jobs at the thrusting investment banks Goldman Sachs and Morgan Stanley. Instead he chose to join a friend of his father's, Sandy Weill. And thus began one of the most famous partnerships in modern US financial services. Weill was an aggressive financier on the rise at credit-card business American Express. Dimon joined as his assistant. When Weill was ousted from American Express Dimon followed him.

In 1986 the pair bought a sleepy consumer-loan firm called the Commercial Credit Company. They used that as a vehicle to mount an impressive series of acquisitions, which in the 1990s culminated with Travelers Insurance. In 1998 the upstart Travelers launched an audacious bid for Citigroup, a bank with a heritage dating back 200 years, to create the world's largest financial concern.

The father–son relationship between Weill and Dimon had always been intense and at one point looked unbreakable. They seemed the perfect team, Weill cutting the deals to buy new businesses and Dimon then hammering these newly acquired organisations into shape. But over time strains developed. In 1995 there was a disagreement about Weill's daughter Jessica Bibliowicz who worked at Citigroup. At the end of the decade Dimon abruptly left Citigroup, bringing a brilliant 16-year partnership to an end. For a while he dropped below the radar, waiting for the right opportunity to come along. Then in 2000 he accepted the job to run Chicago-based Bank One, a sleepy combination of three Midwestern banks that had been cobbled together in the merger mania of the 1990s.

Dimon's early decisions at Bank One showed he had lost neither the decisiveness nor the sure touch he had displayed at Citigroup. He quickly brought many of his own people into management. He cut costs. He made the bank's loan book more robust and moved to make the firm's retail banking more consumer-friendly. By 2003 the firm was posting an annual profit up to $3.5 billion compared to its $511 million loss when he took over three years before. It's scarcely surprising that Bank One should have become an attractive takeover target for JPMorgan just a year later.

By contrast, Dimon's old partner Weill was faring less well. Citigroup was hit by the dot-com bust and the scandals at energy trader Enron and telecoms group WorldCom. Weill eventually relinquished control as chief executive in 2003, aged 69. But Dimon went from strength to strength. In 2004 he oversaw the merger of Bank One with JPMorgan. Two years later he became chief executive of the enlarged enterprise. A year after that he added the chairmanship. Regarding the old JPMorgan bank as old-fashioned, arrogant and insular, he encouraged them to take a leaf out of the book of the less fusty Chase Manhattan staff who had become part of the group following a merger in 2000. He led the drive for less formality by example, regularly chatting to junior staff in the corridors as they went about their business. At weekends he often wore trainers to work and in the bank's elite dining room he would order a hamburger and fries. *Fortune* magazine described him as the 'boy wonder from Queens'.

Behind the informality was a quick mind that insisted on detailed reports on all parts of the bank. He likened running his enormous bank to running a corner shop. It all depended, he said, on stock control and bookkeeping:

> You gotta have good book-keeping. You can't have side books and back books, or whatever kinda books – you have to know where you stand with all your stock. I have always said that we have got to only have one set of books at JPMorgan Chase, and be accurate and comprehensive.

JPMorgan emerged from the 2007–8 crisis largely unscathed. Although it had been an early player in the credit derivatives business back in the 1980s, it had also been quite cautious, holding smaller sums on its balance sheet than rivals. Consequently when the prices of these assets plummeted, as the scale of the sub-prime debacle became clear, it had far less to write off than its competitors. While others shrank in size, merged or, in the case of Lehman Brothers, went bust, JPMorgan soldiered on.

In a way, JPMorgan's resilience in 2007–8 makes its fall from grace just six years later more than a little ironic. For it was precisely the complex world of derivatives it had sidestepped before the great crash that came to bite it in 2012.

It was the Chief Investment Office (CIO) that was responsible for the debacle that unfolded in 2012 and 2013. It was one of the key units within the bank, employing around 425 staff – including 140 traders – and had offices in a number of locations including London and New York. It looked after $350 billion dollars of deposits lodged at the bank. That figure alone would have made the CIO the seventh largest bank in the US.

In charge of the CIO was Ina Drew. Aged 54, with a 30-year career behind her, she was one of the most powerful women on Wall Street, with a reputation as a survivor and one who knew the markets inside out. Traders from other departments would make a point of catching her early-morning talks on market strategy. The daughter of a Newark lawyer and a graduate of John Hopkins University, she lives with her family in the well-do-to but unremarkable suburban area of Short Hills in New Jersey. Her career lay solidly in banking, beginning in 1980 as a trader at Bank of Tokyo Trust and then, via various promotions and company mergers, finding her way to JPMorgan. When Dimon took over the running of the bank he promoted her onto his operating committee of senior executives who reported directly to him. In 2005 the CIO was spun out of the bank's treasury operation and Drew was put in charge of it. Traders say managing risk is about managing your emotions. Drew was seen as a calm sure head.

In good times banks take a long view. They think the economy will perform well and customers will pay back their loans. But banks also need to make plans for when the economy falters and companies default on their debt. Over her career Drew had specialised in planning for the bad times. She bought safe products like government bonds and high-quality mortgages and worked out how they would perform if interest rates rose in a growing economy, or fell in a slowing one. In the 2000s quantitative analysis and other forms of computer-driven mathematical applications began to dominate trading markets. Drew was most at home studying fundamental economic trends.

By the mid-2000s the CIO was looking to branch out into more complex products to hedge the growing and increasingly complex holdings of the bank. Drew began to hire staff who would expand the international reach of her team to trade foreign and corporate bonds, but who also had the quantitative skills to work with complex and riskier credit derivatives. In 2006 she hired Achilles Macris from the UK investment bank Dresdner Kleinwort Wasserstein, where he worked as a proprietary trader. He rose quickly and became international chief investment officer, which meant he ran the London office as Drew's top deputy.

Macris in turn recruited Javier Martin-Artajo as head of credit and equity trading. The Spaniard had worked for Macris previously at Dresdner Kleinwort. And it was Martin-Artajo who was the direct boss of Bruno Iksil, the head trader on the synthetic credit default swap portfolio (SCP) from January 2007 to April 2012 and the man who was to become known as the London Whale.

Iksil was just one of thousands of French traders whose precocious mathematical skills, nurtured by France's highly disciplined education system, proved so attractive to the City of London. Having worked as a proprietary trader at Banque Populaire he moved on to the French investment bank Natixis, where he was head of credit derivatives, before arriving at JPMorgan in 2005. A family man with four children, Iksil would travel to London via Eurostar from his home just outside Paris and he tended to work from home on Fridays. Usually dressed in casual clothes and black designer jeans, he rarely met bank clients and was allergic to wearing ties. Despite his post-scandal high profile a photo of him has never been published.

At JPMorgan he took responsibility for one of the most complex areas of products. In 2008 Lord Charles Aldington, a senior executive of Deutsche Bank in London, was asked to define a collateralised debt obligation (CDO). He told MPs on the Treasury Select Committee: 'I have not come before this committee as an expert on CDOs.' It was a telling moment: so complicated were CDOs that a senior banker did not seem to be able immediately to explain them. Such complexity had lain at the heart of the sub-prime scandal. Now, it seemed, it lay at the heart of an area of JPMorgan that was responsible for investing $350 billion of the firm's deposits.

Revenues for the SCP in the early days were volatile but were always positive by the end of the year. In 2008 the portfolio reported $170 million in earnings. The following year was much better, because the SCP anticipated that General Motors would file for bankruptcy and made a series of highly lucrative bets accordingly. In 2009 the SCP earnings increased more than fivefold to $1 billion. In 2010, as the financial crisis began to ease, the view on credit changed and the SCP earnings shrank to $150 million. The Senate subcommittee that was to look into the whole London Whale episode later observed:

> The overall strategy was to increase protection when people were worried but decrease it when people are not worried, like insurance; as people became less worried after the financial crisis, less credit protection was needed by the bank.

By June 2011 Drew and Macris had come to the conclusion that the continuing eurozone crisis would cause the markets to fall, and that the CIO should therefore increase its credit protection. The SCP bought a great deal of long and short credit protection (long protection provided the SCP with insurance against a fall in the value of investments that were expected to rise; short protection offered similar insurance taken on a fall in the price of assets held). It also purchased securities that had fallen heavily in value, which are known as 'distressed'. By the time it had completed its buying spree the notional size of the portfolio had expanded more than ten times, from $4 billion to $51 billion in 2011.

For his part, in September 2011 Bruno Iksil began to take big positions – large investments – in an index of 100 higher risk companies (known as CDX High Yield 11). His gamble paid off handsomely, making a star of the Frenchman within his part of the Chief Investment Office. Credit default swaps work like insurance and are intended to protect financial institutions against potential losses. Iksil took an enormous bet that a basket of 100 firms in the key CDX High Yield index would not default on payments or go bankrupt. In effect he was gambling on a continued improvement in the US economy. Recovery in Europe was unlikely in 2012.

In January 2012 Iksil backed his judgement by aggressively selling credit default swaps to rival trading firms and clients who thought the economy would turn bad. If that were to happen a number of companies in the index would experience what the industry calls a credit event – a missed payment or bankruptcy. Hedge funds, which play the markets on behalf of rich investors and investment funds seeking high returns, were among those who bought Iksil's credit protection, as a form of insurance. JPMorgan would bill the trading firms, hedge funds and other investors four times a year to keep the cover against future losses in place. Should a number of the corporations in the index fail, the US bank would have to make a substantial payout to the traders, hedge funds and other investors that had bought JPMorgan's credit protection insurance.

Iksil was engaged in two simultaneous strategies, a not uncommon practice in trading rooms. He was at one and the same time selling the credit default swaps or insurance against the meltdown, while at the same time taking a huge bet that the meltdown would actually occur. The assumption was that if he bet big enough on the index going horribly wrong the returns would be far greater than the payout JPMorgan would have to make under the terms of the credit default swap. In the early months of 2012 Iksil built his position on the failure of companies within the index, spending $1 billion in all.

Other traders noticed his activities and awarded him his first nickname, the Caveman, because he refused to back down on his bets. His strategy was a highly risky one and many thought that the Caveman was heading for a spectacular fall. But in November two of the corporations in the index, the US power company Dynegy and later American Airlines, went into Chapter 11 bankruptcy, triggering a $400 million payout to the synthetic credit portfolio (SCP) or index. This apparent triumph encouraged even more reckless behaviour.

Iksil had been fortunate in the extreme, but as the Senate subcommittee later pointed out, his success encouraged further risk-taking:

> The American Airlines gain also appears to have coloured how the CIO viewed the SCP thereafter, as a portfolio that could produce significant profits from relatively low cost default protection. In addition, it produced a favourable view within the Chief Investment Office of the SCP's complex trading strategy that involved combining investment grade and non-investment grade credit index trades, accumulating massive tranche positions, and sustaining a period of losses in anticipation of a large payoff.

Towards the end of 2011 the senior management at JPMorgan had asked the CIO to reduce the amount of risky assets it carried on its books by $25 billion. This was part of a firm-wide strategy put in place in advance of new rules, imposed by international banking regulators in Basel, intended to boost the cash held in banks around the world. It was, however, easier said than done. The simplest and fastest way to cut risk is to unwind positions – in other words, reverse investment strategies – by selling them, and Drew accordingly asked Martin-Artajo how much it would cost to adopt this course with the riskier positions. But when Martin-Artajo reported back a few days later he informed Drew this move would be costly.

As with any commodity, whether it is overripe peaches or gold bars, fire sales never yield the best returns. If the assets held in JPMorgan's Chief Investment Office had to be disposed of rapidly the bank would have to accept whatever price was on offer. Unwinding or reversing around 35 per cent of the trades in the portfolio would, it was estimated, produce losses of about $516 million. It was a scenario reminiscent of the 2011 movie *Margin Call* where actors Jeremy Irons and Kevin Spacey engage in a frantic 24-hour effort to dump rotten assets before the market wakes up to what is happening.

Drew was acutely aware that the loss they were looking at considerably exceeded the $453 million profit the portfolio had made in the whole of 2011. Not surprisingly, therefore, she was not keen to pursue this particular route. But that left her with a series of difficult questions. How could the department's risky assets be reduced? How could adequate default protection be kept up across a range of firms the unit thought would default that year because of the eurozone crisis? And would the new SCP strategy be a way to boost revenues over the next 12 months?

JPMorgan's task force, which later reported on the events of 2012 and 2013, concluded of the situation in which Drew found herself: 'These priorities were potentially in conflict. The requirement that the traders satisfy all of these goals appears to have prompted at least some of the complicated trading strategies that led to the losses.' For its part the investigating Congressional subcommittee observed that, for Drew, 'policing risk conflicted with her interest in generating gains.'

At the start of January 2012 the London traders started to retreat from positions based on risky assets. By 10 January, though, Martin-Artajo was emailing Drew to point out that the move 'has been somewhat costly to unwind'. Drew responded the same day: 'Let's review the unwind plan to maximize pl [profit and loss]. We may have a tad more room on rwa [risk-weighted assets].'

Now, instead of reducing risk, the traders began to expand the portfolio on an ad hoc basis to take advantage of the corporate defaults they were sure would come. Having formerly been told to reduce holdings of risky assets they were now told there was still room to hold more. Not surprisingly, this caused some confusion. Iksil, following the earlier plan to wind down the book, had let protection expire only to discover on 19 January that Eastman Kodak were filing for bankruptcy after 133 years in business. His portfolio lost $2.5 million. Iksil's managers told him not to let a loss like this happen again.

To make matters worse, Iksil and Martin-Artajo were by now using calculations that appeared to minimise losses. The CIO typically marked its derivatives books – that is, placed a value on its current holdings for accounting purposes – in line with the midpoint of market prices over a single day. This technique is known as 'marking to market' and is used by the bank's senior financial management to monitor the state of its health on a daily basis.

But in January Iksil and Martin-Artajo started using more favourable prices, rather than the midpoint, with the goal of making the portfolio look as if it was performing better than it was. It did this in two ways. The bankers could pitch prices at the lower end, making the losses on the Iksil's portfolio appear to be smaller. Alternatively, they could price the assets at the higher end to exaggerate gains.

On 22 January 2012 Iksil acknowledged that $100 million had already been lost and forecast that there was more bad news to come with a potential further $300 million of losses. Iksil, Macris, Martin-Artajo and other key staff at the London office therefore met on 26 January to hammer out a new strategy for the year.

Iksil's proposal was not to shrink the SCP but to expand it with a complex mix of long and short bets on the credit markets. In so doing, he argued, they would be able to take advantage of the one thing they were confident of: that because of the euro crisis, 2012 would be a bad year for firms. His idea won general acceptance. In an email he sent to a colleague on the day of the meeting Iksil ordered that dealers make 'the trades that make sense'.

> Sell the forward spread and buy protection on the tightening move. Use indices and add to existing position. Go long on risk on some belly tranches especially where defaults may realise. Buy protection on HY [high yield] and Xover[2] in rallies and turn the position over to monetise volatility.

If that stream of words seems intimidating to the uninitiated, it doesn't seem to have meant much to the experts either. When in March 2013 the Senate subcommittee asked Drew to explain what the strategy was, she struggled. 'The presentation was unclear, and she could not explain exactly what it meant,' the committee reported. Nor did the CIO's chief risk officer Irvin Goldman seem any less befuddled. He told the Senate that the presentation 'did not provide enough information to clarify its meaning'. This was just the kind

---

[2] A credit index comprising a mix of high-yield (junk bond) and higher-yield investment grade names.

of market gobbledegook that regulators might have hoped the great financial crisis would have stopped in its tracks, having exposed the destructive nature of allowing trades that were little understood.

For his part, CIO market risk officer Peter Weiland was able to shed a little light. 'Mr Iksil,' he said, 'was basically describing a strategy of buying low and selling high.' In other words, he was seeking to do what street traders across the world endeavour to do at their market stalls on a daily basis. But he complicated matters by using a series of different strategies over different time periods. At any point in time, therefore, he might have trades pulling in entirely different directions. The fact that senior staff didn't fully understand this – nor the risks entailed – is a little disconcerting.

Throughout January the Chief Investment Office worked on its plan to replace one crucial risk model, plotting the chances of trades going wrong, with another that might slash the perceived risk it had on its books. The aim was to show that it was pursuing a new, safer strategy.

Among the suggested plans was one contained in a 12 January email to Weiland, Martin-Artajo and Patrick Hagan (a quantitative analyst for the CIO who has a PhD in applied mathematics from the California Institute of Technology). It discussed a new value-at-risk (VaR) model Hagan was working on.

VaR is one of the five risk measures the CIO used to police its activities. It measured the most the bank stood to lose on a given day if trades went wrong. 'Hopefully we get this approved as we speak,' Martin-Artajo told Weiland in the same 12 January email.

In a 23 January email Jamie Dimon personally approved a four-day increase in the firm-wide VaR limit. Dimon acted because the CIO's own VaR limit had broken not only its own but the group's overall VaR limit. Hagan's model, which the company later said was full of errors, produced estimates half the size of the old model and well under the unit's $95 million limit when it was introduced on 30 January.

In February the market continued to move against the portfolio as European conditions eased rather than worsened. During this month traders expanded the notional value of the book by $34 billion. Iksil wrote to a colleague that he was doing all he could to cut risk 'as much as I can in a bleeding book'.

In mid-February, another long-term trading limit called the comprehensive risk measure, or CRM, projected that the portfolio could lose $6.3 billion over the next 12 months. Weiland ridiculed these figures. He wrote an email to Martin-Artajo and other managers on 2 March in which he stated: 'We got some CRM numbers and they look like garbage as far as I can tell.'

In fact this figure turned out to be a remarkably accurate prediction of the portfolio's losses by the end of 2012. By the end of February the portfolio had lost a further $69 million, its second straight month of losses.

The extent of Iksil's trading in credit indexes attracted attention. The founder and managing partner of Saba Capital Management bragged at a February investment conference in New York that his best investment idea was to buy protection on the Markit CDX North America Investment Grade Index – an obscure index Iksil was selling protection against. In effect the Saba executive was teasingly recommending that wise investors should do the opposite of what Iksil was doing.

Later, in April, Bank of America managing director Kavi Gupta, a derivatives trader, wrote a note to clients saying that a growing number of hedge funds were coming into this market to bet against the London Whale. 'Fast money has smelt blood,' Gupta wrote. Iksil himself complained in the same month that his stakes had become so big in what were thinly traded illiquid markets that other traders 'knew' his position and were taking advantage.

Daily losses had spun out of control in March. The corporate bond market Iksil was betting against continued to rally, and hedges he put in place didn't keep pace with his mounting losses. All the while the pressure from Martin-Artajo to report higher values escalated. 'I can't keep this going,' Iksil told Julien Grout, a junior trader, in discussing a month-end pricing adjustment requested by Martin-Artajo, according to a transcript of a call on 16 March 2012. 'I don't know where to stop, but it's getting idiotic.' During the same call Iksil added, 'There's nothing that can be done, absolutely nothing that can be done, there's no hope...The book continues to grow, more and more monstrous.' Iksil posted a year-to-date loss of $161.1 million on 16 March, when his losses were closer to $600 million, according to a separate spreadsheet maintained by Grout.

By mid-March meetings were being held every other day to discuss a portfolio that had clearly spun out of control. Now the team were looking to change tack. Previously they had taken a short position, betting on poor credit conditions, as a hedge against the bank. Now they were focusing on a collection of long bets, backing benign market conditions. No longer was the CIO portfolio acting as a hedge against future JPMorgan losses should corporate clients get into difficulty. It was now taking the same position as the bank itself, which was counting on global market conditions improving. By the end of March the portfolio held an $82 billion long position in a credit index called IG9, which represented half the market and counted on improved conditions.

The crunch point for the London Whale came on 23 March at a videoconference between Drew, Iksil, Macris, Martin-Artajo and others. Macris told Drew of the portfolio's mounting losses, but said they had to continue trading to 'defend their positions'.

Drew, however, was unconvinced. As she later told the Senate subcommittee, 'you buy or sell something based on value, not to defend your position.' She therefore ordered the London office to 'put [the] phones down' and stop trading.

CIO chief risk officer Irvin Goldman followed this up with an email later that day saying that Drew 'does not want any trades executed until we discuss it'. This phrase was underlined and in bold. Unfortunately, because the portfolio was locked into so many losing bets, pulling down the drawbridge didn't stem the losses. By the end of March the minus figure stood at $550 million, bringing losses for the first quarter up to $719 million.

On 30 March JPMorgan's own internal audit unit issued a report criticising the CIO risk management department. On the same day Achilles Macris, the head of the CIO's London office where the trades were carried out, wrote in an internal email that he had 'lost confidence' in his team and that the office was in 'crisis mode'.

In late April Drew was removed from control of the portfolio and a team was sent to London, led by the bank deputy chief risk officer Ashley Bacon, to unwind the complex series of bets. The losses continued to mount. By the end of the month they stood at $2.1 billion for the year to date. By the end of the year they had reached $6.2 billion. After that the firm moved the portfolio into the investment bank and stopped reporting its losses separately.

News of the disasters at JPMorgan had started to leak out. On 6 April 2012 the *Wall Street Journal* and Bloomberg revealed that a trader, unnamed but dubbed the London Whale, had taken such big speculative positions in a number of credit markets that prices had actually moved on the bets he made. Not surprisingly, questions began to be asked outside the bank as well as within, and investors started to voice their concern.

JPMorgan's response, though, was robust. It claimed that the press had misunderstood the purpose of the CIO. Its job was to put in place hedges against the risks that the bank took in its other operations and not to engage in aggressive trading. In a statement JPMorgan claimed its CIO unit 'focused on managing the long-term structural assets and liabilities of the firm and is not focused on short-term profits'.

This message that nothing was amiss was underlined by Dimon himself and his chief financial officer Douglas Braunstein when they hosted a first-quarter earnings conference with analysts on 13 April. Dimon was asked directly whether there was cause for concern about the London Whale news reports. He was dismissive:

It's a complete tempest in a teapot. Every bank has a major portfolio. In those portfolios, you make investments that you think are wise that offset your exposures. Obviously, it's a big portfolio. We're a large company and we try to run it. It's sophisticated, well, obviously a complex thing. But at the end of the day, that's our job, to invest that portfolio wisely and intelligently to – over a long period of time – to earn income and to offset other exposures we have.

Braunstein was also questioned on the purpose of the SCP. He said:

We have had that position on for many years and the activities that have been reported in the paper are basically part of managing that stress loss position, which we moderate over time depending upon our views as to what the risks are for stress loss from credit. We are very comfortable with our positions as they are held today. And I would add that all of those positions are fully transparent to the regulators. They review them, have access to them at any point in time, get the information on these positions on a regular basis as part of our normalised reporting. All of those positions are put on pursuant to the risk management at the firm-wide level.

In the face of such confident denials from the irreproachable Dimon and his right-hand financial controller, analysts decided to give the JPMorgan pair the benefit of the doubt. After all, this was Dimon and JPMorgan and not a bank generally considered to be at the more reckless end of the spectrum. No hard numbers that pointed to losses were provided (a statutory requirement if they knew of any). The analysts chose to back Dimon's assurances, knowing that JPMorgan had built a 'fortress balance sheet' (meaning it should always keep a large reserve of spare capital to cope with unforeseen shocks). Dimon had often said publicly: 'Every five years or so, you have got to assume something bad will happen.' In the case of the London Whale it had.

The Dimon and Braunstein show was enough to calm markets. After taking an initial hit from the news reports the Wall Street bank's share price settled back to where it had been before the storm in the teacup. It would rapidly become clear, however, that traders who had tipped off the media on the unusual trading activity of the London Whale were onto something. And, of course, after Dimon made his statement, losses within the CIO continued to climb.

Not surprisingly, therefore, when Dimon faced shareholders in May 2013 at the company's annual general meeting in the bank's capacious settlements office in the bucolic surroundings of Tampa, Florida, the atmosphere was tense. Dimon himself came under fierce pressure to split his all-powerful job of chairman and chief executive in two. It took a veiled threat of resignation, if investors dared strip him of authority, backed by a letter on 10 May 2013 from the board's senior independent director Lee Raymond – a former chairman and chief executive of oil firm Exxon Mobil – to ensure Dimon's survival. Raymond cautioned that splitting Dimon's roles 'could be disruptive' and was against their best interests.

'An inflexible approach to the question of whether one person can serve as both chairman and CEO is not the right answer,' he said. In the event only 32 per cent of investors supported the proposed split. 'This isn't about good governance; it's about busybodies without a clue, trying to do the dumbest thing slapping and shaming a superb CEO for no practical reason,' commented media mogul Barry Diller. In an internal memo to staff Dimon welcomed the outcome, saying: 'I love coming to work here every day – and hope to be doing it for years to come.'

Some of Dimon's fellow executives, who saw 50 per cent votes against them, did not fare so well. Ellen Futter, president of the American Natural History Museum, received only 53.1 per cent in favour of her remaining on the board. James Crown, president of Henry Crown and Company, a Chicago-based investment firm, gained the support of 57.4 per cent of investors and David Cote, chief executive of Honeywell, scored 59.3 per cent in favour of his re-election. All three were members of the board's risk committee. Anne Simpson, head of corporate governance at the large Californian state employee pension fund Calpers, stated: 'This is borderline rejection, too close for comfort, and I would suggest they step down.' Senior independent director Lee Raymond told around 200 investors to 'stay tuned' for changes to the board composition and structure.

In August 2013, some 18 months after news of the London Whale affair broke, the US authorities brought charges against two of those involved. One was Bruno Iksil's boss, Javier Martin-Artajo, a Spaniard who is resident in the Cotswolds. The other was Iksil's subordinate, Frenchman Julien Grout. Iksil, though, was left off the charge sheet drawn up by the US regulator, the Securities Exchange Commission (SEC), when he agreed to cooperate with the prosecutors in outlining just what had gone wrong at the bank.

Dimon's own response to the $6 billion scandal was to gut the Chief Investment Office. In mid-May 2012 he accepted the early retirement of Drew, after more than 30 years on Wall Street. Two months later the bank fired Macris, Martin-Artajo and Iksil. The firm also accepted a number of other resignations at the unit including Weiland, CIO chief financial officer John Wilmot and CIO risk officer Irvin Goldman. It suspended Grout in July 2012, because it was unsure how strongly he was coerced by senior traders. Grout resigned in December 2012.

At group level Braunstein was demoted from chief financial officer to vice-chairman of the firm. The bank also clawed back $100 million from many of these executives in terms of unpaid bonuses and share options. It was one of the first examples of the post-crisis reforms, which gave boards of directors the job of reclaiming bonuses from executives at fault. Drew accordingly lost $21.5 million – though, of course, this has to be put in the context of generous remuneration over many years.

Dimon installed Craig Delany, a member of the bank's executive committee with a role in mortgage banking, as the new head of the CIO. He was given the task of bringing a 'focus on its basic mandate' of investing in high-quality products like government and corporate bonds and mortgage-backed securities. The internal task force recommended that the CIO strengthen its risk unit, which had failed to challenge the strategies of the department's traders. More than 200 new or restructured risk limits were imposed to toughen its investment policies.

Dimon took a cut in annual pay to $11.5 million. His supporters say it is a testament to his strong leadership that in the financial year of the scandal the bank still posted record full-year net income of $21.3 billion on sales of $99.9 billion. There were those among investor groups and activist funds, however, including the trade union-backed CtW and Britain's Hermes Equity Ownership Services, who lobbied for Dimon to lose his role as both chairman and chief executive of the bank. Their argument was that a strong chairman would be able to submit Dimon to greater scrutiny in the future.

When the Senate subcommittee came to report on the whole sorry business at JPMorgan it revealed failures at many levels, not just within the bank but also among those who were supposed to be regulating it. In other words, it exposed a systemic failure reminiscent of the worst days of 2007 and 2008.

Certainly, the regulators do not emerge well from the London Whale fiasco. According to the Senate subcommittee, Iksil's portfolio was not publicly mentioned until 27 January 2012, at which point it was already almost $100 million down. 'The OCC [Office of the Comptroller of the Currency]', it was noted, 'failed to notice and follow up on red flags signalling increasing CIO risk in the reports it did receive from the bank.'

This was hardly due to a shortage of regulators. There were 65 regulatory staff on site at JPMorgan offices in the US who conducted 'approximately 60 examinations' a year into the different areas of the bank. The OCC also has an office in the City of London, though the Senate subcommittee noted that it 'did not ask any of its London staff to conduct examinations of the CIO's London operations'. Among other things, the OCC failed to pick up on the fact that in the reports received the team under Drew's supervision had broken trading limits eight times in 2011–12, sometimes for weeks at a time.

The regulator knew of the of the large $400 million gain the

CIO made at the end of 2011 'but did not inquire into the reason for it or the trading activity behind it, and so did not learn of the extent of the credit derivatives trading going on at the CIO'. If the regulator had looked into the background to the trade it would have found that it was linked to the American Airlines bankruptcy and that this was not tied to any broader strategy for limiting credit exposure at the bank. This would have led them to conclude that this portfolio was set up to make profitable trades rather than hedge risk.

The OCC first learnt of the huge positions the London Whale had racked up when it saw the press reports on 6 April 2012. It admitted to being 'surprised to read about them'. It asked the bank about the losses but, when it received the same kind of reassurances as had been used by Dimon and Braunstein to brief investors, expressed itself satisfied with the explanations and 'considered the matter closed' towards the end of that month. On those occasions when the OCC did try be more forceful JPMorgan simply pushed back harder. In one exchange the OCC said Drew complained the regulator was trying to 'destroy' JPMorgan's business. In other meetings the OCC said bank executives called its staff 'stupid', or took on a 'combative' tone. By all accounts the Comptroller's office, like almost everyone else lived in awe of Dimon and JPMorgan's unimpeachable reputation.

It was not until May 2012, when the bank disclosed that the portfolio had so far produced year-to-date losses of $2 billion, that the regulator consistently pressured JPMorgan for information. In January 2012 the Chief Investment Office began issuing its own monthly executive management report, a review of the essentials of the business. Previously the CIO review was included the bank's Treasury reports. But the CIO did not send its new report to the Comptroller's office for the first four months of the year, which covers the months that losses at the portfolio began to explode.

The subcommittee concluded: 'It is difficult to understand how the bank could have failed to provide, and the OCC failed to request, basic CIO performance data for a four-month period.' The regulator did receive risk limits covering the five different measures designed to monitor the SCP, which – had they have been read – would have showed that the portfolio breached its various limits over 330 times in the first four months of the year.

The OCC knew the bank intended to change the value-at-risk model for the SCP and that this would produce significantly lower results, but did not take this any further. The subcommittee simply 'found no evidence that the OCC made use of the risk limit reports in its routine regulatory oversight efforts.'

The subcommittee said:

> JPMorgan Chase's ability to dodge effective OCC oversight of the multi-billion-dollar Synthetic Credit Portfolio until massive trades, mounting losses, and media reports exposed its activities, demonstrates that bank regulators need to conduct more aggressive oversight with their existing tools and develop more effective tools to detect and stop unsafe and unsound derivatives trading. In addition, the bank's lack of transparency and resistance to OCC information requests indicates that the OCC has failed to establish an effective regulatory relationship with the bank and must take new measures to recalibrate that relationship and ensure good faith cooperation by the bank with OCC oversight.

It added: 'The question is whether the OCC can recalibrate its regulatory relationship to achieve effective oversight, not only with JPMorgan Chase, but also other large financial institutions?'

The new Comptroller of the Currency Thomas Curry took up his position three days before the first press reports about the London Whale broke in April 2012. He survived the criticism and moved to beef up the regulator, including boosting staff numbers, strengthening its derivatives specialists and making its examinations more rigorous. How successful these measures will be remains to be seen. After all, the London Whale affair itself came in the wake of sweeping and thoroughgoing reforms – the Dodd–Frank Act in the US comprised more than 1,000 pages – that had followed the disasters of 2007 and 2008.

So far as the bank itself was concerned, the Senate subcommittee was scathing on the way JPMorgan handled its key value-at-risk model and sought to use it to minimise the size of losses. It suggested that the new VaR model was brought in with the sole purpose of decreasing the appearance of risk and failed to give an accurate measure of the risks the unit was undertaking. The executive responsible, Hagan, told the subcommittee he was 'rushed' and 'under a lot of pressure' to complete his value-at-risk model. He added that he 'never fully understood the prior VaR and so did not know exactly why his model produced lower results'.

Just how different the two models turned out to be is revealed by the fact that on the day the revised VaR model was approved (30 January), the $132 million figure that would previously have been recorded as the amount of cash at risk that day fell at a stroke to $66 million. Thanks to the new model the CIO never breached its VaR limit of a projected $95 million loss in a day. In May the bank was to scrap this VaR model and return to the old one, saying that it had been found to contain mathematical errors and that it required too much manual entering of data onto spreadsheets – a further potential source of errors. But those preceding months were critical. The subcommittee noted that the mismarking of data 'appears to have begun in late January, accelerated in February and peaked in March' – in other words, the figures were most misleading just at the time when accurate data was most desperately needed.

It's scarcely surprising that the Senate subcommittee should have concluded that although the Chief Investment Office was designed to be a hedging unit it had acted more like a risk-taking department. At a time when the bank was taking a long view of the economy the CIO would move between short and long positions in pursuit of profits. With a really lucrative trade, such as the American Airlines deal in 2011, the CIO could not point to the bank taking a counterbalancing view that reflected its optimism about US recovery.

When it came to views of individuals, the consistent message both of evidence given to the subcommittee and to JPMorgan's own task force, which produced a 129-page report into the scandal, was just how much senior management were trusted to get on with the job. The task force said of Drew, for instance: 'She was viewed by senior firm management as a highly skilled manager and executive with a strong and detailed command of her business and someone in whom they had a great deal of confidence.' The US Senate Permanent Subcommittee on Investigations, which produced a 300-page report into the affair, said Drew 'exercised nearly unfettered discretion as a manager'.

How much people further up the chain of command knew and when they knew it is a matter for conjecture. The subcommittee said of Dimon's 'tempest in a teapot' comment to investors on 13 April: 'The evidence also indicates that, when he made that statement, Mr Dimon was already in possession of information about the SCP's complex and sizeable portfolio, its sustained losses for three straight months, the exponential increase in those losses during March, and the difficulty of exiting the SCP's positions'. Dimon, however, contended that he did not how much trouble the CIO was in until days before the bank disclosed to the market on 10 May that the SCP had lost $2 billion, with more losses expected.

The picture that emerges from the whole sorry mess of the London Whale disaster is of a unit left to its own devices until things had spiralled so badly out of control that intervention became essential. The question, therefore, is why those who worked in the CIO should have taken such risks in what was meant to be a hedging unit.

A clue here is the subcommittee's observation that Iksil, Macris and Martin-Artajo 'were among the most highly-paid employees in the bank', and that their pay tended to rise when the unit made higher profits. The trio's pay was pegged to an internal 'reference group' that was largely made up of 'investment bank employees in positions that were profit-orientated, rather than risk management-based'.

In 2011, their final full year at the bank, Drew earned a total of $14 million, Macris $14.5 million, Martin-Artajo $10.9 million and Iksil $6.8 million, while junior trader Grout took home $1 million. More than three years after the collapse of Lehman Brothers there was no indication that bonus structures which incentivise employees to take irresponsible decisions had been curbed, despite barrowloads of new rules and regulations intended to act as fail-safe devices against risky trades. Under the 'Volcker Rule'[3] the type of risky activity these individuals became involved with would be banned by a bank insured by the US government.

*

[3] This rule is named after former Federal Reserve chairman Paul Volcker. His report sent to President Obama in January 2010 argued for a ban on 'proprietary' in-house trading by the investment banks.

Defenders of big banks in general and JPMorgan in particular would no doubt argue that the London Whale incident is a one-off – an unfortunate incident that won't be repeated. What worries more sceptical observers is that the circumstances and the individuals involved are far from being one-offs. The events of 2012 have echoes of earlier banking scandals, and the culture that created them is still very much in place.

Nor has the London Whale fiasco been JPMorgan's only problem in recent times. While the attention of Dimon and the American regulators was turning towards it in 2012, a lesser eruption was taking place in another part of JPMorgan's empire in London. The difficulty this time was at the bank's London corporate broking arm JPMorgan Cazenove. The New York bank had taken full control of Cazenove, the City's most blue-blooded broking house, in November 2009 in a £1 billion deal. The transaction was seen as bringing together two of the greatest historic names in finance. The majority of Britain's leading FTSE100 companies used the services of Cazenove as their corporate stockbrokers, giving JPMorgan access to a rich vein of British clients.

All looked well until April 2012 when out of the blue the British regulator, the Financial Services Authority, alleged that one of the bank's senior dealmakers had abused his position by passing insider information to clients, and announced that it was fining the individual £450,000 for 'inadvertent market abuse'. The dealmaker accused was no ordinary mortal: in his time Ian Hannam had been responsible for arranging the quotation on the London market of several multi-billion pound companies including brewer SAB Miller and miner BHP Billiton. (He had also had a hand in one or two of the more controversial floats of recent years, including the scandal-riven Indonesian coal miner Bumi that has been at the centre of endless disputes.) Hannam's initial appeal to the

Regulatory Decisions Tribunal was turned down but he decided to take the appeal to the next level known as the Upper Tribunal. Hearings were held in July and October 2013.

'Hannam singlehandedly turned the London Stock Exchange from being a UK equity market into a global equity market,' says one of his key supporters, Neil Bennett of the City advisory firm Maitland. The FSA's charges against Hannam rested on confidential emails sent in 2008 providing details to third parties of the potential sale of Heritage Oil to one of his clients.[4]

In August 2013 JPMorgan again found itself in trouble, this time with regulators in New York over its hiring practices in China. The allegation was that, in order to secure business favours from Chinese-based corporations, the bank had hired the offspring of top Chinese officials. As anti-bribery legislation around the world has been tightened, there has inevitably been close scrutiny of the relationships Western companies have with their clients in China and other emerging markets.

The banking group itself had become aware that something might be amiss, noting in its quarterly filing of accounts with the Securities and Exchange Commission in July 2013 that the SEC's anti-bribery unit was looking for information on 'employment of certain former employees in Hong Kong and its business relationships with certain clients'.

One way and another 2013 was a bad time for JPMorgan. In September it paid a fine of $920 million to settle the US investigations into the London Whale affair. In November it agreed to pay $4.5 billion of penalties to settle allegations that it had mis-sold mortgage bonds to pension funds and other investors. In the same month it shelled out $13 billion to settle accusations that before the

---

[4] On 27 May 2014 the Upper Tribunal upheld the decision of the FCA that Hannam engaged in two instances of market abuse. At the time of writing it is not known whether he will appeal.

credit crunch of 2007–8 it routinely bundled sub-prime mortgages into securities and sold them on as high-quality investments. Dimon had previously sought to claim that responsibility for this rested with Bear Stearns and Washington Mutual, two firms that JPMorgan absorbed in the era of the Great Panic. And in January 2014 the bank admitted that it had failed to alert US authorities to the Ponzi scheme[5] run by serial fraudster Bernard Madoff and paid a further penalty of $2 billion. Over a three-year period JPMorgan went from saint to sinner, paying in total an astonishing $28.7 billion in fines.

JPMorgan's recent record has been a depressing one for that most blue-blooded of all American financial houses. But it's also not a unique one, and it shows how little banking culture has moved beyond the dark days of 2007 and 2008. Former Bank of England governor Lord King has gone so far as to suggest that it may be impossible to regulate the behaviour of the banks and those who work within them. He despairs at the fact that five years on from the crisis the 'too big to fail' problem has not been resolved. The Americans would not run the risk of the dislocation of the US financial markets to allow an institution like JPMorgan Chase to fail because they are simply too big.

For JPMorgan a key issue is whether it really is possible for one individual to rule a vast empire, even if that individual has the track record and charisma of Jamie Dimon. Citibank and Bank of America Merrill Lynch – both of which came to serious grief in the financial crisis – have split the roles of chairman and chief executive at the behest of their investors.

But, arguably, JPMorgan's recent woes are also symptomatic of a more general and ongoing malaise in banking. In the

---

[5] Ponzi schemes illegally use the flow of funds coming from new clients to fund dividends and other promised payouts to existing investors.

post-crisis period the banks faced the challenge of rebuilding weak balance sheets. The perilous combination of the need for greater profits and still lax bonus rules motivated reckless behaviour. This manifested itself in different ways. In retail banking it drove the sale of products that customers had no need of, generating a £18 billion mis-selling scandal in UK domestic banking. It led traders in the investment-banking arms of the banks to bend the rules by seeking to rig and manipulate interest-rate, foreign-exchange, energy and other financial markets, helping to cause the Libor scandal. And for the big international banks, like HSBC and Standard Chartered, it encouraged employees to stretch rules governing money laundering and financial sanctions.

The transition from crisis to repair offered the banking industry a profit and bonus opportunity. Lawmakers and regulators were still catching up with the public mood and were distracted by the need to build new structures, establish stronger rules and improve the quantity and quality of regulation. It was in this atmosphere that the bankers and traders played a game of regulatory arbitrage, finding the weaknesses in the system and exploiting them with scandalous and disastrous results.

# 6

# Fixing the Market: Libor and Interest-Rate Rigging

In his first nine years in office Mervyn King, the fiercely intellectual governor of the Bank of England, showed no inclination to become personally involved in the affairs of the commercial banks. In private he felt free to berate their behaviour in the run-up to the financial crisis of 2007–9. He worried about the way in which high-risk casino-type investment banks had come together with traditionally low-risk, high-street banks, and the tensions in goals that resulted. And he was critical of a pay and bonuses structure that seemed to reward people who took the greatest risks with their institutions, and of strategies that appeared to focus on shareholder dividends rather than the prudent managing of capital and liquidity.

Up until May 1997, when New Labour made the Bank of England independent of government, it had been customary for the governor of the Bank to keep a wary eye on the bankers. King's priorities were very different, and he focused on building the Bank into a monetary institution that enjoyed the same high status for its economic analysis as the pre-euro Bundesbank in Germany. In this he was brilliantly successful. His slightly owlish, bespectacled figure, with its extraordinary ability to explain complex concepts in easy-to-understand terms, was widely respected, and his power to restrain inflation – the scourge of British governments in the late 20th century – acclaimed.

But the morning of Monday 2 July 2012 witnessed a radical departure for the governor. Shocked by the news that had reached him from Barclays Bank over the weekend, he took the rare step of summoning its chairman Marcus Agius and senior independent director Michael Rake – the deputy chairman – to his office. The background to his decision to call in these two senior figures was the revelation that Barclays, among others, had been manipulating the London Interbank Offered Rate (Libor), the interest rate used to set the cost of transactions worth trillions of pounds and dollars across the globe. The immediate cause of his decision was the disclosure that the chief executive of Barclays had *not* resigned.

King's expectation had been that the emergency board meetings held at Barclays over the weekend would result in the departure of Bob Diamond, the buccaneering Barclays chief executive, who had come to be seen as the central figure in the Libor-rigging scandal. Agius, a tall, silver-haired figure with a touch of the old City about him, would keep the ship steady until a new chief executive had been identified and put in place, and would then fall on his sword. In the event, though, what had actually happened was that Agius had decided to resign and Diamond had decided to stay.

At the Monday-morning meeting in the governor's parlour, beneath a portrait of his esteemed predecessor Montagu Norman, King finally exercised the peculiar authority of his office as so many of the previous holders of the office had done. Calmly and carefully he began the conversation by saying that, of course, he had no authority in this area and was not speaking for the government, although the Treasury was aware he was having the conversation. Then the gloves came off.

King told the two men that he wanted them to understand that

Agius's resignation alone could not be regarded as resolving the problem. The regulators had lost confidence in the bank, and the scalp of a non-executive chairman who could not be said to shape the bank's culture was not what was required. Both Agius and Rake questioned King's analysis, at which point the governor reached for his copy of a letter from the regulator which had been delivered to the Barclays board on 10 April 2012. He went through it paragraph by paragraph in an exchange that lasted more than 15 minutes. The regulators, he concluded, had a 'very real problem' and added that 'something has to change'.

At no point during the conversation did King say that Diamond or any other individual should resign but he did urge that when Agius and Rake left the room they should reflect on his comments.

When the stock exchange opened the following day it did so to the tumultuous announcement that Bob Diamond, one of the most powerful of all bankers, had been eased out by his board. King was later to be accused by the Commons Treasury Select Committee of having sacked Diamond and, in so doing, overreached his authority. 'I don't need any more authority to have a conversation' was his response.

The dramatic departure of Bob Diamond from his roomy office in the Barclays tower at Canary Wharf, decorated with photographs of Chelsea FC's triumph earlier that year at the European Cup Final in Munich, was a symbolic moment. If the financial crash of 2007–9 revealed real shortcomings in the way banks handled themselves, the Libor scandal of 2012 that brought Diamond down suggested that they had learned few if any lessons. More than that, it showed the risks inherent in high-street banks that had become investment giants.

And Barclays was, at its heart, a retail bank, taking deposits from customers and lending them out to other individuals and businesses. It had a venerable history, stretching back to 1690 when John Freame and Thomas Gould, both Quakers, established the first London office. The business initially attracted depositors because of the Quaker reputation for integrity. In 1728 the bank moved to its famous Lombard Street address in the City, where it would remain until the group's headquarters shifted a few miles east to Canary Wharf in 2005. In 1736 James Barclay, the son-in-law of John Freame, became a partner in the business.

The bank's growth surged in 1896 as it merged 20 regional banks and became a joint stock bank under the Barclays name. The enlarged business, which employed 1,500, was listed on the London Stock Exchange in 1902, and by 1925 had become one of the country's five biggest banks.

Between 1925 and 1986, the time of the Big Bang in London which deregulated the City and allowed further foreign competition, Barclays continued to expand at home and abroad. Two of its biggest overseas acquisitions at the time were the National Bank of South Africa and the Colonial and Anglo-Egyptian Bank, both in 1966. But at home it continued to demonstrate it was at the cutting edge of banking. In 1966 it launched Barclaycard, the country's first credit card. And in 1985 it followed Midland Bank (bought by HSBC in 1992) in abolishing transaction charges for retail customers who were in credit. Even though the shareholdings of the founding families had faded to virtually nothing, the bank had a system of fast-tracking talented executives, and the names Tuke, Bevan and Buxton cascaded down the generations. John Varley, who was chief executive during the period when the culture went awry, had married into the Pease family – one of the founding dynasties.

After the Libor scandal, Anthony Salz, vice-chairman of N M Rothschild and a former senior partner at the law firm Freshfields Bruckhaus Deringer, was asked to write a report on the bank.

Describing its culture he noted: 'As a bank originally dominated by family interests, Barclays had developed a culture in its early years that was described to us as reflecting its non-conformist origins, but also somewhat based on patronage rather than being meritocratic.' This culture was 'described as family values or simply how things had always been done'. (The report went on to say: 'As the bank grew and the external environment changed, the family-based culture was eroded and something of a vacuum seems to have developed, with individual businesses developing their own way of doing things.')

It was in the aftermath of the Big Bang of 1986, at which time Barclays employed 110,000 staff around the world, that the decision was made to diversify the nature of its business and break into the lucrative but competitive business of raising cash for major corporations on the international money markets and City trading. Stockbroker de Zoete & Bevan and stockjobber Wedd Durlacher were duly purchased to create an investment-banking arm Barclays de Zoete Wedd (BZW). Barclays was now playing in a league dominated by large US players such as Goldman Sachs, Morgan Stanley and JPMorgan, all of whom had a history of trading their own money on the financial markets along with those of their clients.

After running up big losses in real-estate lending, the bank began to expand again in the early 1990s, and in 1994 a further break with the past occurred: the bank took on a chief executive, Martin Taylor, who had no family links to the founders of the bank. Two years later, on 4 July 1996, Boston-born Bob Diamond joined the group from Credit Suisse First Boston.

Diamond was a classic American success story. The dark-haired, elegant banker with an engaging smile and a slight Irish lilt to his accent began life in Concord, Massachusetts, one of nine children born to his Irish-Catholic parents who were both teachers. After a brief academic career at the University of Connecticut he moved into investment banking, working for Morgan Stanley and Credit Suisse First Boston before moving across to Barclays in 1996. Here he transformed the investment bank into an international powerhouse. When I once complained to Agius, who became chairman of Barclays in 2006, about the levels of Diamond's remuneration (and the fact that his employer paid his American taxes), Agius pointed out that Diamond was different from other bankers: he was not some mere employee but an entrepreneur who had built a business within Barclays from scratch.

Diamond's initial task was to run Barclays de Zoete Wedd and the diverse group of businesses that formed its investment bank. Barclays Capital, as it was called, had grown fitfully as it tried to establish itself in a cut-throat environment, and the late 1990s proved a bumpy ride: huge losses were chalked up in 1998 owing to the Russian financial crisis, and exposure to the failed hedge fund Long-Term Capital Management (LTCM) served to make things worse. But Diamond was not deterred. In 2003 he launched the Alpha Plan at Barclays Capital, which aimed to close the gap on its US rivals by more than doubling revenues in four years.

Under Diamond's direction Barclays Capital developed a distinct close-knit leadership team. Salz found the culture at the investment bank 'hard-working, fast, competitive and well rewarded for success'. Diamond hired senior bankers and awarded generous pay packages in a bid to play catch-up with rivals. Between 2002 and 2009 the unit paid out an average of £170 million a year in long-term bonuses to a changing group of around 60 people. Rich Ricci and Jerry del Missier became his most trusted lieutenants. The unit moved from strength to strength, becoming the most profitable part of the bank. Salz noted that: 'In little over a decade, the weight of Barclays' business model has moved from one based on relatively simple consumer products to one whose revenue depends increasingly on far more complex investment banking.'

From his perch in New York Diamond thus transformed Barclays Capital into one of the biggest and most effective traders in international debt, adding along the way an innovative fund management group, Barclays Global Investors. The San Francisco-based firm was the brainchild of a smart American financier, Pattie Dunn[1], who was a pioneer in creating a new form of investment vehicle known as the Exchange-Traded Fund: it was effectively a new type of share that enabled investors across the world to invest directly in stock-market quoted vehicles that traded in all manner of assets from gold to stock indices and shares. By 2005 things were looking good. In the bank's Equality and Diversity Review of that year Varley wrote to staff: 'You've heard me say before that I want Barclays to be a top five bank. I measure that not by stock market size but by capability. In other words, the test is: are we seen by our customers and clients as one of the best (i.e. Top 5) in each of the markets or segments or product areas in which we compete? The answer to that is yes.' It was to be only a matter of time before Diamond replaced Varley at the helm of the bank.

Diamond's greatest coup came in the immediate aftermath of the collapse of Lehman Brothers in September 2008 when he swooped in to buy the healthy American corporate broking and trading part of the bank (including its New York headquarters) for £1.2 billion from the receivers. At a stroke he turned Barclays into one of the world's most powerful investment-casino banks, the profits of which would outstrip that of its Quaker-founded parent. Even before the Lehman purchase the investment bank accounted for 31 per cent of the group's record £7 billion sales in 2007. It would grow to around

---

[1] Dunn died of ovarian cancer in 2011 after a long battle with the illness.

half of the bank's revenues. In a little over a decade Diamond had, almost from a standing start, taken a small investment bank and made it a global player.

Diamond's razor-sharp mind and eye for the main chance allowed Barclays to skate through the financial melee of 2007–9 relatively unscathed. It has to be said, though, that there was one major near miss, and a number of ongoing concerns. The near miss came when, to cement its bold perception of itself, Barclays tried to buy Dutch rival ABN Amro in 2007; it only dodged what would prove to be a highly toxic bullet when Sir Fred Goodwin's Royal Bank of Scotland stepped in and created a consortium to buy ABN Amro for £49 billion.

The ongoing concerns were more general ones, wrapped up with differing perceptions of Barclays' underlying health in the years of the credit crunch. Anthony Salz described this phase of the bank's history in the following terms:

During interviews we were told that at times the executive management and Board of Barclays felt under siege, not only from the volatile markets but also from its stakeholders. The FSA and the Treasury naturally questioned whether Barclays could continue to operate without Government help following the Government's rescue of RBS and subsequently LBG [Lloyds Banking Group, the newly merged Lloyds TSB and HBOS]. In markets there were questions over many banks' asset valuations and Barclays was subject to particular scrutiny.

Barclays was determined not to take government cash and to preserve its independence. The idea of giving the British government a say in its affairs was anathema for a bank with a distinct free-enterprise culture and global brand. In particular it feared that its buccaneering investment-banking approach, already under scrutiny from regulators, might be curtailed.

Instead it went twice to sovereign wealth funds in the Middle East and Asia for money. The bank's first cash call, in June 2008, saw Qatar Holding, Challenger (another Qatari fund) and other sovereign wealth funds, including Temasek of Singapore, invest a total of £4.5 billion in the bank. The initial deal raised merry hell among traditional shareholders, who objected to being excluded from a fundraising in which they felt they should have been given first preference. The second capital-raising in October and November 2008 involved Qatar Holding and Challenger investing with Abu Dhabi a total of £7.3 billion in the bank.

At the time, Barclays saw the Middle East fundraising as essential to survival. The fundraising was orchestrated by the bank's chief financial officer, Chris Lucas. But the big fees paid to intermediaries have come to be seen as a blot on the bank's integrity. In time the FSA (succeeded by the Prudential Regulatory Authority in 2013) and the Serious Fraud Office were to launch investigations into whether Barclays, in part of a complex deal, loaned Qatar the cash to buy the bank's own shares, which contravenes market regulations.

In August 2013 Chris Lucas – a central figure in the mounting investigations into the Middle East fundraising – resigned abruptly, stating ill health, having signalled earlier that he wanted to leave after six years running Barclays' finances. 'I want to do the right thing by Barclays, my family, and myself, and therefore I have reached the difficult decision to step down sooner,' he told shareholders.

As part of its bid to raise cash the bank also sold its fund management arm Barclays Global Investors (BGI) to the giant US asset manager BlackRock for £8.2 billion in June 2009. Bob Diamond, himself a shareholder in BGI, personally pocketed £27 million from the share sale. While this is not a breach of any law or rule, corporate governance frowns upon directors profiting from personal holdings of shares in connected companies, so this particular transaction raised eyebrows. When I queried the issue directly with chief executive John Varley – who was an early backer of the BGI business – he passed it off as of little importance, simply noting that Diamond had been an early investor in BGI shares and was reaping his reward.

The market, the regulators and the government continued to take a strong interest in Barclays during this period. At the end of 2008 Barclays' leverage ratio, the ratio of lending to cash in hand, was higher than that of its UK rivals. The high leverage ratio reflected both the ambition of the bank's lending and the inadequacy of its capital in very uncertain times. In January 2009 Barclays had to take the highly unusual step of issuing a market statement saying it did not have to raise cash. Chairman Marcus Agius and chief executive John Varley jointly stated: 'Our starting point is that Barclays has £36 billion of committed equity capital and reserves; we are well funded, and we are profitable.'

Barclays went on to pass stress tests, which studied whether the bank held sufficient high-quality assets to withstand another shock, in 2009 and later in 2011. But questions still remained over whether the bank had the strength to remain out of government hands. Indeed, the issue was still unresolved in 2013 and would lead to yet another bruising encounter with the regulators. In the words of the Salz review: 'We consider the intense focus on Barclays' valuation and accounting reflected not only attitudes resulting from the growth of its investment bank but also a view that Barclays was somehow failing to tell the whole story, an impression which management was unable to correct.'

Much of the reason for this was the aggressive stance against regulators adopted at Barclays Capital over the value of the assets on its books. Barclays consistently claimed, for instance, that although it held asset-backed securities based on US sub-prime mortgages on its books the quality was far better than those that had caused the financial meltdown. Varley explained to me on several occasions that most of the mortgage securities held by Barclays were 'Alt-A' – alternative mortgages that were more risky that standard home loans but less risky than sub-prime. Similar claims were made by some of the other distinctly opaque assets held on the bank's books.

Concerned that things were not as transparent as they might be, the financial authorities became uneasy, and there was a certain accompanying level of distrust among shareholders. What caused particular worry was the schemes the group put in place to improve its balance sheet, and therefore the financial strength of the business. Briefly summarised, these devices involved shifting risky assets off the books through clever accounting.

The prime example of this questionable strategy was the firm's Protium deal, set up in September 2009. It involved a package of £7.6 billion of mortgage-based assets being sold to a team of 45 Barclays traders who would then run the assets on behalf of the bank through an independent company called C12 Capital Management based in the Cayman Islands. Barclays loaned the cash to C12 to buy the assets and agreed to pay them £26.5 million a year based on performance to run them. The effect of the scheme was to remove these risky assets from Barclays' balance sheet. In an interview with me, during the week that Protium was announced, Varley argued that it was a normal transaction and that it had been approved by the regulators, 'end of story'. Salz, however, disagreed: 'FSA executives told us that there were conversations with Barclays conveying the FSA's view that Protium was a complex transaction with which they were very uncomfortable.'

The group battled the regulators to keep Protium off its books for the next two years. But in March 2011 the US Securities and Exchange Commission said it was 'unable to concur with [Barclays'] conclusion that the non-consolidation of Protium is appropriate'. With both the US and the UK regulators now against it Barclays knew the game was up; in April 2011 it took back £6 billion of Protium assets onto its balance sheet, paying out £55 million as a break fee to C12. Barclays also agreed to buy out £179 million of undisclosed third-party investors in the deal. And it invested £496 million in another C12 fund called Helix. As ever, the accounting was opaque and the pain was taken by Barclays investors rather than the participants in the transaction.

None of this perturbed the ever-bullish Diamond. Other UK bank chief executives attempted to keep a low profile, but Diamond broke ranks, telling MPs in 2011 that the time for 'remorse and apology' over the role of banks during the financial crisis should come to an end. Worries nevertheless persisted about Barclays. The following year FSA chairman Lord Adair Turner held private talks with Agius during which he laid out some of the issues troubling the regulator. He followed this up with a formal letter outlining his concerns over Barclays' 'pattern of behaviour over the last few years'. He listed Protium and five other schemes that were of concern, arguing that the FSA was left with 'an impression that Barclays were [sic] seeking to "spin" its messages in an unhelpful fashion'. The FSA, its chair said, 'urge you and the Board to encourage a tone of full cooperation and transparency between all levels of your Executive and the FSA'. Dated 10 April 2012, the letter was delivered just two months before the Libor scandal broke.

On 18 April Agius replied, yielding little ground and defending the bank's position on most of the points Lord Turner had made. The Barclays chairman argued that the valuations the bank used 'were within the acceptable spectrum. Time and markets have proven these to be less aggressive than suggested.' He made no apology for 'protracted' discussions with the FSA 'because we had very strongly held views'.

Salz was in no doubt that relations between Barclays and its regulators were in a bad way by the time the Libor scandal broke. His report concluded: 'We believe a culture developed within Barclays, quite possibly derived originally from the investment bank, which came across to some as being "clever" or what some people have termed "too clever by half", even arrogant and aggressive. Barclays was viewed by some as pushing the envelope to the limits. This was a view expressed at times by the financial regulators, at least in the UK. It is also true that some shareholders and public bodies shared the same perspective.' It was that arrogance allied to the market uncertainties Barclays faced during the tumultuous years of the credit crunch that led it inexorably into the Libor scandal.

While the technicalities of the London Interbank Offered Rate are complex, the underlying principle is simple enough. Libor, whose origins date back to the 1960s and 1970s, is the benchmark interest rate that banks use to set the cost of major market transactions. Often referred to as the most important number in finance, it underlies some $800 trillion-worth of financial instruments ('about six times the world economy in orders of magnitude of dollars of contracts' according to the chairman of the Commodity Futures Trading Commission (CFTC), Gary Gensler), ranging in sophistication from interest-rate derivatives to mortgages. In other words, the Libor rate determines the cost of borrowing for almost everything from what the largest businesses pay for loans to what families receive for their savings. Banks making Libor-related loans quote the interest rate as 'Libor plus', the plus element being the interest rate on top of Libor calculated on the perceived nature of the credit risk.

For such an important number, the Libor rate is calculated in a surprisingly unsophisticated way. Each day since 1988 16 major banks have been asked: 'At what rate could you borrow funds, were you to do so by asking for and then accepting inter-bank offers in a reasonable market size just prior to 11am?' They then submit estimates of what it would cost them to borrow across 10 currencies and 15 lengths of loan, ranging from overnight to 12 months. What emerges is not one simple figure but a whole directory of rates depending on the currency and the length of time for which the money is being borrowed. The submissions at the time of the disclosure of the scandal were collected by media corporation Thomson Reuters, acting on behalf of the UK trade body the British Bankers' Association (BBA), which strips out the four highest submissions and the four lowest and then averages the remaining eight. Just after 11am the rate is flashed across tens of thousands of trading screens around the world.

The rate is not formally supervised by any national authority – so it is entirely in that sense free-market – and herein lies a core weakness. No one nation has responsibility for it, and the body that oversees its collection, the BBA, has little if any real muscle. As a result, a rate brought in to ensure an independent and impartial process for the handling of unsecured loans by banks is open to manipulation. And, almost inevitably, that is precisely what has happened.

In Barclays' case it emerged that some of the false submissions came in the fevered aftermath of the Great Panic in 2008. (It's worth noting, though, that the New York Federal Reserve, which regulates Wall Street, said it first saw mass-distribution emails in the market questioning the validity of Libor rates as early as 2005.) The Royal Bank of Scotland (RBS) and the Lloyds TSB and HBOS, after a hurried merger, had been bailed out by the government and were therefore perceived as stable.

Barclays did not wish to appear weak by submitting higher Libor rates than its rivals. It was sensitive to the fact that in the summer of 2007 it had been stigmatised by the money markets after it was disclosed to have been a heavy user of the Bank of England's emergency overnight borrowing facilities. It had no wish to feature in the headlines again. By submitting a lower rate than it was actually paying it would send a signal to the City and international markets that it was a robust bank able to borrow and lend at the finest rates. Barclays also made a great deal of money from trading all manner of financial instruments. If dealers had even microseconds of advance knowledge of the rates to be submitted they could adopt trading positions that would generate income, boosting the performance and bonus income of the unit concerned. In the United States several class action suits, groups of potentially harmed clients brought together by lawyers working on contingency fees, are planning to test the case for compensation against banks in the courts.

In a disciplinary notice delivered on 27 June 2012 the Commodity Futures Trading Commission (CFTC), the American regulator of commodity and derivatives markets, reported: 'Barclays' traders located at least in New York, London and Tokyo asked Barclays' submitters [those submitting borrowing costs to the Libor committees] to submit particular rates to benefit their derivatives trading positions, such as swaps or futures positions, which were priced on Libor and Euribor. Barclays' traders made these unlawful requests routinely.'

The traders themselves took a distinctly casual approach to their acts of manipulation: 'always happy to help' and 'done . . . for you big boy' were just two of the email comments exchanged between Barclays' traders and Libor submitters that were later revealed by the CFTC in the US and the FSA in the UK. Perhaps most notorious of all was an effusive thank you in May 2006 emailed by a now former Barclays' employee to a derivatives trader who had responded positively to a request to submit a lower Libor rate: 'Dude. I owe you big time! Come over one day after work and I'm opening a bottle of Bollinger.'

It should be noted that Barclays were not the only offenders. As regulators and prosecutors from Canada to Tokyo started to look into the rigging scandal, some 16 of the world's biggest lenders ranging from America's giant Citigroup to Japan's Bank of Tokyo-Mitsubishi UFJ came under scrutiny. And, judging from some of emails exchanged between traders, there were people in a number of banks who were as blatant in their manipulation of the Libor rate as their Barclays rivals. US and UK regulators established, for example, that at RBS 'misconduct was widespread', with over 219 documented requests to fix the rate and 'an unquantifiable number' of oral requests. The watchdog found the practice, between 2006 and 2010, involved at least 21 traders and at least one manager. When they examined taped conversations and email exchanges the FSA was able to pick up, via the bank's Bloomberg instant-messaging system, just how casual and frequent the abuse was.

On 14 September 2009, for example, a trader, identified as Derivatives Trader B by the FSA, asked one of the bank's Libor submitters, called Primary Submitter B, for a high Libor rate (the industry refers to submitted rates as 'fixings'). But the next day, 15 September, the trader asked for the rate to fall:

DERIVATIVES TRADER B: can we lower our fixings today please
PRIMARY SUBMITTER B: make your mind up, haha, yes no probs
DERIVATIVES TRADER B: im like a whores drawers[2]

---

[2] 'A whore's drawers', which move up and down with great rapidity, is a familiar phrase used by City traders. It refers to high volatility in markets where prices rise and fall with exceptional speed.

On March 2007 the FSA picked up another email exchange between an RBS trader, Derivatives Trader D, and another trader at a rival Libor bank, External Trader A:

> DERIVATIVES TRADER D: please please low 6m [six-month] fix on Monday . . . I have got a big fix.
> EXTERNAL TRADER A: No worries.

At Swiss bank UBS, meanwhile, according to the FSA the following message was sent by a trader to a broker:

> If you keep 6s [six-month yen Libor] unchanged today . . . I will fucking do one humongous deal with you . . . Like a 50,000 buck deal, whatever . . . I need you to keep it as low as possible . . . if you do that . . . I'll pay you, you know 50,000 dollars, 100,000 dollars . . . whatever you want . . . I'm a man of my word.

The UBS missive clearly reveals a banker offering a bribe to their broker. Inter-dealer brokers are independent finance houses who bring different banks together as anonymous buyers and sellers. Brokers make their money from commissions on these trades. Bankers engaged in Libor manipulation often used so-called 'wash trade'. This refers to transactions put through a favoured broker with an equal and opposite trade made soon after. There is no economic benefit to this trade, but the broker picks up a tidy commission. Astonishingly, the FSA found evidence of more than 1,000 occasions of collusion between UBS and eleven brokers at six different brokerage firms, mainly to fix the Japanese yen Libor market.

At RBS, meanwhile, cosy relationships were even cosier. In a

February 2013 disciplinary ruling the FSA described how 'RBS failed to identify and manage the risks of inappropriate submissions' and went on to explain the less than satisfactory seating arrangements that the bank had adopted. 'RBS established a business model that sat derivatives traders next to Libor submitters and encouraged the two groups to communicate without restriction despite the obvious risk that derivatives traders would seek to influence RBS' Libor submissions.'

Given how widespread the abuse appears to have been, it may seem surprising that when the scandal started to hit the front pages Barclays should have come in for particular criticism. After all, to take just one other example, in December 2012 UBS was to be fined £940 million, after the FSA found it guilty of 'extensive and widespread' misconduct, involving at least 45 bankers over the five-year period 2005–10 and 2,000 documented requests for Libor manipulation, not to mention countless verbal ones. But Barclays suffered most because they owned up first. They had made a decision, advised by the legal firms Clifford Chance in London and Sullivan & Cromwell in the US, to settle with the regulators as quickly as possible in order both to remove a shadow over operations and to earn praise for owning up to past mistakes. This was a perfectly sensible decision on the face of it, but it was one that backfired.

In June 2012 American and UK regulators revealed they had fined the British bank Barclays £290 million for attempting to manipulate Libor between 2005 and 2009. At a stroke Barclays found that it had become the lightning rod for all that was perceived to be wrong in the financial community. Diamond himself became a target for criticism, not least because he was so well paid: during his tenure at the top he amassed £100 million in pay and perks. He was eager to portray himself as a new type of banker, a better 'corporate citizen', with a keen interest in developing banking in Africa (I gently teased him with the name 'Safari Bob' in my column in the *Daily Mail*). This was not what the media, however, chose to focus on.

Just 24 hours after Diamond was eased out of Barclays, and on a day when he should have been celebrating American independence with his family, he appeared before the Treasury Select Committee. It was precisely 16 years since his arrival at the British bank. The anniversary was marked by a three-hour grilling, during which many aspects of Barclays' conduct in general and his in particular came in for scrutiny.

But Diamond also had his own bombshell to drop. In the course of questioning by MPs he recalled a phone conversation he had had with Bank of England deputy governor Paul Tucker on 29 October 2008. During the call, Diamond testified, Tucker had mentioned that 'senior' Whitehall figures were concerned at the high Libor figures the bank had been submitting, and that there was a feeling that these should be lowered in a bid to calm the market perception of Barclays' creditworthiness. Unusually, Diamond had taken a note of the conversation, which he had passed to his chief operating officer Jerry del Missier and which Barclays now released.

'Mr Tucker stated the level of calls he was receiving from Whitehall were "senior", the note recorded, 'and that while he was certain that we did not need advice, that it did not always need to be the case that we appeared as high as we have recently.' Del Missier understood this to mean that Diamond, with government backing, was telling him to lower its Libor submissions. The order was passed on to his rate submitters.

The suggestion that someone in Whitehall had demanded that Barclays act to lower a free-market interest rate set the hares running. Just a week after regulators had uncovered the rigging of the most important number in finance, Diamond was now saying that the central bank, backed by government, had told Barclays to manipulate its submissions as far back as 2008. Diamond might have been seeking to clear his own name and put some distance between himself and the Libor affair but in the process he had drawn Paul Tucker into the scandal and set off a witch-hunt for a Whitehall 'meddler'. Chancellor George Osborne saw a chance to make some political mischief at the expense of his Labour predecessors. He claimed that ministers in the previous Labour government, including Ed Balls, now Shadow Chancellor, were directly involved in the Libor scandal.

In July 2012, as a result of a freedom of information request, Labour MP John Mann obtained a series of emails that cast new light on who the mysterious Whitehall figure may have been. The exchanges were between Paul Tucker and the Cabinet Secretary Sir Jeremy Heywood, a former investment banker at Morgan Stanley in London. In the 2008 emails Heywood expresses concern that rates of borrowing for US dollars have fallen faster than those for sterling. In one of the exchanges Heywood asks Tucker if he has heard Libor is high 'because Barclays is bidding it'. Tucker responds that the Bank of England is monitoring the situation.

Paul Tucker, at the time the front-runner to replace Sir Mervyn King as the governor of the Bank of England, found his reputation on the line. He requested a hearing before the MPs' committee as soon as possible, and duly appeared the following week. Asked if government ministers had requested that he lean on Barclays he replied, 'Absolutely not.' Since his call to Diamond had not been recorded – and in fairness it was just one of many calls he had had to make that day – and since there was no note-taker present (the usual protocol when sensitive calls are made from government departments), nothing could be proved either way. But the fact that Tucker could not produce conclusive proof to counter the somewhat flimsy evidence put to him, combined with a somewhat stuttering performance before the committee, damaged him. He wasn't helped by the fact that an email he had written to Diamond on his appointment as chief executive was produced, describing the American as 'a brick'.

Tucker had done an immense amount of work for the Bank of England and had been closely involved both in repairing banks and in trying to police them more closely, but the Diamond affair cost him, not least because it contributed to his being passed over as the next governor in November 2012. A Barclays official was later to tell me that Tucker was sunk by a file note from Diamond that was highly unusual. In his period as chief executive it was one of just two phone calls that the astute Barclays boss translated into a note for the file.

Tucker never quite gave up on his belief that he could be the next governor and didn't learn that he had been passed over until hours before the Canadian Mark Carney was unveiled by George Osborne in November 2013. His experiences over Libor had, however, taught him an important lesson. The backup staffing provided to the Bank of England's governors and deputy governors was inadequate. Like government ministers they needed to be properly staffed with 'private offices' whose duty it was to take notes of every phone and personal conversation so there was always a formal record.

In immediate terms the fallout from the Libor scandal involved both loss of personnel and loss of cash for Barclays. The bank not only witnessed the departure of Bob Diamond, but also those of Marcus Agius and of Jerry del Missier, who resigned the same day as Diamond after 15 years with the group. A few months later, in April 2013, Rich Ricci resigned after 19 years at the bank. He had waived his bonus in 2012, but nevertheless landed £18 million that year from selling 5.7 million shares he gained as part of annual bonuses and incentive schemes from previous years. With his string of racehorses at the annual Cheltenham Festival (he named one of them 'Fatcatinahat') and his penchant for heavy tweeds and trilby hats, American-born Ricci had cut quite a figure. So far as financial penalties were concerned, Barclays agreed to pay a fine of £290 million to the US and British authorities in June 2012.

For Barclays the Libor scandal raised some profound questions that went beyond fines and assessment of individual conduct. Sir Hector Sants, who served as chief executive of the FSA for five years before moving to Barclays in December 2012 as head of compliance, put it this way to me in an interview at the Barclays tower at Canary Wharf:

I think that history will say the more interesting issue to do with Libor is not the discovery of wrongdoing in a group, whether it is 100, or 200, it's not thousands of people. What is interesting is that Libor was the tipping-point in respect of . . . the dissatisfaction of society with banks. So it absolutely catalysed the sense that banks were not acting in the interests of society. And it persuaded the senior management of banks, which I think Barclays has been at the forefront, to recognise that change is necessary . . . Executives at Barclays realised that Libor was a watershed moment in their need to change culture.

The person chosen to lead cultural change was new chief executive Antony Jenkins. Significantly, he came from the less tainted retail side of the bank. Conservatively dressed and clean-cut, Jenkins first joined Barclays in 1983 before leaving in 1989 for a lengthy stint at American competitor Citigroup. He returned in 2006 as chief executive of Barclaycard before taking on wider retail responsibilities. The retail side of Barclays also came to be tainted on this occasion by the mis-selling of payment protection insurance (PPI) to people who did not need it. Jenkins maintains that by the time he took charge of the retail side the mis-selling was all but over.

He was joined by a new chairman of the bank, City grandee Sir David Walker. Walker was a former deputy governor of the Bank of England and a City regulator, who had spent many of the 'boom' get-rich-quick years of banking working for the investment banker Morgan Stanley. Together, Walker and Jenkins, supported by Hector Sants, embarked on an internal and external communications offensive designed to demonstrate that Barclays had learned the lessons of the past and was set on a new course. Jenkins told me at a lunch in the autumn of 2012 how he wanted to make Barclays the 'go to' bank and to effect cultural change so as to build a more ethical structure. He provided the first indications that some of the more contentious activities – such as the bank's tax restructuring work – would probably be closed down.

This was of a piece with a declaration he made in October 2012 soon after taking over the helm: 'You will see at Barclays we will make significant progress in the coming months and at Barclays that will start to rebuild trust. I'm on record as saying that the industry and to some extent Barclays did lose sight of the customer and it's our job to put the customer back at the centre of everything that we do.'

The changes were implemented in the following months. In January 2013 Jenkins told all of the bank's 140,000 staff to sign up to a new improved code of conduct or leave. He added that bonuses would not just be assessed against financial rewards, but against new 'purpose and values' criteria.

Jenkins told staff: 'There might be some of you who don't feel they can fully buy into an approach which so squarely links performance to the upholding of our values. My message to those people is simple: Barclays is not the place for you. The rules have changed. You won't feel comfortable at Barclays and, to be frank, we won't feel comfortable with you as colleagues.' Just in case the message was not getting through to staff and other stakeholders visiting its Canary Wharf headquarters, Jenkins ordered the installation of five enormous free-standing signs in the vast glass entrance-hall space of the building. They went up in January 2013, emblazoning the message that Barclays' workers would be expected to show respect, integrity, service, excellence and stewardship in all their activities. And in case anyone missed the message on entering the building the same words were painted onto the stainless-steel elevator doors. Inside the lifts, along with Barclays share-price movements, videos played showing all the charitable work being done by the group and its staff. The desire for cultural change was being drummed in at every level.

In February 2013 Jenkins followed through with his undertaking to me that he would close down the bank's controversial tax unit, Structured Capital Markets, which helped big businesses avoid tax. Barclays said it would continue to advise clients on their tax arrangements, but would not engage in activities where the main purpose is to avoid tax.

'There are some areas that relied on sophisticated and complex structures, where transactions were carried out with the primary objective of accessing the tax benefits. Although this was legal, going forward such activity is incompatible with our purpose. We will not engage in it again,' the new chief executive said.

Jenkins also proceeded to extract Barclays from other more controversial activities. In April 2014 the bank announced that it would put an end to its involvement in commodity and energy trading. The move followed a series of disciplinary actions brought against banks for manipulation. In July 2013 American rival JPMorgan Chase was accused of being involved in manipulation of the power markets in California. It announced in January 2014 that it would be selling all of its commodities businesses. Paradoxically RBS had sold its commodity-trading operation RBS Sempra to JPMorgan in February 2010.

In an effort to get a better picture of what had gone wrong at the bank and driven it towards unethical practices, Barclays also set up the Salz review, which – at a cost of £14.8 million – duly produced a 236-page report, 'An Independent Review of Barclays' Business Practices', in April 2013. As is the nature of such internal studies it was circumspect in its language and avoided some of the searing criticism and testimony that was emerging from the public hearings of the Parliamentary Select Committee. But it was based on a very thoroughgoing probe into the bank's innermost secrets. The bank's new chairman Sir David Walker said it made 'uncomfortable reading'.

In essence the report confirmed the view Sir Mervyn King had expressed in his testimony to the Treasury Committee in the summer of 2012 that Barclays had sailed 'close to the wind' too often. It blamed a 'win at all costs' attitude within Barclays Capital, a senior leadership team that 'disliked bad news' and a culture that 'lacked openness' which flowed from this. The high levels of pay at the investment bank, combined with a lack of other ways of measuring success, led to 'an enormous challenge to prevent a cultural drift toward a sense of entitlement'.

Barclays was not alone in seeing the need for a moment of self-examination. So intense was the outcry over the Libor scandal that in July 2012 the Coalition government, which (like its Labour predecessor) had previously refused a commission on the financial panic, had second thoughts. Prime Minister David Cameron announced that a review would be undertaken to demonstrate and ensure that the UK had the 'toughest and most transparent rules of any major financial sector'.

The joint Parliamentary Commission on Banking Standards that was then formed was headed by Andrew Tyrie MP, the astringent chair of the House of Commons Treasury Select Committee. Among those joining him was the former Chancellor of the Exchequer Nigel Lawson and the future Archbishop of Canterbury Justin Welby, who had once been a City trader. All too often governments set up commissions to kick awkward issues into touch. If that was the hope here, it certainly didn't work. The commission proved to be both combative and thorough; its stars, arguably, were the new Archbishop with his strong moral compass and the former Chancellor, a believer in laissez-faire economics, who clearly felt that the financiers had let capitalism down.

The commission's 600-page report, published 11 months later in June 2013, looked closely at the events and personalities involved in the Libor scandal, and came to some radical conclusions. 'Recent scandals', it observed, 'have exposed shocking and widespread misconduct . . . taxpayers and customers have lost out.' Part of the answer, it argued, was to introduce a new law to make it a criminal offence to engage in 'reckless banking'. 'The fact that recklessness in carrying out professional responsibilities carries a risk of a criminal conviction and a prison sentence would give pause for thought.'

The call for change was duly accepted by Chancellor George Osborne, who announced to the Commons that he accepted the report's main recommendations and that he promised legislation to make them law. The new banking act, which made reckless banking an offence carrying a seven-year sentence, was passed in December 2013 and came into effect in the spring of 2014.

Also to come under scrutiny in the months after news of the Libor scandal broke was the regulatory authority which had failed to stop it – the FSA. Set up only a few years earlier in 1997 in an era of soft-touch regulation, it was broken up in April 2013 and replaced by the Financial Conduct Authority (FCA), which was given the task of regulating behaviour and practices in the City. A new Prudential Regulation Authority (PRA) was also established under the stewardship of Andrew Bailey at the Bank of England to ensure the safety of the larger financial institutions.

As a parting gift the FSA recommended to its successors that they should 'establish clear internal roles and responsibilities relating to Libor'. It added that they should ensure 'that staff are sufficiently inquiring and challenging and they maintain the necessary breadth of perspective'.

So far as the acronym at the core of the scandal was concerned, Chancellor George Osborne asked chief executive of the FCA Martin Wheatley to look at what should be done about Libor itself. He duly produced a report in September 2012, in which he argued that while the benchmark need not be scrapped altogether, it should be radically reformed. Libor, he suggested, should be covered by an Act of Parliament and those trying to manipulate it should be prosecuted. The BBA should lose the right to administer the rate, and an application process for a new body to run the benchmark should 'immediately' begin. To make Libor itself more robust, Wheatley proposed that the number of banks involved in establishing it should be expanded from the current group of more than 20, and that calculations should be based on current transactions rather than estimates. Finally he argued that the submissions from individual banks should no longer be published on the day of the Libor rate, but held back for three months so that banks quoting high rates would not come under immediate pressure over their creditworthiness.

Baroness Sarah Hogg, a former adviser to Prime Minister John Major, was given the task of finding a new administrator for Libor now that it was to be removed from the BBA. The decision made waves at the London Stock Exchange. In June 2013 it was announced that the future administration of and trading on the Libor market was to cross the Atlantic and become the responsibility of the New York Stock Exchange Euronext. The LSE bid is understood to have failed because it was in partnership with the British–Canadian market information service Thomson Reuters, which previously had worked with the sacked BBA.

So far as individuals and companies affected by the manipulation of Libor were concerned, there was anger but no clear way forward. Various civil actions were launched in the immediate aftermath of the Libor scandal, seeking financial redress on the part of plaintiffs as diverse as US stockbroker Charles Schwab and the East Coast port city of Baltimore. But it's far from clear whether the actions will prove successful. Plaintiffs will have to demonstrate that the attempts by individual banks to rig the rate definitely succeeded over the period of the contracts they drew up. They will also have to prove that as rates moved up or down, they themselves always suffered and did not gain from a particular miscreant rate.

Even so, as recently as 14 March 2014, the US bank regulator the Federal Deposit Insurance Corporation (FDIC), in its capacity as receiver of 38 banking institutions that failed between 2008 and 2011, filed a massive new lawsuit in the Southern District of New York against the US dollar Libor rate-setting banks and against the British Bankers' Association and related entities. It charged that between 2007 and mid-2011 the defendants conspired to manipulate the US dollar Libor rate.

Banks have certainly been made to pay for their behaviour. Barclays settled for a £290 million fine. RBS was fined £390 million by

US and UK regulators in February 2013. Germany's largest financial group Deutsche Bank, which suspended five traders as a result of its own internal inquiry, added over £500 million in March 2012 to its fund (now standing at £2 billion) to settle legal actions brought against it; much of this cash is earmarked for Libor settlements.

At the same time a number of bankers have resigned or lost their jobs. There have also been a handful of arrests. Director of Britain's Serious Fraud Office David Green, for example, launched an investigation into Libor manipulation in the course of which, in December 2012, Thomas Hayes, a former trader for Citigroup and UBS, and Terry Farr and Jim Gilmour of the inter-dealer broker RP Martin were arrested. Inter-dealer brokers are generally smaller financial firms that sit at heart of the City of London and transact wholesale trading among City firms. It was charged that these individuals had sought to manipulate trades in the Japanese yen Libor market. All appeared in court in May 2014 and pleaded not guilty.

In September 2013 the London-based inter-dealer broker ICAP, headed by former Conservative Party treasurer Michael Spencer, was fined $87 million by the US and British authorities for its role in Libor rigging. The US Department of Justice charged three former ICAP derivatives brokers with conspiracy to commit wire fraud and two counts of wire fraud – offences that carry penalties of up to 30 years. At the same time the British regulator the Financial Conduct Authority and the US Commodity Futures Trading Commission ordered ICAP Europe to pay fines of £14 million and $65 million respectively.

Michael Spencer, who transformed ICAP from a small, little-known money broker into the world's largest inter-dealer broker was chagrined by the affair. As one of the Conservative Party's biggest City backers it was a shattering blow to his reputation and that of his firm. In a phone call to me he apologised profusely for what had happened. He assured me everything had been done to make sure that compliance was tightened, so there could be no repeat of the regulatory lapses.

At one level, it looks as though the Libor scandal is now a thing of the past and that lessons have been learned. Offending banks have been fined. Individuals have been held to account. Libor itself has been overhauled and new regulation put in place. Doubts, however, remain about the underlying nature of a sector that could have allowed this to happen.

In the first place, it is worrying that it should have taken so long to unearth an abuse that certainly dates back to 2005, when there was evidence that Barclays had tried to manipulate both Libor and its euro area equivalent Euribor. The New York Federal Reserve did actually raise concerns then. By the spring of 2008, at the height of the Great Panic, worries over the validity of Libor rates were spreading throughout the market as banks scrambled to find short-term funding. There might not have been specific suggestions of wrongdoing but a number of reports in the *Wall Street Journal*, the *Financial Times* and Bloomberg News at this time openly questioned the accuracy of the benchmark. In April the British Bankers' Association brought forward its annual review of the Libor process, and in December of the same year updated its governance, though it made only cosmetic changes to the benchmark. (Critics say this was only to be expected as the BBA is a lobby group fully funded by banks based in the UK.)

At the time, the FSA's banking sector team talked to the BBA about ways to bolster the benchmark, including a suggestion that banks who submitted false returns should be expelled from the panel. It did not, however, insist that changes be made. An FSA minute of a meeting between the FSA and the BBA on 28 April

2008 noted: 'It was evident that [the BBA representative] doubted whether the Libor fixing process would change significantly after the review.'

When a review commissioned by the FSA was released in March 2013 its report pointed out that the BBA's December 2008 paper on Libor 'did not refer to whether it had found lowballing [bids deliberately pitched at rates under those being set in the market] and it led to no banks being removed from a panel'. It added: 'We conclude, with the benefit of hindsight, that there was opportunity for the FSA to have pressed the BBA for a more radical outcome with more wide-reaching proposals.'

For his part, Mervyn King had no doubt that the Libor market was totally dysfunctional, particularly during the chaotic aftermath of the collapse of Northern Rock in September 2007 and Lehman Brothers a year later in September 2008. The spreads – that is, the difference between the rates at which banks would lend and borrow from each other – rose to enormous levels. In normal conditions the spread would be expressed in basis points, 100 to each 1 per cent. But as the crisis took its toll and banks proved reluctant to lend to each other the spreads climbed into double-digit full percentage points. So concerned did the British Bankers' Association become about the data, which was adding to market volatility, that it ceased to publish and distribute the figures.

As King told the Treasury Select Committee, 'Libor is the rate at which banks don't lend to each other.' Even so, although the Bank of England was aware that Libor had become a meaningless number, no one had reported to it on what were later deemed to be illegal actions. In June 2008 Timothy Geithner, then President of the New York Federal Reserve (later to become US Treasury Secretary), was so concerned about the rate that he emailed Sir Mervyn King to suggest ways in which Libor-setting could be toughened up. Sir Mervyn passed on the memorandum to the FSA. King and his colleagues at the Bank, including his then deputy Paul Tucker, were later criticised for not acting on the Fed's complaints more wholeheartedly. It was, however, King's view, and that of other central bankers, that it was not their job to interfere in Libor because it was at its core a private contract. For its part, the FSA later said that it had no record of the Geithner email.

What emerges from all this is a sense that key people knew that Libor wasn't working, but that no one thought to look under the bonnet to see just what was going on. When the Financial Services Authority published its Internal Audit Report on Libor in March 2013, after an examination of 97,000 documents dating from between 2007 and 2009, it stated: 'The FSA should have considered the possibility and likelihood of lowballing (particularly in the period from April 2008), rather than assuming the only problems with Libor were those caused by structural issues in the Libor fixing process interacting with deteriorating market conditions.' The FSA ruled that it should have been 'more inquiring and challenging' with the weight of information that came across its desk. A number of mass-circulation emails should have alerted the body, such as an unnamed broker report on 29 November 2007 which included the following comment:

Increased talk that Libors were actually being slightly understated given that banks did not want to post a rate above the pack; others thought it had been a finger in the air exercise for some months.

An unnamed bank on the Libor panel noted on 27 November 2007: 'Conditions are deteriorating in all currencies. GBP cash is regularly devoid of offers, and Libor rates quoted are "increasingly meaningless".'

A compliance officer at a bank that was not on the Libor panel made the following observation to their FSA supervisor on 1 April 2008:

> The issue is that the Libor rate is daily being set at least 25bp [basis points] to 30bp below what can be obtained in the market. This has the impact of distorting the market as a number of products are based on the Libor. If the contributor banks are quoting these below market rates then surely they should be made to lend at least a certain amount at these rates.
>
> It appears to us that something is wrong when a panel of contributor banks is supplying Libor at below what the banks can achieve in the market. It may be worth the FSA investigating to see if the contributor banks are making profits on the back of these quotes.

In other words, people in authority might have been suspicious but they also didn't want to know. And those who were perpetrating the manipulation of Libor must have known that what they were doing was at the very least questionable, but they carried on doing it anyway. In the words of Terry Smith, the pugilistic analyst and fund manager at the City firm of Tullett Prebon, speaking as the Libor crisis unfolded: 'It is an illusion that an act cannot be prosecuted as a crime just because there is no specific piece of legislation that proscribes it. We have perfectly good laws and they need to be applied.'

One might have expected two of the key players in the Libor debacle – Barclays and UBS – to have kept out of the headlines since then. However, neither has been particularly fortunate on that front. On 17 June 2013 Barclays was fined $487.9 million by the US Federal

Energy Commission for alleged manipulation of electricity prices in the American West in the years 2006–8. The bank vowed to contest the fine. Traders involved on the alleged offences were, however, dismissed.

In July 2013 the reformed bank became involved in a nasty dust-up with the new banking regulator the Prudential Regulatory Authority, headed by Andrew Bailey. In one of his last acts as governor Sir Mervyn King had authorised the PRA to write to Barclays to inform it of what it considered to be an enormous £12.8 billion capital shortfall. Barclays initially sought to resist the move and chose to criticise the Bank of England and the PRA for seeking to impose stringent rules too rapidly when it was wholly unnecessary. The new board headed by Antony Jenkins looked to be displaying some of the old arrogance that had made it so unpopular at Westminster, in government and among the general public.

But this time the bank blinked first. In the last week of July 2013 it was announced that Barclays would supplement its capital through a £5.8 billion rights issue of shares to existing investors – one of the largest fundraisings in the history of the City of London. It would also raise a further £2 billion of capital through the issue of so-called 'contingent bonds' that would have the same characteristics as ordinary shares if the bank were to run into difficulty. And it promised to shed from its balance sheet £60 billion to £80 billion of assets by June 2014, without cutting off lending to small businesses and households.

The truth was that Barclays had not totally vanquished its liking for risk-taking despite all the fine talk of integrity and respect when Jenkins had taken the helm in the wake of the Libor scandal. The bank's accounts were still heavily laden with hard-to-value investment-banking assets of the kind that caused so much anguish during the financial panic of 2007–9. Promising a new culture was easy enough. But delivering a more ethically anchored institution when Barclays is so dependent on its investment banking-casino banking arm for income was a wholly different kettle of fish. And while Jenkins doesn't command the level of remuneration that Bob Diamond enjoyed, his 2012 pay – if considerably less than the £20.9 million package that his predecessor earned in 2011 – was still a more than respectable £8.6 million. In February 2013 he waived his £1 million bonus for 2012 saying the bank had had a 'difficult' year.

As for UBS, the fine levied on it for its Libor shortcomings came on the top of a string of misfortunes for the Swiss bank. It suffered large losses on toxic debt during the 2008 crash; it sustained a £1.4 billion loss from a trading fraud committed by London-based trader Kweku Adoboli; it had to agree a £500 million settlement of a tax-evasion investigation in the US and also costs and claims related to sales of residential mortgage-backed securities. As at Barclays, wholesale changes were made amongst the bank's executives. But UBS's activities seriously undermined Switzerland's reputation as a place where bankers behaved with discretion, secrecy and integrity. Given all these various misdeeds, the usual mantra that is used on such occasions – 'Lessons have been learned' – rings a little hollow.

# 7

# The Perils of Global Banking: Money Laundering

Among Britain's swaggering breed of pre-crisis bankers Stephen Green, the chairman and chief executive of Britain's biggest bank HSBC, always seemed a little different. Fiercely intellectual, somewhat diffident, he exuded a sense of high moral standards in a profession all too often besmirched by greed, wrongdoing and a disregard for the well-being of customers. As one might expect for a man in his position he had followed a fairly typical career course, serving first at consultants McKinsey before moving onto the old Hongkong and Shanghai Banking Corporation in 1982. But he had also been ordained as an Anglican priest, and was rather proud of the fact that he was the first practising banker ever to have the privilege of preaching at St Paul's Cathedral, in the heart of the City of London.

When I interviewed him in 2009, at the time of the publication of his second book *Good Value* – a moral defence of capitalism that was nominated for the prestigious Goldman Sachs/*FT* Business Book of the Year prize – he expressed disgust for the worst excesses of his fellow bankers. Green evoked that oldest of City aphorisms 'our word is our bond', adding, 'The idea that you can play fast and loose with that is immoral.'

I left Green's spacious office in the HSBC tower at Canary Wharf feeling that he and his bank were different. True, HSBC had been caught up in the sub-prime debacle through its November 2002 purchase of US Household Finance Corporation, the 'trailer-park' lender that made mortgage, car and credit-card loans to sub-prime borrowers. But this deal had been the brainchild of Green's predecessor Sir John Bond and the new chairman was acting to clean things up. Consequently, when in December 2010 Green was selected by Prime Minister David Cameron to be the UK's new trade minister and was elevated to the House of Lords as Baron Green of Hurstpierpoint, it looked a good appointment. Green brought expertise and moral authority to the role. Thanks to his HSBC background, he also had the reputation, knowledge and influence to make a real impact on Britain's weak trade relations with China and the other fast-growing emerging democracies of Asia. This, after all, was HSBC territory.

HSBC always did seem a steadier, better balanced and more carefully controlled bank than many of its compatriots on Britain's high streets. To that extent its exposure to the fallout from its $15.5 billion acquisition of Household seemed a blip, albeit a large one: the unit would lose a staggering $50 billion over six years before in was closed in 2009. It is testimony to the strength of the rest of the HSBC operations, from its British branch-banking network (the former Midland Bank) to its domination of Hong Kong's booming markets, that it could survive such losses with barely a tremor. As a result, HSBC never came under the sustained pressure that threatened the survival of the Royal Bank of Scotland (RBS), Lloyds Banking Group and to lesser extent Barclays.

HSBC's great strength and resilience lay in the global nature of its footprint. A major force in the UK, it is also a major player in the US, even though down the decades it has struggled to challenge the likes of JPMorgan Chase, Citigroup and Bank of America Merrill Lynch. That said, HSBC Bank USA (HBUS) held assets of $290 billion on 31 December 2013 and serves about 3.8 million customers through 240 branches.

But the most important area for the group is its Global Banking and Markets unit. In effect this is HSBC's investment bank, fighting for the same territory and business as the likes of Goldman Sachs and Barclays. Through this unit HBUS is able to offer the group as a whole access to the US market, the largest economy in the world. Just as critically, it is able to offer access to the US to its Far Eastern clients, in the bank's Asian heartland. Through its New York operation HSBC can handle international wire transfers, clear a variety of US dollar payments and provide foreign-exchange and hedging services. It can also service the American needs of over 80 affiliates and 2,400 separate finance houses across the globe. Such a worldwide reach – from the UK to the US via such newly wealth-creating markets as China, Singapore, India, Mexico, the Middle East and Africa – means that even at the height of the credit crunch HSBC's sheer scale ensured that storms in some of its territories did not shake its empire as a whole.

To that extent its profile was rather similar to that of Standard Chartered, chaired by Sir John Peace, the inspiration behind credit-checking agency Experian, and led by another McKinsey alumnus Peter Sands. Standard Chartered may not have had the UK high-street presence of HSBC but it was an impressive international player nevertheless. Indeed, it turned out to be one of the few major UK banks actually to expand through the financial crisis, largely because it does most of its business in Asia, the Middle East and Africa, areas of the world that were not too badly damaged by the financial storm of 2007 and 2008. The bank was able relatively easily to withstand its only little local difficulty when its own off-balance-sheet enterprise 'Whistle Jacket', which had invested in toxic debt built on sub-prime mortgages, was liquidated. For his part, Sands went on to play an advisory role in the recapitalisation of the other high-street banks in 2008.

Given the reputation these two banks enjoyed it seems peculiarly ironic that they should have been seen to stumble just as other, less prudent banks were edging back from the brink. The fact is, though, that while both HSBC and Standard Chartered rarely troubled the headlines in the tumultuous years of the credit crunch, in 2012, just as the furore of the financial crisis was starting to fade from view, they both found themselves directly in the line of fire. After lengthy and painstaking investigations, US regulators decided to fine the two institutions $2.6 billion. Unlike their rivals they were not found guilty of manipulating Libor, rigging the foreign-exchange market, issuing dodgy products, or indulging in questionable off-balance-sheet enterprises. Instead both were found guilty of offences that seem on the surface a thousand miles away from normal international commercial banking operations: money laundering and sanctions busting.

For HSBC it was the bank's involvement in Mexico that proved to be particularly toxic. Back in November 2002 the bank had bought Mexico's fifth largest bank, Banco Internacional, from rival Grupo Financiero Bital for $1.1 billion, changing its name to HSBC Mexico (HBMX). At the time the unit served around 6 million customers and employed 15,400 staff. Mexico seemed a good prospect in many respects as a fast-growing economy and as part of the NAFTA (North American Free Trade Agreement) zone. But it was also a country where drug trafficking had become a major part of the economy. In the words of the US State Department in the year that HBMX was formed:

The industrial-scale drug trade has transformed narco-trafficking into one of Mexico's deadliest businesses . . . These organisations have demonstrated blatant disregard for human life as the executions of law enforcement personnel, government officials, and innocent bystanders have increased . . . In recent years international money launderers have turned increasingly to Mexico for initial placement of drug proceeds into the global financial system.

The way that such drug gangs as the Arellano Felix Organisation, the Carrillo Fuentes Organisation and the Gulf Cartel operated was to take the dollars earned from sales of drugs in the US and physically smuggle them across the border back into Mexico. The gangs would then deposit the exported dollars in Mexican banks or foreign-exchange houses (called Casa de Cambios) where money-laundering rules were not so rigorously enforced as they are in the US or where the bank staff could be physically intimidated. Once accepted as legitimate funds, the cash would be sent back to the US via plane or truck transport or would be sold back to US banks. Drug dealers would then be free to use 'laundered' dollars to fund deals, and buy legitimate businesses, on both sides of the border. The State Department reported that by 2012 drug gangs were laundering 'as much as $39 billion' a year through Mexican and US finance houses.

HSBC were aware of the dangers. An audit of Brital carried out in July 2002, prior to its purchase by HSBC, revealed that 'high risk clients receive no special monitoring coverage'. It also pointed out that the Mexican unit had set up accounts for tens of thousands of customers in the Cayman Islands, and that 41 per cent of the accounts reviewed 'lacked full client information'. The audit concluded that 'the target organisation does not have a strong compliance culture'.

In an email to colleagues on 10 July 2002 HSBC head of compliance

David Bagley recognised the scale of the problems the firm was taking on. He stated: 'Sandy [Flockhart, HBMX chief executive] acknowledges the importance of a robust compliance and money laundering function which at present is virtually non-existent . . . There is no recognisable compliance or money laundering function at Bital at present . . . Sandy thinks it is important to look at both issues affecting Mexico City, but also closer to the border where there appears to be substantial cross-border flows of monies, including USD [US dollars] in cash.'

Given these huge known compliance problems one might wonder what possessed the HSBC board and senior management to sign off on the Mexican transaction. The strategy of investing in emerging and newly wealth-creating markets was sensible enough. In this, HSBC, Standard Chartered and other UK corporations including Vodafone and distiller Diageo were as one and, on occasion, all had to accept certain local conditions that were less than ideal. But Mexico was different. Here the problems were so deep-seated and the reputational risk accordingly so high that to some outsiders it is surprising that HSBC should ever have wanted to get involved. There was a political dimension to all this, too. The beneficiaries of money laundering were people who were quite prepared to commit acts of violence against people working for the US Drugs Enforcement Agency. Anything HSBC did or did not do in Mexico, therefore, was likely to be closely scrutinised by powerful figures over the border in the US.

As the new bank bedded down there were some worrying indications of miscreant behaviour. In 2007 HSBC Mexico sent $3 billion in physical cash back to its US affiliate. A year later this leapt 25 per cent to $4 billion – more than any other Mexican bank even though HSBC Mexico was only the fifth largest bank in the country. During the period January to September 2008 HSBC Mexico repatriated $3 billion: 36 per cent of the total volume of the hard-cash dollar market between Mexico and the US. This figure was also double what the largest bank in Mexico, Banamax, had sent to the US in this period.

In February 2008 Mexican regulators met with HBMX's new chief executive Paul Thurston (who had taken over from Sandy Flockhart) and told him of their concerns. They said their Financial Intelligence Unit (FIU) found that 'in the majority of the most relevant ML [money laundering] cases' they had investigated in 2007, many were carried out through HBMX. Vast sums of dollars were pouring into HBUS from its affiliates unchecked. An investigation by a US Senate subcommittee, headed by Senator Carl Levin, noted in 2012 that 'for a three-year period, from mid-2006 until mid-2009, the US unit accepted more than $15 billion in physical US dollars from other HSBC affiliates, but failed to conduct any AML [anti-money-laundering] monitoring of the bulk transactions.'

The reason for this state of affairs was that it was HSBC policy at the time to assume that any affiliate that was 50 per cent or more owned by the group met the firm-wide anti-money-laundering standards. In the case of HBMX this was a rash assumption for the US arm to make, particularly as US regulations explicitly direct all American banks to carry out due diligence before opening an account for any foreign financial institution.

On 15 March 2007 the US Drug Enforcement Agency and the Mexican government raided the home of Chinese-Mexican businessman Zhenli Ye Gon, a long-standing HBMX client. There the authorities found over $205 million in US dollars and $17 million in Mexican pesos, firearms and international wire transfer records. Ye Gon owned three Mexican pharmaceutical firms – Unimed Pharm Chem, Constructora e Inmobiliaria Federal and Unimed Pharmaceutical. Since his firms had reported no gross income for the three years from 2005 to 2007 he was, not surprisingly, accused of having 'significant unexplained wealth'. A couple of months later, in July 2007, he was arrested and imprisoned for aiding and abetting the manufacture of methamphetamine. US prosecutors dropped the charges in 2009 after key witnesses recanted their testimony, but as late as January 2014 Ye Gon was still confined to a US jail despite Mexico's attempts to extradite him to stand trial on the other side of the border.

Ye Gon's account at HSBC Mexico had been opened when the bank was run by Bital. He went on to move $90 million in 450 transactions using HBMX and a number of other major banks and finance houses. HSBC compliance staff told the Senate subcommittee that they had ordered the account to be closed somewhere between 2003 and 2004, and that they were surprised to find the account still open when the case hit the headlines in 2007. In the words of HBMX chief executive Paul Thurston to Sandy Flockhart, now promoted to Latin American regional head, and others in March 2007: 'This is a very serious, and high profile, case which has potential reputational damage to the HSBC Group, and must be given the highest priority.'

In the course of a review of HSBC Mexico's anti-money-laundering controls in March and April 2007, which Thurston personally oversaw, he laid out the unit's weaknesses. Among other things he found the business had a 'lack of adequate documentation and filing systems which remain from the former Bital days'. He added that the bank had a 'lack of a compliance culture'. These were much the same criticisms HSBC had made about the Mexican unit when it had bought it five years earlier.

HBMX's Cayman Islands office also came under scrutiny. This was a shell office run from Mexico, but with no staff actually stationed on the Caribbean island. Inherited from Bital, which had opened the business in 1980, it allowed customers to open an account without having to vouchsafe many personal details. In fact, an internal 2008 survey not only found that a large proportion of accounts lacked the details regulators would expect to see, but that 15 per cent of the files contained no information at all. Such an arrangement was obviously attractive to wealthy Mexicans wishing to shelter from Mexico's high tax regime. But, as one HBMX compliance officer told the subcommittee, it was also more than a little appealing to 'organised crime'. The business grew rapidly from 1,500 accounts with an undisclosed balance in 2005, to 60,000 accounts with assets of $2.1 billion at their peak in 2008. As HBMX chief executive Luis Pena said in a 28 November 2008 email to a colleague: 'Cayman and Mexican dollar accounts provide us with $2.1 billion of cheap funding.'

Under pressure from regulators in 2008 HSBC Group began to monitor these accounts more closely. In July 2008 the bank found that one account was being used to make large regular payments to an aircraft hire firm called Cabello Air Freight in Miami. The US firm was reportedly involved in the supply of aircraft to drug cartels. Since then HSBC has closed thousands of these accounts. It is not clear from the evidence to the Senate subcommittee that Cabello was among the accounts closed. Nevertheless, in 2012 the Cayman Islands branch still held 24,000 accounts with a combined balance of $657 million.

Some indication of the compliance problems HSBC faced in Mexico emerges from their dealings with the Casa de Cambios, which are there ostensibly to provide foreign-exchange services. One such, Casa de Cambio Puebla, which was a client of the bank, saw $11 million of its assets frozen in Miami and London in May 2007 following allegations from the US that it was involved in money laundering for drug gangs. It had been noted that in just three years, between 2005 and 2007, the firm's banknotes business had grown almost tenfold from $18 million in 2005 to $113 million.

A few weeks later, in July 2007, HSBC Group compliance expressed the view that the account with Puebla should be closed. HSBC Mexico compliance initially queried this. Later in the month chief executive Paul Thurston agreed that such action was necessary. Yet the account was not actually closed until November, some four months later, following the receipt of a warrant from the Mexican attorney general seizing all funds in the Puebla account.

The delay highlights the fact that compliance procedure at head office and the Mexican bank was not always fully aligned. Even when an order had been given by a senior officer, there was no cast-iron guarantee that it would be automatically carried out. Why this should be so is down to a mix of complicated factors. It's quite possible that the executives in some of the local banks were loath to turn business away. They wanted to ratchet up profits and personal bonuses. But it's also an unfortunate fact that intimidation and the fear of what ruthless and murderous drug cartel members might do to bankers who did not play ball was a significant consideration. The kidnapping of bank staff was widespread. Employees were also regularly offered bribes by gangs.

To make matters worse, as HSBC Mexico struggled to turn round the poor compliance culture it had inherited from Bital, it found itself beset by staff problems. In 2005, for example, the bank accepted the resignation of HSBC money-laundering deterrence director Carlos Rochin after a staff whistle-blower hotline disclosed that reports of monthly meetings of the money-laundering committee had been made up and sent to the local regulator. The false reports had been concocted by a junior employee under the direction of Rochin, who had been brought in by HSBC to beef up compliance.

In a July 2005 email John Root, HSBC Group head of compliance for Latin America, told colleagues after a May visit to HSBC Mexico:

'Projects are started but seldom completed.' In December 2005 HBMX produced a 55-page compliance report which concluded that the unit was still 'Below Accepted Levels'. Among other things, the study pinpointed a failure to track foreign remittances, to pick up on accounts that raised alerts, and to identify risky clients.

The report was finally issued in the spring of 2006. In a May 2007 email to other compliance colleagues John Root discussed its findings. He said: 'The one that sticks out is apparent lack of monitoring of the (relatively few) AML [anti-money-laundering] staff in the field. This raises a "red flag" in a place like Mexico, where the drug cartels are very powerful and ubiquitous.'

On 17 July 2007 Root sent a withering email to HBMX head of compliance Ramon Garcia Gibson, criticising 'rubber stamping unacceptable risks' at the unit's compliance committee meetings. Root added: 'I am quite concerned that the committee is not functioning properly. Alarmed, even. I am close to picking up the phone to your CEO [Paul Thurston].'

On 23 February 2008 Thurston wrote to HSBC's then group chief executive Michael Geoghegan and told him that compliance at the Mexican unit was still below standard. And the issue had become more pressing because 'with [Mexican] President Felipe Calderon declaring war on the drugs gangs, crime and corruption the judicial authorities have heightened the focus on financial investigations'.

Thurston added: 'HSBC has historically, and continues to have, a worse record than the other banks, so we have become a focus of attention. The new head of the FIU [Mexican Financial Intelligence Unit] has told us that his staff have told him that HSBC has been the most difficult bank to obtain accurate and timely data from for the past four years.'

Thurston also told Geoghegan that in order to try to cut back on lax compliance he had introduced 'stronger disciplinary procedures' against 'branch managers who continued to open accounts without all of the necessary customer information'. He added that the unit received 'more than 1,000 letters per week' from the Mexican banking regulator, the CNBV, asking for missing account information.

Later in February 2008 HSBC head of compliance David Bagley conducted an exit interview with HBMX anti-money-laundering director Leopoldo Barroso who was scathing about the compliance unit. In his notes Bagley wrote that Barroso 'thought that there was a culture that [was] pursuing profit and targets at all costs and in fact had seen no recent improvement in the standard of controls or the types of decisions being taken'. Barroso added that the department was 'at least' 35 people short.

In a 19 February 2008 email Geoghegan shared his concerns about the lack of compliance progress at HSBC Mexico with a number of senior colleagues, including his group chairman Lord Stephen Green. According to Carl Levin's Senate subcommittee Lord Green had been warned about serious problems in the Mexican operation as far back as 2005 by a whistle-blower, but HSBC 'made no effort to identify any suspicious activity [until] mid-2009'.

On 26 November 2008 Geoghegan travelled to Mexico City for a high-level meeting with the CNBV. The regulator told him and other senior staff around the table that it was greatly concerned about a number of issues at HSBC Mexico. These included the amount of cash at the unit's Cayman Island branch, poor compliance procedures and the amount of money HSBC Mexico was passing back to the US. CNBV and US regulators were concerned this was drug money, it was stated. Mexican regulators even had a tape of a known drug lord recommending HSBC Mexico as the place to bank.

Geoghegan acted quickly. That night he sent an email to HBMX president Emilson Alonso in which he said: 'It occurs to me: we should stop any dollar remittances or accept any dollar payments unless they are done via a customer's account. We should stop shipping dollars.' The following day HSBC Mexico pledged to stop buying or selling dollars at any branch by 1 December. And it would no longer accept dollar cash deposits to any dollar account at any branch by 1 January 2009.

Two days later, on 28 November 2008, Geoghegan sent another email to local compliance staff saying that 'if there are persistent breaches' of customer information documents 'in a particular branch, the branch will be closed and all staff dismissed regardless of how much business we will lose on account of it'. In January 2009 HSBC Mexico earmarked two branches for closure.

Alonso queried the changes. But HSBC Group head of compliance David Bagley replied in a 9 June 2009 email: 'The inherent AML [anti-money-laundering] risk in Mexico is still very high and there are not many other parts of the Group that have what is effectively a drugs war being conducted on the streets.' A week later HBUS moved its risk rating for HBMX from its lowest to its highest notch.

The Senate subcommittee report acknowledged the difficulty the centre had in controlling the Mexican operation. 'HSBC Group executives and compliance personnel worked to build a compliance culture, but repeatedly faced a workforce in Mexico that disregarded the Group's AML policies and procedures, delayed obtaining required KYC [Know Your Customer[1]] data, delayed closing suspect accounts, and delayed reporting suspicious activity to regulators.'

In early 2009, under pressure from regulators, HSBC Group took drastic measures, including prohibiting HBMX branches from buying or selling US dollars, shutting entire branches with chequered histories, and scheduling for closure thousands of accounts with

---

[1] Standards that provide information to a bank about its customers.

incomplete KYC documentation. Even with those actions, HSBC Group acknowledged internally that HBMX 'continued to pose a high risk of money laundering to the Group'.

HSBC's Mexican problems did not end with the regulatory intervention of 2009. In 2011 it was found to be at the centre of a money-laundering scam that used travellers cheques. Over a three-month period from April to June 2011 some 188 sequentially numbered cheques, issued by an unnamed US bank, were negotiated for payment at the same HBMX branch in Mexico. The cheques carried illegible signatures so that they provided no information about the payees. On fourteen occasions over that three-month period, two men made purchases in batches of travellers cheques which, each time, had a combined value of $10,000–$140,000 in all. Over a three-year period, from 2009–11, those two men bought travellers cheques from the same HBMX branch with a combined value of $1.9 million.

Much of the material detailing HSBC's problems in Mexico did not fully emerge until 2012. (In fairness to HSBC, the Senate subcommittee report did then praise the bank for 'handing over vast swathes of relevant information even when it did not paint the bank in a favourable light'.) Shareholders, analysts and customers thus remained largely ignorant of the bank's run-in with the US authorities for some time, even though the bank was under scrutiny from an array of regulators including the Office of the Comptroller of the Currency (OCC), the Department of Justice, the Office of Foreign Asset Control and the Federal Reserve. References to the Mexican stand-off with regulators hardly registered in the published annual reports of HSBC for 2010 and 2011. The annual reports record that 43 branches were sold in Mexico in 2010 and a further 77 in 2011, but much of their focus is on the higher levels of fees being achieved for use of cash machines and credit cards.

2012 proved to be HSBC's *annus horribilis*. In February the firm revealed in its annual Securities and Exchange Commission filing in the US that it might face 'significant' penalties from a number of US regulator investigations that were coming to a head. The bank looked to be in rude health, having posted a profit increase of 15 per cent to £13.8 billion earlier that month. But in its filing there was a note of caution: 'It is likely there will be some form of formal enforcement action which may be criminal or civil in nature in respect of some or all of the ongoing investigations.' Just how damaging to HSBC's reputation for integrity the charges were likely to be was not disclosed.

A new senior management team at HSBC headed by chairman Douglas Flint, a down-to-earth Scotsman, and chief executive Stuart Gulliver were, however, coming to grips with compliance, not just in Mexico but globally. An internal note stated: 'We must adopt and enforce adherence to a single standard globally that is determined by the highest standard we must apply anywhere.' It pointed out that that would often mean conforming to very tough American rules, but that if other jurisdictions demanded high standards then HSBC was ready to meet them. None of this was shouted from the rooftops, or from large signs in the bank's entrance (à la Barclays headquarters at Canary Wharf), but quietly promulgated to senior staff. Discovery of the note prompted Carl Levin's often bruising Senate subcommittee to suggest that HSBC could be setting a benchmark for other significant financial institutions across the globe.

The appearances in the public stocks started on 17 July 2012 when the bank's executives were ordered to come before the US Senate's Permanent Subcommittee on Investigations, the committee that had been so active in holding American banks in general and Goldman Sachs in particular to account for their role in creating the instruments and conditions that led to the Great Panic. The timing could not have been worse for HSBC so far as media attention in the UK was concerned. It was the same month that Barclays, Bob Diamond and the Libor scandal all made the headlines. Banks were very much back under the spotlight.

On the same day the subcommittee issued a coruscating report on HSBC. It accused the bank of being a conduit for 'drug kingpins and rogue nations' in Mexico, Saudi Arabia and Iran, among others, from 2001 to 2009. As the hearing began David Bagley, the head of compliance since 2012, resigned, ending a 20-year career at the bank. Such was the scale of the bank's operations it could be argued that his job was a virtually impossible one. By sacrificing himself, however, he at least temporarily eased the public pressure on the top echelons at the bank. His departure statement was spare: it was the 'appropriate time', he said, for 'someone new to serve as the head of group compliance'. For her part, HBUS chief executive Irene Dorner sought to detoxify the hearings by apologising 'for the fact that HSBC did not live up to the expectations of our regulators, our customers, our employees, and the general public'. As banking apologies go, this was a fulsome one.

The subcommittee's reference to Saudi Arabia and Iran show that Mexico was not the only country to be giving HSBC a headache, and it also provides a hint of just how tricky global compliance can be for a bank of HSBC's size and complexity. Mexico presented one very particular set of challenges, Saudi Arabia and Iran a completely different set. In Mexico the challenge was drug trafficking. In Saudi Arabia and Iran the challenge was terrorism.

HSBC's connections with Saudi Arabia are long standing. It has relationships with major banking institutions, with assets in the tens of billions of dollars, which date back a quarter of a century.

For HSBC the problems in Saudi Arabia began in the wake of the 9/11 terrorist attacks on the US in 2001. In March 2002 a list of names was found in the Bosnian offices of a Saudi organisation designated at that time as a terrorist organisation by the US Treasury Department, although subsequently delisted. On the assumption that some names at least were probably Al Qaeda donors a CD-ROM and computer hard drive and hundreds of documents were taken away.

In 2003 a CIA report into Saudi financial groups, certain of which HSBC had connections, concluded that some of them had been used by 'Islamic extremists since at least the mid-1990s as a con-duit for terrorist transactions'. The report suggested that the Saudi organisations concerned were aware and condoned the terrorist links. The report also noted that in the year 2000 couriers for certain Saudi organisations 'delivered money to an Indonesian insurgent group Kompak to fund weapons purchases and bomb-making activities'. It added that terror groups 'ordered operatives in Afghanistan, Indonesia, Pakistan, Saudi Arabia, Turkey and Yemen' to use certain of the Saudi institutions with which HSBC had historic links.

A Saudi financial group also held bank accounts for a Saudi non-profit group. In 2003 HSBC's own Financial Intelligence Group said this Saudi non-profit group had been linked to al-Qaeda and other terror-group plots to assassinate President Bill Clinton and the Pope, as well as the 1993 attack on the World Trade Center.

Abdulaziz al Omari, one of the 9/11 hijackers on board American Airlines Flight 11, had bank accounts with connected Saudi institutions, as well as several other terrorists on that deadly mission.

HSBC's relationship with Saudi finance was cemented via the purchase by former chairman Sir John Bond of the US Republic Bank of New York in May 1999, a bank that happened to have had wealthy Saudi financial clients since the 1970s. HSBC operated a wide range of financial services with Saudi groups including asset management and trade financing, as well as supplying large amounts of physical dollars. In addition it did business with a prominent money-exchange firm.

HSBC's initial response to concerns expressed in 2002 about possible terror links at some of its business associates in the oil-rich Middle East was to transfer a key account in March of that year from HSBC International Private Banking to HSBC's Institutional Banking Department based in Delaware, a unit better able to monitor account activity. In the same month an HBUS banker wrote to colleagues: 'The most recent concern arose when three wire transfers for small amounts ($50k, $3k and $1.5k) were transferred through the account for names that closely resembled names, not exact matches, of the terrorists involved in the 9/11 World Trade Center attack . . . The profile of the main account reflects a doubling of wire transfer volume since 9/11, a large number of travellers checks but with relatively low value and some check/cash deposits.' Despite the potential 9/11 connection the banker added that 'maintaining our business with this name' was 'strongly supported' by senior figures at HSBC Middle East and HBUS.

But by 2005 the mood had changed – in the US, at least. On 28 January HBUS head of compliance Teresa Pesce sent an email to colleagues. She said: 'After much consideration, Group compliance has recommended that the US business sever ties with these clients based on the current regulatory environment and the interest of US law enforcement . . . Please make appropriate arrangements.' The view in Britain and elsewhere, however, was different. Units such as HSBC Middle East continued to trade with Saudi affiliates. The London Banknotes unit, which for the previous 20 years had sent US dollars to these Saudi associates, lobbied to have this lucrative business reinstated.

In May 2005 HSBC Group compliance gave a little ground when it said that since associates in the Kingdom had recently upgraded compliance procedures regional units could trade with the Arabian bankers if they wished. Saudi associates seemed to come back in from the cold even if HBUS still held out against the business. A lawsuit brought by 9/11 families, which included Saudi financial organisations in its line of fire, was dismissed by a US judge. And all the while London Banknotes and HSBC Middle East pressed for normal trading conditions to open again.

On 17 November 2006 HBUS Banknotes head Stephen Allen, based in London, wrote to colleagues that an associate in Saudi Arabia 'has now run out of patience waiting for us to re-start our banknote trading relationship and unless we can complete the kyc [Know Your Customer] formalities and advise them accordingly by the end of November, they will terminate all product relationships with the HSBC Group – which I believe to be substantial'.

A month later, in December 2006 a Saudi Arabian institution started buying US banknotes from HSBC again but only after senior executives threatened to cut off all business ties. The decision caused waves inside HSBC. One senior institutional banker, Beth Fisher, refused to sign off the agreement. Another, Alan Ketley, showed reluctance and added a series of detailed conditions to his approval.

Over the next four years, between 2006 and 2010, a Saudi associate bought around $25 million US dollars a month from HSBC, amassing $977 million during that period, while only selling $8 million. The obvious reason for this disparity was that the bank had elected to hoard dollars. But it was to emerge that some of that currency, in the form of travellers cheques, leaked to people with connections to terrorist groups.

Once the contents of the damning 2003 CIA report into the

activities of Saudi financial institutions was published in the US in 2007, adverse publicity began in earnest.

HBUS ended its relationship with Saudi associates for the second time in September 2010 when the group decided to exit the US banknotes business worldwide. The decision came a week after US bank regulator the Office of the Comptroller of the Currency (OCC) sent the bank a long letter criticising its banknote anti-money-laundering arrangements. The Senate investigators in their July 2012 report charged that senior staff in HSBC's US and Group divisions 'were aware' of evidence building up against a Saudi financial concern 'but approved or maintained the accounts anyway'. The firm's key test seemed to be 'how much revenue an account would produce'.

The Senate subcommittee that was so critical of HSBC's involvement with Saudi Arabia also highlighted its activities in Iran. Here again was a country that raised red flags among the international community. Its support of terrorist groups such as Hezbollah and its nuclear research have won opprobrium from the United Nations and have led to the imposition of sanctions by Washington and other Western democracies. Yet of the more than 28,000 transactions valued at £19.7 billion that took place between 2001 and 2007 and that the US Treasury Department Office of Foreign Assets Control classed as 'sensitive', 25,000 valued at $19.4 billion involved Iran.

As if Mexico with its drugs cartels and the Middle East with its political turmoil weren't enough of a headache for HSBC, it also found itself in hot water in the unlikeliest of countries: Japan.

The bank's relationship with this most civilised of countries dates back to 2001 when the regional Hokuriku Bank became a client of HBUS. A modest enterprise which can trace its origins back to 1877, Hokuriku had some 185 branches and employed 2,800 in 2013.

From 2005 it began to send HBUS enormous amounts of dollar travellers cheques, amounting to $290 million by October 2008. At one point in 2008 it was sending between $500,000 and $600,000 per day. These travellers cheques were in denominations of $500 or $1,000 and came in sequentially numbered batches, signed and countersigned by the same person with an illegible signature. All the cheques were made out to one of 30 firms or individuals who all claimed to work in the used-car trade. When the OCC bank examiners looked into the issue it identified one particular used-car dealer, SK Trading,[2] as receiving travellers cheques to the tune of $500,000 daily. In the period November 2007 to October 2008 SK Trading and the other 29 entities connected to the used-car trade received a total of $61 million in remittances.

The OCC established from the form attached to the cheques that the cash was for a 'business purpose'. SK Trading's website claimed the business was based in South Korea and that it had been founded in 1984. Further digging, however, revealed that the firm was linked to individuals with Russian surnames who sent cash either from Russian banks or accounts in the British Virgin Islands. And that Russian connection immediately rang alarm bells.

The US regards Russia as a country of 'primary money laundering concern', its highest risk category. According to a 2008 US State Department report: 'Russia remains vulnerable to such activity because of its vast natural resource wealth, the pervasiveness of organised crime, and, reportedly, a high level of corruption.' The report quoted Russia's own financial intelligence unit, which estimated that Russians might have laundered as much as $11 billion in 2007.

It was officials dispatched by HBUS to Russia who established the

---

[2] Not connected in any way with UK-based SK Trading in Edgware.

links in the chain connecting HSBC to a Russian bank via SK Trading. Hokuriku, for its part, proved a less useful source of information. Arguing that bank secrecy laws in Japan placed restrictions on how far it could help, the Japanese bank was only able to provide very basic information such as the occupation of the person at the centre of a transaction, the nature of business being undertaken, or the company involved. The Senate subcommittee had no doubts about what had been going on. HBUS, it concluded, 'enabled a number of Russians engaged in suspicious activity to use a relatively small Japanese bank with weak AML controls to gain access to over $290 million in US dollars in less than four years.'

HBUS has two centres where it processes travellers cheques: in Brooklyn and Buffalo in the state of New York. Processing clerks are supposed to check manually for large numbers of sequentially numbered cheques and set them aside for further review by a compliance officer. In practice, though, because the clerks felt their main priority to be to process as many cheques as possible by the centre's 5pm deadline, they tended simply to pass cheques through the system. The process of double-checking was seen as cumbersome. It involved contacting an officer in another building, waiting for a response and then acting on it. All of these tasks had to be achieved, ideally, before the 5pm deadline.

It was not until May 2012 that HBUS finally closed its account with Hokuriku.

In 2005 chairman Stephen Green robustly defended the bank against allegations, in a Bloomberg article, that the bank was involved in money laundering for Iran and other Middle Eastern countries including Libya, Sudan and Syria. 'This is a singular and wholly irresponsible article on the bank's international compliance procedures,' Green said.

The Senate subcommittee that looked into all this, though, came to a rather different conclusion. In addition to activities in Mexico, Saudi Arabia, Iran and Japan, the subcommittee also found that HBUS carried out transactions for a number of countries against which America has a sanctions programme. These included Cuba, Sudan, Burma and North Korea. In 2012 HSBC agreed to pay US regulators a $1.9 billion fine in settlement of the money-laundering charges – a sum four times that levied on Barclays for its rigging of the Libor interest-rate market.

HSBC's new chairman Douglas Flint, who replaced Stephen Green in 2010, along with chief executive Stuart Gulliver, moved rapidly to detoxify the bank. In the troubled Middle East the number of compliance staff doubled to 3,500 over two years. The bank's 2012 annual report stated that the global cost of compliance had doubled since 2010 to more than $500 million. HSBC also told shareholders recently that it has spent $290 million on 'remedial measures' and plans a review of its customer files across its entire group. It is an exercise expected to cost $700 million over the next five years. The bank has also sought to claw back tens of millions in deferred bonuses from some of the key executives involved. Most importantly, Gulliver has overturned the decentralised structure.

The bank which advertised itself to the world as the 'local bank', offering something different to every community in which it operated, has become the centralised bank. All management functions are now focused in its Canary Wharf headquarters in London and, to a lesser extent, its main business centre in Hong Kong. Financial functions, IT, marketing and the company's website – its window to the rest of the world – are being brought home. It is change management that has been brought about quietly. Even so, the bank faces a major challenge: it is, after all, one of the largest banks, if not the largest. Its assets are a colossal $2.5 trillion, a sum larger than the total wealth of the British economy. It has over 89 million customers in over 80 countries and around 250,000 employees. Ensuring perfect compliance in every territory is an ambitious, if necessary, goal.

HSBC was not alone in clashing with American enforcers over money laundering. Britain's lesser-known emerging-markets bank Standard Chartered also found itself in the dock.

Standard Chartered is unusual in that although it is based in London almost all its operations are overseas. It is a dominant presence in Singapore, a rival to HSBC in Hong Kong, and has a big presence in India, the Middle East and Africa. The City of London office is used largely to provide sophisticated financial services to global clients. It has a long and venerable history. Chartered Bank, formed by Scottish businessman James Wilson (who also set up *The Economist* magazine), which was established in 1853, played an important role in the development of major trade routes in the East, following the opening of the Suez Canal in 1869. The bank's ultimate bedfellow Standard Bank was founded in 1862 in Cape Town Province of South Africa to finance the running of diamond fields around the town of Kimberley.

In the 1990s Standard Chartered developed an unfortunate reputation for making big mistakes. In 1992 Mumbai bank workers were found to have diverted depositor money to speculate on the Indian stock exchange. The affair cost the bank £350 million, one-third of its market value at the time. In the same decade it came under pressure over bribery charges in Malaysia and the Philippines where it had considerable interests. The weakness of the franchise made it a constant source of merger speculation, with the Royal Bank of Scotland among the potential suitors.

Under the leadership of Lord Mervyn Davies as chief executive from 2001 to 2006 and then chairman (2006–9) its reputation was transformed and it came to be viewed as a sure-footed bank that exported UK financial service skills to the rest of the world. The transformation that took place under the stewardship of the diminutive and unpretentious Welshman was continued by his successor Peter Sands, who stepped up from finance director in 2006. Sands had been one of the key architects of the 'Balti bailout' – the informal name given to the 2008 part-nationalisation of the Royal Bank of Scotland and Lloyds, thrashed out over a takeaway curry at the Treasury. In the wake of banking meltdown elsewhere he played up Standard Chartered's 'boring' tag, aware that this would go down well with investors looking for a safe place to put their cash. If that suggests, though, that he had a similar personality to his very accessible predecessor, the truth is that the two men were very different. Sands, who has a shock of floppy white hair, was possessed of a very apparent self-confidence.

In August 2012 the bank presented another strong set of interim results with profits before tax up 9 per cent at $3.9 billion. Sands' comment was that the business 'may seem boring in contrast to what is going on elsewhere, but we see some virtue in being boring'.

Just two weeks later, however, things became rather less boring. Towards the end of the month New York's Department of Financial Services, headed by the aggressive young prosecutor Benjamin Lawsky, accused Standard Chartered of carrying out 60,000 'secret transactions' with Iran worth $250 billion between 2001 and 2007. The Department of Financial Services described Standard Chartered as a 'rogue institution'. It added that the bank's actions 'left the US financial system vulnerable to terrorists, weapons dealers, drug kingpins and corrupt regimes, and deprived law enforcement investigators of crucial information used to track all manner of criminal activity'.

Standard Chartered initially took a hard line, saying it 'strongly reject[ed]' the position taken by Lawsky. The bank said '99.9 per cent' of its trades with Iran were compliant with US law, with only $14 million of its deals falling outside these rules. It added that it thought Lawsky's interpretation of events was 'incorrect as a matter of law'. Behind the scenes it engaged in an intense campaign to bring investor, media and political opinion on side. Lawsky was disparaged as an investigator simply trying to make a name for himself and his department and a lesser figure than those who served on the powerful Senate Permanent Subcommittee on Investigations in Washington.

Initially, StanChart was successful in winning friends to its side. But as further detail of the nature of the alleged offences emerged – at a time when much of the world was seeking to isolate Iran – doubts about Sands' judgement in seeking to resist regulators surfaced. By the end of the year the bank's resistance had faltered, under pressure from 30,000 pages of detailed evidence, and it caved in. Fines of $667 million in total were paid to three US agencies – New York's Department of Financial Services, the Federal Reserve and the Department of Justice.

Senator Carl Levin, chair of the Senate subcommittee that played such a pivotal role in exposing HSBC's misdeeds, was full of praise for Benjamin Lawsky and New York's Department of Financial Services for the tough stance it adopted against Standard Chartered:

> The agency also showed that holding a bank accountable for past misconduct doesn't take years of negotiation over the size of the penalty; it simply requires a regulator with backbone to act. New York's regulatory action sends a strong message that the United States will not tolerate foreign banks giving rogue nations like Iran hidden access to the US financial system.

*

Ever since the Iranian revolution that toppled the pro-Western Shah and installed a radical Muslim government in 1979, the US has imposed financial sanctions on Iran. These were stiffened under Presidents Ronald Reagan in 1983 and Bill Clinton in 1995. In the 2000s the United Nations tightened the noose and other countries, including Britain, imposed similar sanctions. Yet when in 2001 Iran's central bank Markazi approached Standard Chartered to act as its recipient bank for dollar proceeds from daily oil sales of $500 million made by the National Iranian Oil Company, Standard Chartered accepted the role. An email of 19 February 2001 from Standard Chartered's head of inbound sales to colleagues called the appointment 'very prestigious' because 'in essence SCB [Standard Chartered Bank] would be acting as Treasurer' to the central bank.

Standard Chartered also thought a deal with such a high-profile Iranian organisation would lead to further opportunities inside the country. Indeed, it later picked up similar clearing work for Iranian private lenders Bank Saderat and Bank Melli. The central bank, Markazi, told Standard Chartered that a vital part of the arrangement was that its daily dollar proceeds should be processed speedily through the financial system.

The reason why Markazi was so keen to see dollar proceeds dealt with quickly was that existing routes were proving slow and laborious. Between 1995 and 2008 the United States allowed Iran to conduct U-turn payments through the US financial system. These enabled dollar payments from banks outside the US to be made to another bank outside the US. Such payments would be cleared inside America before leaving the country again. The Americans stipulated that the Iranian bank behind the funds had to be identified on the documents that came with the payment. In reality, though, when these payments came into a US bank's clearing house it was mandated to hand them over to the US regulator, the Office of Foreign Assets Control. Here the payment might be reviewed over weeks, months or years; it might even ultimately be rejected. Markazi was looking for a way around a mechanism that stymied Iran's access to cash. Standard Chartered understood this when it took on the contract.

On 23 March 2001 an email from Standard Chartered's group legal adviser told colleagues: 'Our payment instructions [for Iranian clients] should not identify the client or the purpose of the payment.' What Standard Chartered proposed was a method they called 'repair', which they carried out on the documents that accompanied the wire payments. This entailed stripping the message of any data that referred to Iran and replacing it with false entries. The repair, it was proposed, would be carried out by Standard Chartered staff, or else the payments would be sent back to the Iranian bank to be doctored and resubmitted.

The payments came through Standard Chartered's New York office, which cleared $190 billion of payments a day for international clients. Standard Chartered produced a number of manuals for staff to make sure Iranian payments were 'repaired' correctly. One such document was called 'Quality Operating Procedure Iranian Bank Processing'. As the business grew New York's Department of Financial Services found that Standard Chartered 'automated the process by building an electronic repair system with "specific repair queues" for each Iranian client'.

In 2006 US regulators started to pay more attention to this area. Standard Chartered's chief executive for the Americas began to get cold feet and sent the following email to group colleagues in London on 5 October 2006:

Firstly, we believe [the Iranian business] needs urgent reviewing at the group level to evaluate if its returns and strategic

benefits are . . . still commensurate with the potential to cause very serious or even catastrophic reputational damage to the group. [S]econdly, there is equally importantly potential of risk of subjecting management in the US and London (eg you and I) and elsewhere to personal reputational damages and/or serious criminal liability.

Shortly after this warning was issued an unnamed group director famously poured scorn over these concerns. He is reported to have said: 'You fucking Americans. Who are you to tell us, the rest of the world, that we're not going to deal with Iranians.' (Sands later insisted that this had been inaccurately reported.)

During this period the New York's Department of Financial Services said that Standard Chartered convinced accountants Deloitte & Touche to 'water down' a report for US regulators on the bank's anti-money-laundering controls. In June 2013 (after StanChart had admitted to wrongdoing) Deloitte's Financial Advisory Services was fined $10 million and banned from acting as a consultant in New York for one year by the Department of Financial Services for not carrying out an independent audit. The rest of the Deloitte group was unaffected by the ban.

In September 2006 New York regulators asked Standard Chartered to supply data on Iranian U-turns for the past 12 months. The figure was 2,626 transactions worth $16 billion. The CEO of the Americas argued against releasing the full figure in a 5 October 2006 memo to the group. In the event Standard Chartered released only four days of U-turn data to the regulators.

In November 2008 the US Treasury Department banned U-turns, because it had come to the conclusion that the system was being abused. Meanwhile, US regulators maintained their investigations into Standard Chartered, and this in time led to a 2012 fine of $340 million. The charge sheet produced by New York's Department of Financial Services did not spare Standard Chartered's blushes.

> Motivated by greed, SCB acted for at least ten years without any regard for the legal, reputational, and national security consequences of its flagrantly deceptive actions. Led by its most senior management, SCB designed and implemented an elaborate scheme by which to use its New York branch as a front for prohibited dealings with Iran – dealings that indisputably helped sustain a global threat to peace and stability. By definition, any banking institution that engages in such conduct is unsafe and unsound.

Standard Chartered stated that it had stopped these kinds of transactions with Iran in 2007. It also said that it had carried out a 'comprehensive review and upgrade of its compliance systems and procedures', hiring new senior compliance staff both in New York and in the Middle East.

Despite the fine and the internal changes, though, a measure of defiance was apparent. In a visit to the *Daily Mail*'s offices in late 2012 Sands minimised the nature of the offences, suggesting that the numbers had been wildly exaggerated. In March 2013 Standard Chartered's affable and normally frank chairman Sir John Peace again attempted to play down the scale of StanChart's infringements. In a phone conversation with reporters on 5 March the bank's boss said: 'We had no wilful act to avoid sanctions; you know, mistakes are made – clerical errors – and we talked about last year a number of transactions which clearly were clerical errors or mistakes that were made . . .'

The suggestion that sanctions busting and the alteration of documents might be described as clerical errors was a red rag to a bull so far as the US regulators were concerned. They saw it as an attempt by the bank to evade responsibility, even though it had previously been prepared to admit responsibility, pay a fine and agree to mend its ways. Fears were raised that StanChart could face new regulatory action. It was even suggested that it might lose its banking licence. The fact is that Standard Chartered had picked a fight with the wrong people. Unlike their supine British counterparts at the FSA and the Serious Fraud Office the Americans take regulation and enforcement extraordinarily seriously. Jobs at the Securities and Exchange Commission and in regulators' and prosecutors' offices go to the best and brightest in the land keen to make a reputation for themselves. Such enforcement jobs are seen as a path to prosperity in the private sector or one of the steps up the ladder to political power.

The Manhattan District Attorney demanded an apology, and on 21 March Peace had no choice but to retract his unguarded words. 'My statement that SCB "had no wilful act to avoid sanctions" was wrong, and directly contradicts SCB's acceptance of responsibility in the deferred prosecution agreement and accompanying factual statement,' he said. 'To be clear, Standard Chartered Bank unequivocally acknowledges and accepts responsibility, on behalf of the Bank and its employees, for past knowing and wilful criminal conduct in violating US economic sanctions laws and regulations, and related New York criminal laws, as set out in the deferred prosecution agreement.'

A spokeswoman for the Manhattan District Attorney's office was satisfied with the *mea culpa*. 'We demanded a public repudiation and they complied,' she said.

The assault on British banks by enthusiastic American regulators was seen by some at the start of 2013 as a case of the US deliberately targeting overseas institutions while protecting its own. Coming as it did in the wake of the fierce criticisms of BP, or British Petroleum as President Obama insisted on calling it, following the Deepwater Horizon disaster in the Gulf of Mexico in 2010, the accusation had a certain superficial plausibility.

But a closer examination of the facts does not bear out the conspiracy theory. If Standard Chartered was in the firing line then so was RBS's large American subsidiary Citizens which was being monitored for money laundering. More to the point, those who accused the Americans of being Anglophobe missed the fundamental fact that while foreign banks have felt free to operate in some of the most politically sensitive markets in the Middle East, US banks in the post-9/11 era have not. The US War on Terror is still being fought, not just physically but in the financial markets. There is a ruthless determination to cut off funding to Iran and more directly to terror groups including al-Qaeda, Hezbollah and Hamas. By tracing and closing down the sources of finance the US authorities seek to sever the financial lifelines to foreign terrorism. Standard Chartered saw a relationship with the Iranian central bank as a great business opportunity. The US saw it as trading with the enemy.

One could perhaps argue that the US authorities have been tougher on UK banks than on their own. In 2010, for instance, US bank Wachovia, a unit of Wells Fargo, paid only a fairly modest $160 million for laundering money for Mexican drug gangs. But it is well to remember that in HSBC's case money laundering extended to several countries and that the bank's initial responses in terms of compliance were unimpressive. As for Standard Chartered, it made the mistake of leaving a paper trail of deliberate compliance avoidance. It could not have been worse.

Following the collapse of WorldCom and then Enron in 2003, American enforcers and prosecutors threw the book at all those involved, executives and advisers, resulting in stiff prison sentences. In the banking crisis prosecutors took a different route. They regarded the safety and stability of the banking system as more important than bringing individuals and banks to court. Most of the financial cases that have been brought in the US, post-crisis, relate to insider dealing rather than poor financial practice or reckless banking.

In December 2012 Lanny Breuer, the head of the Justice Department's criminal division, said publicly that he had considered prosecuting HSBC, but had rejected the idea because he was concerned that legal action might affect the bank's long-term prospects, and might have an impact on jobs and the wider American economy. His comments reinforced the view in some quarters that a handful of international lenders were regarded as both too big to fail and too big to jail. But that certainly doesn't mean that they were regarded as untouchable. In July 2010, for example, the investment bank Goldman Sachs accepted a record-breaking $550 million fine from the Securities and Exchange Commission. In what became known as the 'Abacus' transaction in 2006–7 Goldman, at the behest of renowned hedge-fund manager John Paulson, created a derivatives product based on a bet that the value of sub-prime mortgages would fall. The investment bank then sold the securities to other clients, including ABN Amro (which became RBS) without informing them of the underlying purpose of the securities it had created. 'This settlement is a stark lesson to Wall Street firms that no product is too complex, and no investor too sophisticated, to avoid a heavy price if a firm violates the fundamental principles of honest treatment and fair dealing,' argued the SEC's enforcement director Robert Khuzami. Even blue-blooded JPMorgan was to find itself being heavily fined: over the London Whale affair in 2012 and, the following year, over the wrongful selling and trading of sub-prime mortgages by Bear Stearns and Washington Mutual – two banks it rescued during and after the financial crisis. This latter offence carried with it the biggest regulatory settlement of all time: a $13 billion penalty.

In fairness to HSBC it has to be said that even its critics would acknowledge that its culture is essentially cautious and prudent. Its top figures – often internal appointments steeped in the traditions of the bank – have generally been quick to correct errors once they have been pointed out. The mistakes of men such as Stephen Green were those of naivety and incuriosity rather than of the venal kind so often seen elsewhere. But the whole money-laundering scandal does show how even the best-intentioned banks can go seriously off course in their search for easy profits. Many banks can be said to have betrayed their customers and clients. Some would argue that HSBC – and Standard Chartered – went one step further. Their actions, in the eyes of their critics, helped criminals and undermined the national security interests of Western democracies.

# 8

# Mis-selling in the High Street:
# PPI and Other Scandals

In 2008, 50-year-old Hertfordshire-based bus driver Michael Hampton was looking for somewhere new to live. He searched high and low and eventually lighted upon a modest one-bedroom furnished flat in Sawbridgeworth. To secure it he needed to stump up a three-month deposit at a cost of £2,500, and so turned to the Abbey National[1], where he had banked for ten years, to negotiate a £5,000 loan that would cover both the deposit and the cost of buying some basic household items. Abbey National, simply known as Abbey at the time, duly offered a loan that would be paid back over five years, with monthly payments set at £122. In addition Abbey sold him a payment protection insurance (PPI) policy. The monthly premium for that was £43. Over five years it would cost him half the value of the original loan. But, as Abbey pointed out, PPI would insulate him from default in the event of illness.

Hampton later recalled just how hard a sell he was given by the bank's saleswoman in a face-to-face interview: 'She kept pointing out to me that it was in my best interests to take the personal protection insurance. She insisted my application would be looked on more

---

[1] Abbey National was bought by Spain's Santander in 2004.

favourably if I took out the insurance. I needed a home to live in so I took out the loan with the PPI.'

Over the next five years Hampton continued to drive the 510 route from Harlow to Stansted Airport or the local 2, 3 and 4 bus routes around Harlow, clocking up in the process 12 years of service with the bus and train company Arriva. He also managed to keep up with his combined £165-a-month payments as the financial world crashed around him and Britain headed into the Great Recession.

A key benefit promised by payment protection insurance is, of course, that it pays out if the policyholder is struck down by sickness. What Hampton didn't appreciate, though, was that his employer already had in place a good scheme to cover precisely that eventuality. Arriva offers up to eight weeks' sick pay to all its workers. And as Hampton's length of service grew to ten years he became entitled to 26 weeks' sick pay. During the five years he paid the premiums on the PPI, Hampton already had more than enough cover via his employer.

By June 2013 Hampton had moved to new accommodation. In preparation for doing some decorating, he had a clear-out of his papers and in the process came across his original loan documents. These reminded him of a recent TV programme hosted by personal-finance guru Martin Lewis, the multimillionaire founder of consumer website Moneysavingexpert.com, in the course of which Lewis had talked about the mis-selling of PPI and advised people to claim money back from those who had provided the insurance.

Hampton had just two payments left on his loan but nevertheless decided to act: 'I thought I would give it a go. I printed off the complaints templates from the website, followed them, and sent them off.' It proved to be a shrewd move. Five days later Santander, which had rebranded the Abbey under its new ownership, wrote back to Hampton offering £2,628.61, which he accepted. 'I was aware of the fuss over PPI from around 2011, he later recalled. 'But by the time I wrote to them I think they knew they were fighting a losing battle. I thought I would be in for months of going back and forth, but it was all over within a week.' Hampton added:

It makes me feel angry to think that my own bank could rip me off like that. It has made me a more wary customer. The gas and electricity prices have just begun to go up. I will wait until all of the big energy companies have put their prices up by January, then I will switch to the best one for me. There is no point switching now, only to find you have jumped to a more expensive company.

Hampton's first encounter with PPI was in 2008. But it had actually been around for a number of years before that, and concerns about its appropriateness for customers had been expressed for almost as long. It has proved to be an expensive business, first for customers and then for the institutions that mis-sold the product, and what it has also demonstrated is that while poor banking practice in recent times has often been most closely associated with investment banks, it has unfortunately spilled over into retail banking, too.

In the boom years for the UK economy, from the mid-1980s to the mid-2000s, it was the investment arms of banks that were expected to take the biggest risks, for the biggest gains. It was an open secret in any universal bank that the highly paid and incentivised investment bankers regarded their retail-banking counterparts as cautious and uninspiring. If there was a business opportunity the bank could take advantage of, you had to rely on an investment banker to spot it, went the theory. The retail units of banks were regarded as the simplest parts of the business, taking in depositors' cash and lending it out as mortgages or consumer and business loans.

Fashions began to change in the early 1990s as retail bankers, too, started to come under pressure to make a greater contribution to profits. Responding to this, they started to focus on increasing the number of financial products they sold to individual customers, knowing that every product would involve lucrative fees and payments to the bank. Local managers at institutions such as NatWest, owned by the Royal Bank of Scotland, took on the new challenge with alacrity. Indeed, so enthused did retail banks become with the idea of selling new products, they came to the conclusion that modern banking needed retail skills of the kind nurtured by grocers like Tesco and Asda. It's not surprising in this context that the appointment of former Asda executive Andy Hornby to a senior role at the Halifax should have been regarded as an inspired move.

In this brave new world the retail arms of banks became an engine room full of millions of customers, who could be lured into buying enticing new products. And they were captive customers, too: despite the advent of easy switching the average person changes their bank only once every 26 years – less often than they move house. Bill Michael, UK head of financial services at accountants KPMG, said banks 'treat customers like captive geese. Captive geese that can be force fed, or sold more product to – whether appropriate or not.'

PPI policies have been sold in the UK since the 1990s. At their heart they encapsulate a simple proposition, and they can be a useful product if sold to the right person, providing peace of mind for those taking out insurance policies, mortgages, unsecured personal loans or credit-card debt. They only became problematic when bankers started to take the view that they could become a moneymaking scheme in themselves, and so began to sell them aggressively to meet the challenge of high sales targets and the potential reward of healthy commissions. The goal, preached from the top, was that branch banking staff, private bank managers and loan officers had a duty to load up the customer with as many products as possible.

This aggressive selling was part and parcel of the culture of the pre-crash era. In the period leading up to the financial crisis of 2007 and 2008 interest rates were, as I have pointed out before, at historically low levels. Vast quantities of money were thus swilling around the wholesale money markets and there was intense competition for business. At the same time, the interest-rate spread – that is, the difference between what it costs the bank to fund itself through retail deposits and the money markets and the interest rate that it charges customers for loans – had shrunk from its previous 2–3 per cent level. In other words, banks were falling over each other to offer deals, and then weren't making that much from them. True, some income was derived from the so-called endowment effect – money sitting in current accounts doing nothing for the customer but utilised by the banks. However, this in itself was not sufficient. In an era when the British were obsessed with the idea of 'free banking', profits had to come from somewhere.

The result was that in much the same way as investment bankers were incentivised to take huge risks in their dealings in products such as sub-prime mortgages, so the retail bankers were enticed into selling a product that, more often than not, the customer did not need. Payment protection products could add 20–50 per cent to the cost of a loan, depending on its precise nature and duration. That was an attractive proposition in the late 1990s. It became even more so after the terrorist attacks of 9/11 in 2001, as low rates became even lower.

The former head of Abbey (after its purchase by Santander), Antonio Horta-Osorio, recalls just how shocked he was when in 2006 he joined Santander UK and lifted the lid on its vast bundle of unsecured personal loans. As he later told me at the elegant

Gresham Street City headquarters of his current employers Lloyds:

> I arrived in August. My first decision in September [2006] was to close the sale of unsecured personal loans. The spread on these loans was 3 per cent and the provision [the amount the bank would set aside each year in case the loans went wrong] was 3 per cent. So the bank was completely losing money because it was break-even without costs. Even worse three years down the road those retail loans at 3 per cent margins had losses of 6 per cent a year, so the first thing I did was close those unsecured loans.
>
> When I arrived at Santander UK people told me don't worry about the 3 per cent loss provisions on unsecured lending. We sell the customer payment protection insurance that is very profitable. That is why I closed unsecured lending. PPI had become so profitable that it was giving a subsidy to unsecured lending.

'The product was flawed, completely flawed,' he concluded.

As RBS testified to the Parliamentary Commission on Banking Standards in June 2012:

> For much of the period in question, personal loan rates were so low that they did not (alone) cover the cost of credit for the customer. In other words, the low personal loan rates for all customers would not have been possible without the cross-subsidisation from PPI sales to some customers.

Former Lloyds Banking Group chief executive Eric Daniels, who was at the helm when the group became the UK market leader in PPI sales, admitted: 'There is no question that the rate on credit cards and personal lending was far below the economic value of those products.'

Whatever justification banks may have felt they had for pushing PPI onto customers, the way many handled it is open to serious question. Customers often signed up for loans unaware that the PPI paperwork would be added later without their knowledge. Some staff told customers they could not approve a loan or credit-card application unless insurance was attached. Others were able to persuade people who would never qualify for a payout – the self-employed, for example – to sign up. Staff were provided with scripts for their high-pressure sales pitches, and were left in no doubt that loans without PPIs were not good for the bank. Few if any mentioned to prospective customers that, thanks to consumer protection legislation, a borrower who did get into difficulties would always be given more time to sort out their financial affairs, regardless of whether they had PPI or not. That snippet of information alone would have put paid to the suggestion that PPI was an urgent necessity.

As chief executive of the Financial Ombudsman Service (FOS) Natalie Ceeney testified in December 2012: 'A consumer would say, "I really don't want PPI," but the reply would be, "I'm sure you do. It's in your best interest," and that would go on four or five times. We have heard some scripts where "pushy" is a mild description of the sales approach.'

In 1998 *Which?* magazine started to highlight some of the problems with PPI. It wasn't just that insurance wasn't always being sold to the right people, it pointed out. If it did suit a particular person's needs and they then needed to make a claim, they often found the procedure both slow and immensely complicated. Not surprisingly some came to the cynical conclusion that the system was designed not to pay out at all. Estimates emerged that banks paid out just 15 per cent of their income from PPI to claimants, making PPI more lucrative than car or home insurance. In total 34 million PPI policies were sold between 2001 and 2012, generating sales of £5 billion a year for the industry at their height.

Following the *Which?* report increasing numbers of consumer and government watchdogs turned their attention to PPI. The FOS raised concerns with banks in 2001. Citizens Advice brought a super-complaint about mis-selling to the Office of Fair Trading (OFT) in 2005.[2] In the same year the regulation of the sale of general insurance, including PPI, moved under the wing of the Financial Services Authority. But the FSA adopted a distinctly and characteristically light-touch approach. 'We are not a price regulator,' said Sir Howard Davies, the former deputy governor of the Bank of England who chaired the FSA from 1997 to 2003. It's perhaps not surprising that the FSA came to be dubbed the 'Fundamentally Supine Authority' in some quarters.

Three separate reviews of PPI were conducted by the FSA, which commissioned market research groups to buy PPI policies from banks and other lenders as a means of verifying the way the product was sold and identifying problems. In 2005 its first study found poor practices. A 2006 report unearthed 'major weaknesses which go to the heart of the culture surrounding PPI sales'. And in its final 2007 report the FSA found 'little or no improvement in the disclosure to customers of the price and policy details, or the eligibility and suitability for the customer'. In June 2013 the FSA's former managing director of retail markets Clive Briault was to recognise that the regulator did not 'appreciate the full extent of the profit made by a few high-street retail banks'.

The Office of Fair Trading, a competition watchdog, pursued its

[2] Super-complaints are cases brought by a recognised consumer organisation about a market feature it thinks is of significant harm to consumers; the OFT then has to investigate the issue.

own probe and referred a Citizens Advice super-complaint to the Competition Commission in 2007. The Commission duly carried out an investigation and finally, in 2009, recommended a ban on selling PPIs alongside credit products and a ban on single-premium PPI (this is where the cost of the insurance is added up front to the loan, and prevents the customer from switching to another insurance policy at a later point).

The first great wave of PPI claims was now starting to arrive at the banks. FOS chief executive Natalie Ceeney notes: 'The volumes before 2007 were tiny. What happened around 2006–7 was the big publicity – there was the super-complaint, all the consumer groups started talking about it and there were the Competition Commission and the OFT inquiries – so the volume went up.'

The Competition Commission's findings were challenged by Barclays and Lloyds at the judicial Competition Appeal Tribunal in 2009. The tribunal ruled that the Competition Commission had to conduct further analysis to establish whether a point-of-sale ban would inconvenience customers. Meanwhile papers written by the FOS and the FSA in 2010 made it clear that these bodies expected lenders to look back years into past policies to see if they had been mis-sold. Worried by this course of events the British Bankers' Association (BBA), the banking industry trade body, which is dominated by the high-street banks, decided to commence legal action for full judicial review in December 2010. It still believed that attack was the best defence.

If the BBA's stonewalling seems reprehensible, it's worth recalling the parlous state many high-street banks were in by 2010. Take Lloyds, for example – the bank that Antonio Horta-Osorio was to join as chief executive in January 2011 and a serial offender in the mis-selling of PPI. It had weathered the first storms of the 2007 credit crunch well. Indeed, in August of 2007 it was ready to rescue

Northern Rock if the Bank of England had provided the right kind of support in terms of willpower and some guarantees. But then in 2008 its chief executive, the American Eric Daniels, along with his chairman Sir Victor Blank, gave the green light to a merger with the beleaguered Halifax Bank of Scotland (HBOS). Daniels saw the deal as a route to dominance in Britain's crowded mortgage and current account markets. Blank, with his connections to New Labour, was able to smooth the way with the then Prime Minister Gordon Brown, who swept aside the normal requirement that such a huge transaction – which would give Lloyds more than a 30 per cent share in some markets – should be referred to the Competition Commission for scrutiny.

On 17 September 2008 the Lloyds takeover of HBOS was announced. Time constraints meant that the deal was done with minimum due diligence, but it wasn't long before Daniels and Blank discovered that HBOS's finances were far from secure, and that its bad debts were on a scale that could hole the previously stable Lloyds TSB beneath the waterline. Just a month later, therefore, on 13 October 2008, as part of its rescue operation for the UK banking system, Gordon Brown's government injected £17 billion into the merged bank, acquiring a 43.4 per cent share stake. Hours earlier the cash machines at HBOS branches had run out of cash and the Bank of England had covertly had to inject tens of billions of pounds to keep the merged bank afloat.

The government's Lloyds stake was subsequently transferred to a new agency, United Kingdom Financial Investments (UKFI), which was intended to act at an arm's length from the Treasury. 'When Lloyds bought HBOS', Horta-Osorio later said in an interview with me, 'I told the executive committee of Santander UK, "This is a snake eating a poisonous bull and the bull is going to affect the snake." I would never have bought HBOS. I would have bought the branches and the deposits but not the loans. This was especially true of the loans of the Bank of Scotland.[3] In such a context of financial disaster, it was only too tempting to attempt to kick the PPI question into touch.

The judicial review finally got under way in January 2011 when the BBA took the FSA to the High Court. The BBA's chief executive at the time, Angela Knight, privately thought it was a bad judgement call, and in January 2013 was to tell the Parliamentary Commission on Banking Standards that she had 'grave concerns' about bringing the action at a time when the country was still living with the financial crisis banks had sparked. 'Given the nature of the situation at the time,' she said, 'given the very high attention on PPI and the fact that there were some really serious issues out there, I could not personally see that a case was necessarily going to do anything in that respect.' UK banks nevertheless unanimously supported the judicial review, knowing that if it went their way it would save billions of pounds in compensation.

In the event, the outcome was deeply disappointing for the banks. In April 2011 the High Court ruled in favour of the FSA's demand that compensation be paid. The BBA responded by saying it would consider appealing this ruling.

Meanwhile, in early 2011 Horta-Osório had attended his first executive meeting at Lloyds Banking Group as a non-executive director. He was shocked by what he heard. 'It had a complacent structure and was going towards the brink again. The bank had £300 billion of wholesale funding in a £700 billion banking portfolio. It had £150 billion of wholesale funding servicing a long-term mortgage portfolio,' he later recalled. In other words, Lloyds was making the same fundamental mistakes that had brought about the

---

[3] HBOS consisted of two parts. The retail operation largely traded under the Halifax name and Bank of Scotland was largely an investment and commercial banking operation.

crisis in the first place: borrowing short term in the money markets to finance mortgage lending over 25 years.

In May 2011, just two months into his new job as chief executive of Lloyds, Horta-Osorio made a decision that would have huge financial implications not only for his bank but for the whole of the UK banking industry and the broader economy. He decided to end the 13-year battle the banks had waged with consumer groups and City watchdogs over PPI. On 5 May he announced firstly that Lloyds would pull out of the BBA's legal fight jointly funded by the industry, and secondly that it would set aside £3.2 billion to pay legitimate claims for compensation for mis-selling. In so doing, he hoped he could draw a line under the PPI business and end any uncertainty about Lloyds' future.

A week later the BBA capitulated: 'In the interest of providing certainty for their customers, the banks and the British Bankers' Association have decided that they do not intend to appeal.' It was a retreat on an epic scale. Three other major high-street banks announced they would set aside cash for compensation. Barclays set aside £1 billion, HSBC £269 million and RBS, the second biggest player in PPI with an 18 per cent share, said it would add £850 million to the £200 million it had already earmarked to pay claims.

Consumer-affairs campaigners at *Which?* – one of the first organisations to highlight the PPI problem – were furious about the long campaign of resistance. Chief executive Peter Vicary-Smith said: 'PPI was mis-sold and complaints about it were mishandled on an industrial scale for well over a decade. It was a colossal error of judgement by the BBA to have brought this case in the first place, which has even further diminished the banking industry's reputation in the eyes of consumers.'

Adam Scorer of Consumer Focus said: 'The entire episode is an embarrassment for our high street banks.' In a prescient statement that warned how difficult the task of paying claims would be he added: 'Refunding billions of pounds to millions of people will be a mammoth undertaking and to get it wrong would add insult to injury.'

No one, however, had fully recognised the scale of the compensation that would be required. The FSA estimated in 2011 that PPI claims for banks and other firms – ranging from Tesco Bank to the Co-operative Bank and Land of Leather – would come to around £4.5 billion. By early 2014 the estimate had risen to an astounding £20 billion and was still climbing. RBS, which quickly raised the amount it had put aside for potential PPI compensation by almost £1 billion, acknowledged that 'the costs of PPI redress and its administration are subject to a degree of uncertainty'. That £20 billion figure dwarfs the bill for the mis-selling of private pensions in the 1990s – £13.5 billion – and comfortably beats the bill of £15 billion that was notched up for the faulty sale of endowment mortgages over much the same period. PPI was officially Britain's worst consumer scandal of all time.

If PPI mis-selling supported one industry, putting everything right has created a new one. According to a survey by employment group Manpower, 20,000 new jobs had been created to deal with PPI claims by March 2013. Lloyds alone has been responsible for 7,000 of these. Manpower UK managing director Mark Cahill said: 'On face value, you'd think we were in the midst of a boom, but many of the jobs created here are the direct result of the mis-selling of PPI and interest rate swaps.[4] These scandals have spawned a new industry to deal with the fallout.'

---

[4] Interest-rate swaps were sold by the banks to small and medium-sized enterprises. It was not properly explained that if economic or financial conditions changed they could result in large losses that might jeopardise the business.

The scale of existing and potential complaints is eye-watering. In the period 2006–11 some 16 million PPI policies were sold, Citizens Advice reported. By April 2011 the FSA said it had received more than 1.5 million complaints since it took over regulation for this area in 2005. Immediately after the banks lost their judicial review the High Court told them to deal with another 200,000 complaints they had put on hold until the case was resolved. This was the tip of the iceberg.

Further claims began to pile into banks, hitting 7,000 a day during 2012. The Financial Conduct Authority (which succeeded the FSA in April 2013) said 4.3 million complaints about PPI were made by consumers that year alone. During this period banks were sending out up to 10,000 compensation cheques a day, with an average payment of £2,750.

And then there were the claims management companies (CMCs), who sought to reach potential clients via advertising campaigns and phone calls. Millions of text messages were sent out, over and over again, in a bid to get more people to seek redress. Banks felt ever more beleaguered, having to take on extra staff in call centres as it became clear that the Financial Ombudsman Service (FOS), a government arbitrator, was itself having to employ more than a thousand extra staff to handle the torrent of disputes between customers, CMCs and banks. Banks soon found themselves in a race with CMCs, desperately sending out letters to ask customers to contact them directly rather than seek the services of an agent whose fees could amount to 25 per cent of any eventual payout. The number of CMCs mushroomed to around 800 which at their height spent £24 million a year on advertising, much of it on daytime TV. The avalanche of texts and unsolicited phone calls showed no sign of abating as late as the spring of 2014.

In December 2012 the Advertising Standards Authority ordered

Mumbai-based CMC Data Supplier to stop sending out millions of 'unsolicited and misleading' texts to phones in the UK after a complaint brought by a group of three people. One typical text said: 'Our records indicate you may be entitled to £3750 for the accident you had. To claim for free just reply CLAIM to this msg. To stop text STOP.' The text was misleading. Handling by claims companies is never free since they take a percentage of the sum delivered.

The ASA noted in its judgement: 'We also understood that none of the recipients had recently had accidents or considered themselves to be eligible to make a PPI claim, and that the texts did not identify who the message had been sent from.'

Banks complained that they were being swamped by bogus claims and blamed the CMCs. Lloyds chief·executive Antonio Horta-Osorio said he had received calls suggesting he was eligible to claim PPI compensation from his own bank. He added that one in four claims that come into Lloyds are from people who never had a PPI policy with the bank.

One study by Arriva showed that 75 per cent of the people it had surveyed had received an unsolicited message from a CMC. CBI director-general John Cridland wrote in *The Times* in November 2012: 'I firmly believe we need to draw a line under PPI', adding that 'banks are sending out tens of thousands of compensation payments and cheques and there is a real sense that the ball is now firmly in the court of ambulance-chasing management companies.' A survey by Citizens Advice in March 2014 found that up to £5 billion had been creamed off by CMCs and 39 per cent of consumers who had used them were not aware that it was possible to pursue the claim for free.

By October 2013 more than 2.5 million people had been paid £8 billion in compensation. At Lloyds, the biggest seller of PPI, provision more than doubled from £3.2 billion to £6.7 billion. In

January 2013 the BBA therefore called for a deadline of April 2014 for new PPI claims. The bank body said it was prepared to pay for a year-long advertising campaign to let consumers know about this new deadline. So intense was the activity of the CMCs that there was even some sympathy for the very banks that had brought the tsunami of claims upon themselves.

Not all banks were behind the scheme to set a deadline; it was feared that another burst of publicity would simply lead to a new wave of claims. The FSA's response to the BBA was lukewarm. It stated that it would not set a deadline without public consultation, adding: 'Our key priority is to ensure consumers are protected, so the FSA Board would need to be convinced that any proposals would be in the interests of consumers.' In testimony before the Treasury Select Committee in February 2014 Martin Wheatley, the chief executive of the Financial Conduct Authority (the successor to the FSA) remained sceptical about the benefits of setting a deadline: 'We have had that discussion [on setting a deadline] many times over three years. Our question is: would there be significant consumer benefit to taking away consumer rights? It's an equation.'

If the claims process has seemed to be unnecessarily long-drawn-out, this is largely to do with the way in which PPI was mis-sold in the first place. Quite simply, many people did not know they had been gulled into buying a PPI policy with their loan, and because consumers have six years to complain after being sold the policy, there is still plenty of time for new complaints to be made. Thanks to the involvement of CMCs and the FOS it's also much harder to throw out undeserving claims straight away – they have a habit of lingering on.

The banks are exasperated by the CMCs, arguing that they simply harvest as many customers as they can, and then send their details to all the major lenders claiming they were mis-sold insurance. CMCs, however, are quick to defend themselves, claiming that clients who took out loans a number of years before may have forgotten which institution actually made the loan. Anthony Sultan, chairman of CMC-industry body the Claims Standards Council, is unapologetic. Pointing out just how many years it has taken for banks to reach this stage he argues: 'If they had held up their hands, there would not be all this activity.' FOS chief executive Natalie Ceeney largely agrees with Sultan: 'The reason the claims management industry has been able to thrive is because [of] detriment built over so many years while banks, in the case of PPI, said, "No, there is not an issue" [and] because banks had not done a good enough job of investigating cases.'

If recent events are anything to go by, such continuing criticism of banks has some justification. In the summer of 2013 *The Times* sent an undercover reporter into a PPI claims handling agency for Lloyds who revealed some worrying details about the ways in which business was transacted. According to the journalist, new employees were told that if they rejected claims very few would end up being taken to the FOS (in fact, of the complaints that are rejected by Lloyds and then submitted to the FOS, 84 per cent are upheld by the arbitrator, the highest percentage of any major lender). Claims handlers were also told to assume that no Lloyds sales staff had mis-sold any PPIs – an interesting assumption given that Lloyds' own boss had been such a critic of the bank's misconduct.

Lloyds responded to criticism by terminating its contract with accountancy firm Deloitte, who ran a 1,300-strong complaints unit from Royal Mint Court in the City of London. The bank vowed to retrain staff 'in line with our policies and procedures'. The Parliamentary Commission on Banking Standards was unimpressed. 'If substantiated,' it pronounced, 'these allegations would demonstrate a woeful failure to meet the standards expected by the FCA and by this commission. Major banks and some senior banking executives remain in denial about the true extent of PPI mis-selling. Over a significant period of time they ignored warnings from consumer groups, regulators and parliamentarians about PPI mis-selling. They used legal challenges to frustrate and delay the actions of the FSA, the FOS and the Competition Commission.'

It's hard to find any good news in the whole sorry mess that has been the PPI scandal. But there has been one marginally positive unintended consequence. According to analysts at the National Institute for Economic and Social Research an estimated £5 billion had been paid out to claimants by May 2012. If the final figure is in the region of £20 billion it will end up boosting growth by more than 0.2 per cent of GDP. And if that's the case, then the scandal has the potential to rival or beat the short-term impact on growth of the London Olympics. The point is that households are much more likely to spend the money than the banks are. A study by economists at Berenberg Bank found a strong correlation between the pattern of PPI payouts and sales of new cars. Politicians may have argued that the banks have been slow to lend in the wake of the financial crisis. But through PPI repayments they have inadvertently been putting cash back into household budgets up and down the country.

Ordinary retail customers were not alone in being mis-sold products by the banks. As the row over PPI ebbed and flowed, it emerged that many of the 4.5 million small and medium-sized enterprises (SMEs) up and down the land also had cause to believe that their local high-street bank was not playing fair with them

The relationship between banks and SMEs has been part of the bedrock of the British economy for decades. In other Western democracies, such as the United States, finance for small businesses comes from a variety of sources including many intermediaries who specialise in this form of lending. Most British SMEs, however, do not have access to alternative forms of finance, other than their own families. Consequently they are almost wholly dependent on the high-street banks for the services they need, whether they're looking for working capital, or a loan for new equipment or premises and expansion. My wife's family still remembers the crucial loan of £10,000 made by Lloyds Bank to her grandfather which helped an immigrant shopkeeper build a chain of department stores up and down the land. Payroll, procurement, foreign exchange, property investment and everything else that the company needed was always transacted through Lloyds from then on.

From 2001 onwards the business arms of the retail banks began to sell interest-rate protection, or interest-rate hedging products (IRHP), to tens of thousands of small businesses which came to them for loans. The product looked, on the surface, to be useful. The hedging or insurance product would provide interest-rate protection, allowing the borrower to keep repayments on a loan stable if interest rates happened to rise. To an extent, IRHP was a little like PPI: it was designed to make borrowers feel they were better protected against unforeseen circumstances – in this case a rise in official or market interest rates.

There's nothing particularly new about the principle of hedging products. In biblical times olive or pomegranate farmers would sell the product to an intermediary, at a known price, ahead of the harvest. In so doing they were able to remove the uncertainty about future income should, for instance, inclement weather cause the crop to disappoint or fail. In the case of interest-rate swaps – the insurance protection sold by the bank to protect the borrower against an interest-rate charge – small-business advisers at a branch bank were encouraged to introduce firms who wanted loans to the investment-banking or 'casino' arm of the bank. Here they were generally offered a choice of two types of product: caps where rates can rise up to a specified level and the protection will still work; and a 'structured collar' – a deal by which the interest rate can fluctuate between agreed levels without triggering increased repayment levels.

Unfortunately, the two products were structured to meet only one potential change in the economic landscape – rising interest rates. They wholly failed to take into consideration the impact that falling interest rates might have. Yet that is what happened in 2008 as the financial crisis hit the global economy. Now central banks rushed to slash interest rates to record low levels. The Bank of England, for example, cut its key bank rate by 1.5 percentage points in October, following this move with four further cuts until the official bank rate hit 0.5 per cent in March 2009. It still stood at that level five years later. In August 2013 the new governor of the Bank of England, Mark Carney, made it clear that he would like to hold rates at that level until 2016 at least so as to provide a period of certainty for borrowers. It was an undertaking that Carney had to rescind in 2014 as Britain's economy roared away at a 3 per cent clip and the unemployment rate fell below his original target of 7 per cent. Interest rates will start to rise in 2015, but in small increments and very gradually.

As interest rates tumbled in the aftermath of the financial crisis the monthly payments on interest-rate hedges perversely climbed. At a stroke 40,000 small businesses – from fish-and-chip shops to small hotels and pubs – that had been encouraged to protect themselves from surging interest rates between 2001 and 2008 found themselves under new financial pressure. They realised now that the downside[5] of the products they had signed up to had not been properly explained. As with PPI, many complained that they

[5] In financial markets the 'downside' is the risk that the investor or borrower could lose money should the tide of sentiment or interest rates move in a way that was not expected.

had been told by their bank when they applied for a loan that they could only have it if they took out an interest-rate swap too. To make matters worse, the very economic woes that put pressure on interest rates also caused a dramatic 7 per cent plunge in economic output in 2009 from a peak reached the previous year. Small businesses faced the double whammy of low interest rates, for which they were not prepared, and disastrous commercial conditions.

Complaints escalated. Banks already embroiled in PPI and Libor scandals were keen to settle early. They knew they needed to avoid damaging their reputations any further. In June 2012 Barclays, HSBC, Lloyds and RBS reached an agreement with the Financial Services Authority to compensate affected businesses from set-aside funds totalling £3 billion.

That's not to say that all felt immediate acquiescence was either necessary or desirable. The chairman of one major high-street bank I spoke to in 2013 was openly unrepentant about the sale of hedging contracts for small businesses. In his view it was a case of *caveat emptor* – businesses buying hedge products should have known better:

> I think the hysteria about the swaps thing is overdone. I don't have any sympathy for the people who were actually sold these things where the two parts of the deal [the loan and the hedge] are separate. But people can easily say, 'I didn't realise that if rates went down I wouldn't get the lower interest rates.' You get terrible things in financial services where the risk moves outside the range of probabilities. It's what we call tail end risks.

He did conclude, however, 'I don't think PPI or swaps show up retail banking in a particularly good light.'

After a two-month review the FSA reported in January 2013 that

90 per cent of the interest-rate swap contracts looked to have been mis-sold. The designated chief executive of the Financial Conduct Authority, Martin Wheatley, described the hedges as 'absurdly complex products'. He said these contracts were sold to businesses as 'no-cost' insurance, but had in fact turned out to be huge liabilities. Wheatley added: 'Where redress is due, businesses will be put back into the position they should have been without the mis-sale.'

The tone of the British Bankers' Association on this occasion was suitably penitent. Its new chief executive, the former journalist Anthony Browne, declared: 'Where customers have suffered unfairly the banks have all agreed that they will put it right.'

Firms designated by the FSA (replaced by the FCA) as 'non-sophisticated' – those with less than £6.5 million in annual sales, fewer than 50 staff, or assets worth less than £3.3 million – now qualified for automatic redress. Others, it was decided, would have their cases reviewed by an independent monitor. If the firm did not agree with this decision it could challenge it in court. Rather than risk embarrassing court battles banks have preferred to reach out-of-court settlements, some of which have been as high as £16 million.

The problem so far has been that the actual paying-out process has been painfully slow. Between July 2012 and autumn 2013 just 32 firms received £2 million in compensation. Martin Wheatley felt this amounted to foot-dragging. 'The industry is deceiving itself if it imagines that a total of 32 offers accepted, totalling two million pounds, is adequate progress,' he said in October 2013. He told banks to speed up the process.

What the initial mis-selling of policies and the subsequent delays in settling disputes has meant in practice for many small businesses is well illustrated by the case of Colne Valley Golf Club owner Jennifer Smith. Along with her brother and son she bought the golf course for £1.2 million in 2001. The 200-acre site in the village of Earls Colne, Essex, includes an 18-hole golf course, a clubhouse and a function room for weddings and parties. The small local club has around 400 members who pay £800 a year – good going for a village with a population of just under 5,000. Non-members can turn up and have a game for between £25 and £35.

The business was struggling when the trio of family members purchased it. But they were not worried; they felt it would thrive with a bit of investment and between them they had an impressive management record. Jennifer's brother ran a successful motor business, while Jennifer had started a tea shop in 1984 that grew to 11 outlets around Essex by the time she sold up in 2000. Before that she had worked in the hotel trade. As for her son, Thomas, he had been a greenkeeper at a number of top courses such as The Belfry and West Sussex golf clubs. Smith says: 'I handle the catering and Thomas works on the golf course. The idea was that we would build the business up and I would pass it onto him – I was getting ready to retire.'

The first few years of the business went well. Facilities began to be improved and the membership grew. 'We were buzzing,' Smith said. Unfortunately her brother Goodwin had been diagnosed with multiple sclerosis in 2000, and by 2007 he was making it clear that he wanted to sell up his share of the business to the two other family members.

By this time Jennifer had spent £75,000 to obtain planning permission to build a small 14-room hotel beside the clubhouse and wanted to take this further. She therefore went to her local Barclays, where she had banked for over 10 years, for a loan. She was offered £1.3 million at 1 per cent above base rate to be paid back over 15 years.

Towards the end of the negotiations her bank manager introduced her to a colleague from Barclays' investment bank BarCap. The BarCap adviser, her regional bank manager, Thomas and Jennifer then met for about an hour at the golf club in late December 2007. The advisor took the pair through a presentation for a structured-collar interest-rate swap, which would keep payments even if interest rates fluctuated between 4.75 per cent and 6 per cent over seven years. In December 2007 the UK interest rate was 5.5 per cent, and had not been as high as 6 per cent since February 2000.

The interest-rate swap covered only half the length of the loan, because Jennifer was coming up to retirement, and the original plan was that after seven years in this business she would sell her property portfolio and use part of the proceeds to pay off the rest of the loan. Jennifer felt pressured. 'I felt really excluded at that meeting,' she said. 'I didn't understand it. My son didn't, although he may have pretended to. I wasn't even sure if my local manager did, because he barely said a word. There was no mention that the firm would have to pay if rates went down. They constantly talked about rates going up . . . In the past when I have taken out loans, I have always had a floating rate. I have always gone with the market. If it goes with you that is great. If it goes against you, well, you just have to work a little bit harder.'

Jennifer worried over the loan terms for several months, but eventually signed. Why did an experienced businesswoman sign a deal she didn't fully understand? 'At the December meeting the BarCap advisor called me old-fashioned and said that this is how loans are constructed these days,' she explained. 'But the most powerful thing he said is that without this swap, we were not going to get the loan.'

For the first year after the loan things went well. Jennifer was able to buy out her brother and continue to invest in the business. However, when interest rates dropped between 2008 and 2009 this changed. The interest the golf club was paying on the loan had been £11,000 a month, but in January 2008 another £4,000 was taken out of the firm's account by Barclays.

Jennifer did not know why this was, and thought it must be a mistake. She phoned her local bank who, she says, also thought it might be an error. But after they checked they told her that once the base rate fell below the level agreed she would have to make extra payments. The agreement signed only provided protection if rates fluctuated in the range 4.75 per cent to 6 per cent. Bizarrely, if market interest rates fell below the lower point of the range the cost to the bank customer actually rose because the other party to the contract, which had taken on the risk of rising interest rates, became the beneficiary. To break the agreement at this time would have cost the club £290,000. '£4,000 was our profit so that was that part of the business gone straight away.'

The club cut two jobs and reduced the hours of others it employed. The number of casual staff was also pruned. Plans for the hotel and all other capital spending stopped. The business survived through cash injected into it from a separate £300,000 personal loan Jennifer had taken out. She also had the income from the tea-shop business she had sold out of years before, because she still owned the commercial properties and rented them.

As the pressures mounted, the bank put the business under special measures in January 2009. This meant the firm's spending and business plans were controlled by a nominee of the bank, the accountants KPMG. 'KPMG told us we used too much fertiliser and we had to cut down,' Jennifer recalls. 'We did this and the greens became diseased and we had to go back to what we had done before. They told us to put up prices but people stayed away, so we had to put them down again.'

For the first time in her business career, her cheques were

bouncing. She said she had used a local bakery supplies firm for over 20 years, but after two cheques bounced they refused to trade with her again. 'That was the worst period, between 2008 and 2009. I really thought I would go under, I thought I would have a nervous breakdown.'

Jennifer unilaterally suspended interest-swap payments in January 2013, telling the bank 'to come and take the keys' if they did not agree. The bank has not taken over the business, but each month the £4,000 she would have paid is added to the outstanding loan.

The golf club held a three-hour meeting with accountants Deloitte, who acted as an independent adjudicator in May 2013 after the business had put in a claim for £250,000 in damages. This figure includes payments, reviews and consultants' fees the bank insisted the club pay after the interest-rate swap went bad, as well as compensation.

In October 2013 Jennifer was still awaiting a decision. She said: 'The issue still affects us. Members at the club heard in 2012 that the issue had been settled, so they ask why haven't we refurbished the changing rooms. I tell them the case is still ongoing, and they think you are spinning them a line.'

The affair has damaged her business and affected the family. 'The business has lost its momentum, and it will be hard to get that back. We are a close family, but there have been tensions between the three of us and our wider families over this.' The lesson Jennifer has learned from the affair is simple and perhaps, obvious: 'Don't sign something you don't understand.'

A study of the Royal Bank of Scotland's lending policies to small and medium-sized businesses by former deputy governor of the Bank of England Sir Andrew Large, issued on 1 November 2013, isolated some of the weaknesses in the system. Looking at the way in which RBS operated, he found that there was no single central point where responsibility was taken for small-business lending, even though this was such an important area for the bank: RBS, through its NatWest branch network, claims to have more customers from the sector than any other bank. He also found that the credit approval process was slow, and that only 25 per cent of inquiries by SMEs turned into actual loans. Given how important SMEs are to the state of the British economy, this is a worryingly low statistic.

Shortly after the Large report was released I met Business Secretary Vince Cable, a stern critic of the banks, at a commemorative event. Cable was disturbed by the findings of the Large report and the failure of the 84 per cent state-owned RBS to play its role in the recovery of the British economy. He mentioned to me that there was 'more to come'. On 25 November 2013 Lawrence Tomlinson, the 'entrepreneur in residence' at Cable's business department, issued his own devastatingly critical report on RBS's lending practices. Until the appearance of his report the existence of Tomlinson as an adviser to Cable was barely known. His main claim to fame was his involvement in the creation of the care home services concern LNT Group.

Tomlinson's report claimed that he had received a large body of evidence about RBS's turnaround arm Global Restructuring Group (GRG) and had uncovered 'very concerning patterns of behaviour leading to the destruction of good and viable UK businesses'. The charge was that RBS had engineered good businesses into default both to generate revenues for the bank through fees and to sell devalued property assets to its property arm West Register. The report stated:

The profit-making nature of GRG significantly undermines its position as a turnaround division, in which good businesses should be restructured and returned to normal banking. The temptation to get hold of assets and take additional profit from these businesses to boost GRG's balance sheet is clear.

The charges made in the Tomlinson report, together with some of the heated language suggesting that RBS's behaviour bordered on the fraudulent, could not go unanswered. The Financial Conduct Authority immediately announced an inquiry. And RBS's new chief executive, the languid New Zealander Ross McEwan, called in Clifford Chance, one of the City of London's 'magic circle' firms of top lawyers, to review evidence that the bank's GRG arm had acted improperly. Clifford Chance interviewed 138 small-business customers in the GRG recovery unit and 45 employees and reviewed 1,200 files amounting to 400,000 documents to see if it could turn up any support for the Tomlinson charges.

In its assessment, released on 17 April 2014, Clifford Chance found there was 'no evidence to support the damaging and serious allegation' that GRG 'was guilty of systematically setting out to defraud small business'. In a response to the Clifford Chance rebuttal McEwan expressed relief at the outcome of the inquiry, saying 'trust in RBS was put at risk by the allegation of systematic abuse made by Tomlinson'.

Clifford Chance did not give RBS and the GRG unit a wholly clean bill of health. It found cases where the customers felt the fees lacked clarity. It also reported that a 'handful of customers' had made derogatory comments about the behaviour of RBS staff. The bank also revealed that it would be closing the property arm at the centre of the Tomlinson charges, West Register, because of 'the damaging perception that the bank had a conflict of interest when it purchased property as part of a restructuring process'. In essence it was an acknowledgement that the highest standard had not been observed in the state-owned bank.

One senior City enforcer, director of the Serious Fraud Office David Green, told me in April 2014 that he had very serious concerns about the use by big companies of top City lawyers to conduct internal inquiries in parallel with official inquiries. A practical result of the internal inquiries was that the City lawyers had the first crack at interviewing key witnesses. It could then be argued by the target company and the lawyers that the testimony of the individuals concerned had 'qualified privilege' and official investigators could not gain full access. Green's comments provide some insight as to why it has been so hard for regulators to act forcefully against banks and bankers.

The PPI, IRHP and small-business lending scandals arose in particular circumstances – banks seeking to guarantee profits in a period of economic turmoil and low interest rates saw opportunities and grabbed them. When it all turned sour, the usual mantra 'Lessons have been learned' was chanted. The problem is that each point in the economic cycle seems to bring in its wake evidence of poor practice and questionable dealing.

Take, for example, the sale of interest-only mortgages during the boom years of the housing market. It may seem obvious, from the description, that an interest-only mortgage is precisely what it says it is. But many people who took out this product appear not to have been properly advised that at the end of the mortgage period they are still left with a responsibility to repay the capital sum borrowed.

Premium accounts, which require the customer to pay a fee for services of between £5 and £25 a month, also have a question mark over them. Varying in their precise detail from offer to offer, they often give higher interest rates and better deals on overdrafts than standard current accounts. They frequently include a range of other services including car, mobile phone and holiday insurance. Around one in five adults or 10 million people have been persuaded by the banks to adopt these accounts since they were introduced in the 1990s, and the market is currently estimated to be worth £1.5 billion a year. The number of premium accounts on offer has grown from 39 in 2007 to 70 in 2013.

They sound very attractive, but they are not always the wonderful value for money that they seem. The insurance element, for example, might seem worth having, but the services on offer can often be bought more cheaply elsewhere. Moreover, consumers may have already acquired much of this insurance through domestic home policies or by ticking boxes when they make their travel bookings. A survey by *Which?* in 2011 found that 30 per cent of people who have been encouraged to take up premium accounts use none of the services at all. Premium accounts may be good for the banks, but that does not mean that they are automatically good for individual customers.

The way in which new business is drummed up is also less than ideal. Telesales staff for banks typically ring up affluent customers and offer to 'upgrade' them to 'added-value accounts'. The monthly charges are often added to statements as administration fees, and do not clearly spell out what the customer has bought. FSA policy director Sheila Nicoll voiced her concerns in 2012: 'These products are often referred to as upgraded accounts but if you end up paying for an element you can't claim on it's money down the drain.' *Which?* concluded that these accounts are 'rarely worth the money'.

According to the Financial Ombudsman Service complaints about premium accounts have been rising strongly. In September 2013 it reported that complaints had climbed by 75 per cent over the previous year and were now running at 3,500 per annum. This was despite the fact that earlier in the year the rules had been tightened. Customers were claiming back their annual fees and interest, and often receiving £2,000 or more to settle their claims.

The new rules introduced in March 2013 by the Financial Services Authority stipulated that the bank selling the account must check whether the customer was eligible for the policies in the package and must share the information with the customer. It should also send the customer a letter each year setting out the requirements and benefits of each insurance policy. The Financial Conduct Authority, which took over from the FSA, will continue to administer these changes.

In December 2012 Lloyds suspended branch and phone sales of these accounts while it retrained staff, though it allowed customers to take up an account via its website. Santander stopped selling new accounts in March 2012, and then announced in July 2013 that it would move existing premium package customers to other retail accounts. Santander retail banking director Reza Attar-Zadeh said: 'We want to simplify what we offer. A smaller range of products means we can focus on better service.'

Former Lloyds chief executive Eric Daniels complained to the Parliamentary Commission on Banking Standards: 'We thought that, with our consistent and constant dialogue with the regulators, we were on the side of the angels. We had thought we were listening and responding. I would characterise our board and management as being responsible and responsive during this period.'

All this is well and good. But it is worth bearing in mind the words of the Parliamentary Commission on Banking Standards: 'The interest rate swap and PPI mis-selling debacles both highlight how banks appeared to outsource their responsibility to the regulator.' It's hard to avoid the conclusion that a similar state of affairs operated with premium packaged accounts. And that sense that banks have spent years teetering on the edge of what is acceptable and what is reprehensible – and then all too often coming down on the wrong side – has not gone away.

# 9

# The Enforcers: The Struggle to Create a New Financial World

In the summer of 2013 Andrew Bailey, the deputy governor of the Bank of England, along with his team of supervisors, joined the top brass of the Co-operative Bank for an awayday at the magnificent stone edifice of the 1816 Rookery Hall country house hotel outside Crewe in Cheshire. As head of the Prudential Regulatory Authority (PRA) it was Bailey's responsibility to establish whether the Co-op Bank had sufficient capital to withstand a crisis and if not, how its owners, the Co-operative Group, intended to remedy the matter. Whenever it was questioned about resources the Co-op always maintained that it could put its hands on all the capital and liquidity it needed because the cash resources of the group were in the billions.

After an intense day of scrutinising and trying to understand the Co-op's balance sheet better, Bailey and his team of inspectors were invited to join the chairman of the bank, the well-upholstered and florid-faced Rev. Paul Flowers, for dinner in the hotel's plush dining room. Flowers, as the host, sampled the wines ordered by his colleagues, rejected them with a flourish and proceeded to order the finest and most expensive vintages on the wine list. It was a signal to Bailey and the other members of his team that the ethical bank seemed to have a somewhat profligate culture.

The inspection of the Co-op Bank was part of a wide-ranging exercise to establish the capital and liquidity needs of the UK banking system. Until the Bank of England could be satisfied that the UK banks were sufficiently capitalised and had de-risked their balance sheets then the twin goals of making the banks safer and securing greater lending to growing businesses could not be achieved. Bailey and the PRA came to the startling conclusion that Britain's top banks and building societies needed to raise a further £27.1 billion in new capital if they were to meet the guidelines set by banking supervisors at the Bank for International Settlements in Basel. The biggest shock was the finding that Barclays needed £12.8 billion of new funds to fulfil capital requirements and meet rules on the amount of lending it could do by midway through 2015. The report also reconfirmed an already identified capital shortfall at the Co-op Bank.

The precision of the PRA exercise shows just how far attitudes to the regulation of UK banks have shifted since the storms of 2007 and 2008. Then, the soft-touch approach that had become so popular in the 1990s still prevailed. The former chief executive of the Financial Services Authority Hector Sants told me in an interview at the Canary Wharf headquarters of Barclays in 2013: 'It was driven by a very strong view that came out of the self-regulatory community that you let the City get on with it. With responsibility split between the Bank of England [and the FSA] it was also driven by a government and public policy philosophy that it was good to encourage the financial sector and that overbearing regulation would have a negative effect.'

Now, just a handful of years later, the mood had changed. In opposition David Cameron and Shadow Chancellor George Osborne were only too aware of the failings of the country's financial machinery and felt overhaul was required. In 2008 Osborne asked

Lord (James) Sassoon, scion of one of the most distinguished banking dynasties who had spent much of his career at investment bankers S. G. Warburg before working in the Treasury under Gordon Brown, to assess past failings and come up with a new model. Sassoon, who now runs the London operations of the Far Eastern trading house Jardine Matheson, was horrified by what he found. 'There has been a massive regulatory failure in this country and lots of other places in the build-up to 2007–2008,' he told me in an interview in 2013.

Sassoon's proposed solution was in some ways a surprising one. His view was that the Bank of England had not performed well in the lead-up to the credit crunch. Nevertheless, he felt that it should now resume the central role it had had before 1997. It was a case not so much of rewarding the bank for previous failings as requiring it step up to the plate. The result was a radical restructure on the lines Sassoon suggested, picking up on some of the ideas already aired by witnesses before the Treasury Select Committee. In April 2013 the regulation of significant financial institutions, both banks and insurers, was formally moved from the Financial Services Authority to a new arm of the Bank, the Prudential Regulatory Authority, with a new deputy governor, Andrew Bailey, at its head.

The neglected financial stability arm of the Bank was reconstituted as the Financial Policy Committee with the governor in the chair and another deputy governor, Jon Cunliffe (who replaced Paul Tucker in 2013), in charge. A former Treasury mandarin, Jon Cunliffe continued the tradition of having at least one senior Whitehall figure in a senior position at the Bank. And if that implies that Cunliffe was given a post for which he had no financial experience, it is worth remembering that in his previous post as Britain's ambassador to the European Union he had gained first-hand knowledge and experience both of the euroland crisis and of European efforts to tighten up financial regulation. His committee was given the task of scrutinising such UK developments as the housing-market bubbles and such global trends as the explosive growth of the shadow banking system.

Meanwhile the beefed-up Bank of England gained a new governor, Mark Carney, sometimes referred to as the George Clooney of central bankers because of his matinee-idol looks. He was an understandable choice to replace Lord (Mervyn) King when the latter retired in July 2013 after two gruelling terms in office. In his previous role as governor of the Bank of Canada Carney had steered his native country smoothly through the financial crisis of 2007–9 despite the proximity of and close financial relationship with its near neighbour the United States. He could rightly boast that although emergency liquidity had to be provided when the markets froze over, no Canadian banks needed to be recapitalised during the financial crunch.

In 2011 Carney was catapulted by the Group of Twenty[1] powerful nations into the role of chairman of the Financial Stability Board, which was charged with introducing a new framework of global financial supervision designed to prevent a repeat of the Great Panic. The new governor's knowledge and confidence when it came to matters of financial stability had been its own recommendation.

When I interviewed him in Nottingham, on his first road trip as governor in August 2013, Carney (speaking in a characteristic rapid-fire manner) declared that 'the core of the banking system has been substantially repaired. It is not as strong as we ultimately need it to be. There were a series of fault lines. I would say one of them was the banking system, but we've repaired that. The second

---

[1] The Group of Twenty (G20) nations represent 85 per cent of the world's output. One of the proposals to emerge from the leaders' London summit in April 2009, led by Gordon Brown, and the successor summit at Pittsburgh later that year, was the conversion of the existing Financial Stability Forum into a more intrusive Financial Stability Board.

was there was no transparency: you couldn't really tell what was going on in the system. We've improved the transparency around bank reporting.' But he acknowledged the job wasn't done. 'We still need to make a lot of progress in derivatives markets, huge markets, multi-trillion markets,' he said.

'One of Carney's deputies, Andrew Bailey, a Bank of England insider, was given the very precise role of making sure that significant banks and financial groups operating in Britain are safe. A plumpish figure, Cambridge-educated Bailey exudes a mild-mannered, calm Britishness. He is widely regarded as one of the best and the brightest to emerge from the Bank's own hierarchy in recent times and his easy-going exterior hides a steely determination to fix British banking for once and for all.

Under the stewardship of Andrew Bailey the Prudential Regulatory Authority has warned that 'firms should not . . . approach their relationship with the PRA as a negotiation.' It has stated that it is there to make judgements about the soundness of banks, and will not be fobbed off by counterarguments, or pressure from senior bankers or the government of the day as has so often happened in the past. Bailey has proved true to his word, dealing firmly with the Co-operative Bank, for example, and insisting that Barclays and other high-street banks act with urgency to bring their balance sheets up to scratch. In July 2013, having stated that Barclays own fundraising plans were inadequate, he forced an unwanted £5.8 billion rights issue of shares to existing investors.

The reformed and renamed FSA, now the Financial Conduct Authority, is taking no prisoners either under the leadership of chief executive Martin Wheatley, who has very clearly stated that the new body has 'the power to shoot first and ask questions later'. Set up to ensure that financial institutions treat customers fairly, the FCA investigates economic crime and has the power to veto new products. Its focus on customers was demonstrated in its first major report under Wheatley's stewardship, in May 2013, when it warned people with interest-only mortgages, due for repayment by 2020, to start taking urgent remedial action. Its teeth were shown in December 2013 when it fined Lloyds Banking Group £28 million for offering improper incentives to employees – from bottles of champagne to a system of career snakes and ladders – for selling rotten products to customers.

Not that everything has gone the FCA's way. In late March 2014 some accused it of acting rashly when a decision to review some 30 million insurance and pensions policies, held by 'zombie' life companies that are largely closed to new business, was leaked to a newspaper, causing havoc on the stock market. The insurers called for Wheatley's resignation. The Chancellor George Osborne said he was 'profoundly concerned' by events. The Treasury Select Committee opened hearings.

Whatever teething problems there may have been, the multilayered new regulatory authority has shown a gritty determination not to be bullied by vested interests, and a strong resolve to tackle some of the most deep-rooted problems in the banking system, financial services and markets. It has talked tough and acted tough.

The obstacles it faces, however, are profound. Issues stretching back years have still to be tackled, and new scandals continue to crop up. Just one example among a host of others demonstrates the ongoing nature of the banking problem – the rate-rigging scandal that has enveloped some 15 global banks and the Bank of England's own trading desk. Then there's the endless saga of the Co-operative Bank, which has kept the PRA so busy. There's the continuing fallout from various mis-selling schemes. And there is concern about a housing market that looks dangerously overheated.

Each time there's a crisis the regulatory authorities have shown a willingness to engage with it directly. It was partly to meet the shortcomings revealed by the rate-rigging scandal, for example, that in March 2014 Carney persuaded Nemat Shaflik, the Egyptian-born and British-educated former deputy managing director of the International Monetary Fund, to join his top team at the Bank of England as deputy governor in charge of overall policing of the markets. But such flexibility also adds to the complexity of a system that is already complicated. The Bank of England may now be at the centre of all things, but it is surrounded by satellite authorities that inevitably sometimes overlap in terms of jurisdiction. Some have pointed to the dangers of regulatory arbitrage, with powerful City institutions playing off one arm of the Bank or regulatory structure against another. Some have even suggested that the all-powerful nature of the new Bank of England – akin now to the independent Federal Reserve Board in the United States – does not sit comfortably with a constitutional set-up that has traditionally seated power in Whitehall and Westminster. Despite constant scrutiny from Select Committees of the Commons, it could be argued that the nation's approach to its economic well-being is to an extent slightly undemocratic.

As to the ultimate effectiveness of the new set-up, the jury is out and will remain so for some time.

So far as regulation in the US is concerned, early decisiveness has to an extent become mired in later controversy. Certainly, when it came to recapitalising the banks, the US authorities ultimately proved to be more rigorous and determined than their UK counterparts. Banks were subjected to forensic stress tests and billions of dollars were made available via the government's $700 billion Troubled Asset Relief Programme (TARP), which had been signed into law on October 2008 by President George W. Bush. By the middle of

2013 just over $400 billion of the TARP fund had been drawn on, and all of the major lenders had paid back their funds with interest. Not, it has to be said, that the picture is unremittingly sunny. By January 2014 some 83 smaller and medium-sized US banks owed the taxpayer $2.1 billion. The Government Accountability Office (GAO) reported that $1.5 billion of outstanding TARP funding was concentrated in ten institutions. Sixty of the banks concerned had fallen behind in their dividend payments and 47 were classified as problem banks by the Federal Deposit Insurance Corporation, the regulator of America's second-line banks.

Regulation subsequent to that initial flurry has proved trickier, though it got off to a promising start with the setting up in May 2009 of a ten-person Financial Crisis Inquiry Commission appointed by President Obama and Congress. The Commission, headed by Paul Angelides, the former State Treasurer of California, reported in January 2011. It worked in parallel with the Senate Permanent Subcommittee on Investigations, headed by Senator Carl Levin, which released its own findings under the title 'Financial Crisis: Anatomy of a Financial Collapse' in April 2011 after taking extensive evidence. The two studies then came together to form the backbone of the Dodd–Frank 2010 financial reform act.

This massive piece of legislation aimed to deal with every aspect of the crisis, from consumer protection to supervision of the credit-rating agencies to the 'Volcker Rule' designed to stop financial firms taking huge bets on their own account (in other words, it banned banks from risky but potentially lucrative trading using their own cash, rather than their clients'). The bill gave the government the power to seize and shut down large troubled financial companies. It handed the Federal Reserve extra powers to protect borrowers against abuses in mortgage, credit-card and other types of lending. It introduced new rules for bringing the derivatives market under government oversight. It also gave shareholders more say over how company executives are paid. It was a genuinely revolutionary document, the most important series of financial reforms since Franklin D. Roosevelt's New Deal in the 1930s.

In July 2010 Congress passed the Dodd–Frank. In its wake a number of large new regulators were created: the Office of Credit Ratings, which oversees ratings agencies; a new public watchdog called the Consumer Financial Protection Bureau; the Financial Stability Oversight Council (FSOC) whose job is to oversee all other financial regulators; and the Office of Financial Research which has been set up to assist the FSOC. President Obama's view of the legislation was that it would 'protect consumers and lay the foundation for a stronger and safer financial system, one that is innovative, creative, competitive, and far less prone to panic and collapse'. Christopher Dodd, the veteran Democrat Chairman of the Senate Committee on Banking, Housing and Urban Affairs who was so instrumental in creating the bill, added: 'More than anything else, my goal was, from the very beginning, to create a structure and an architecture reflective of the 21st century in which we live, but also one that would rebuild trust and confidence.'

Passing the legislation, however, turned out to be rather easier than getting it implemented. Such was its complexity that it required 50,000 pages of rules to see principles put into action. Enthusiasm for it evaporated amid the rancour of the Obama presidency. By July 2013 two-thirds of the 398 separate rules had yet to be enacted.

The following month President Obama gathered together his most senior finance officials at the White House, including chairman of the Federal Reserve Ben Bernanke and Treasury Secretary Jack Lew, as well as the chairs of the Securities and Exchange Commission and the Commodity Futures Trading Commission (CFTC), Mary Jo White and Gary Gensler. His message was simple: step up the pace on getting this bill into place. 'The President commended the regulators for their work,' the White House declared following the financial summit, 'but stressed the need to expeditiously finish implementing the critical remaining portions of Wall Street reform to ensure we are able to prevent the type of financial harm that led to the Great Recession from ever happening again.'

Fine words, but easier said than done. In fact, regulators faced resistance on two fronts. Republicans have held up progress on the act and have refused to agree new budgets for financial agencies given the task of policing Wall Street. They argue that this wide-ranging law unconstitutionally gives great powers to regulators to govern by fiat and whim. Texan Jeb Hensarling, who is also chairman of the Financial Services Committee in the House, said in August 2013: 'Dodd–Frank is a complex piece of legislation that is harmful to our floundering economy and in dire need of repeal.' At the same time, the well-funded banking lobby has voiced its desire to see key parts of the bill watered down or thrown out. Dennis Kelleher, the chief executive of finance reform group Better Markets, said in September 2013: 'Some version of some paid mouthpiece of Wall Street is at virtually every regulator every hour the regulator is open.'

Other financial industry groups have gone so far as to take the CFTC to court in a bid to amend rules that set limits on derivative contracts. Even less partisan figures have been critical. Alan Greenspan, the Federal Reserve chairman for more than 18 years, said of Dodd–Frank in March 2011: 'Regulators are being entrusted with forecasting, and presumably preventing, all undesirable repercussions that might happen to a market when its regulatory conditions are importantly altered. No one has such skills.' He added: 'Is the answer to complex modern-day finance that we return to the simpler banking practices of a half century ago? That may not be possible if we wish to maintain today's levels of productivity and standards of living.'

By April 2014 a total of 280 Dodd–Frank rules making requirement deadlines had been passed, but only 152 (54.3 per cent) had actually been met with the rules finalised; 128 had been missed altogether. Some 98 (24.6 per cent) of the rules had still to be proposed by the various regulators involved. Fears were not unsurprisingly being expressed, among supporters of the bill, that large parts of the legislation were being left in limbo. Former Federal Deposit Insurance Corporation chairman Sheila Blair said: 'The longer you wait to finalise the rules, the more they get watered down, the more exceptions that get built in, people's memories about the crisis start to fade and the pressure isn't there.'

If all the controversy implies that the authorities have been stymied into inaction, that is certainly not the case. Barclays settled with the US authorities over the Libor scandal in June 2012. Both Standard Chartered and HSBC were challenged and fined by US regulators over money laundering. And if that seemed to suggest that US authorities were happy to act, but only against non-US banks, the very American JPMorgan was then faced in 2013 with a series of fines, penalties and compensation demands to quench a series of fires that ranged from the London Whale affair to the wrongful selling of mortgage securities (the charges here dating back to the financial crisis). The shifting of the regulatory sands was acknowledged by JPMorgan's chairman Jamie Dimon in a 32-page letter to shareholders in April 2014. The normally taciturn Dimon described the bank's wide-ranging legal cases with multiple regulators as 'the most painful, difficult and nerve-wracking experience that I have ever dealt with professionally'.

The response of a number of key bankers has been to anticipate potential problems rather than wait for them to explode. Goldman

Sachs, for example, decided to close down its 'high frequency' stock market trading when the practice was exposed in a book by the American financial chronicler Michael Lewis. Fear of the harm that law enforcers and regulators might choose to inflict on even the largest of Wall Street firms proved a powerful countervailing tool.

Nevertheless, the authorities in the US still face considerable challenges. They have an advantage over their British opposite numbers in that, rather than having to create completely new regulatory authorities with all their attendant teething problems, they have been able, for the most part, to use the same key regulators who have been in place since the Depression of the 1930s – and before. But they are all now operating to new powers and extensive and complicated rule books. Britain, with its principle-based approach, tends to fall short when the principles are insufficiently clear or direct. The US, with its rule-based regulation, tends to be a victim of the complexity such rules lead to, not to mention the internal wrangling they involve.

If the US and the UK have managed to grasp at least some of the many nettles that strew their path, the European tendency has been to avoid them. Such indeed was the scale of the uncertainty and inaction in the crucial years 2009–11 that many large institutional investors became highly sceptical whether a large number of eurozone banks would even survive. Worried that nations were ignoring the huge debts they had amassed, investors acted to push up interest rates on the borrowings of weaker eurozone countries. The market view at the time was that a partial break-up of the eurozone was inevitable if weaker countries were to regain control of their currencies. These nations, the thinking ran, could then devalue, making their exports cheaper and more competitive.

Fund managers, who controlled vast sums in centres like Boston, Zurich or Hong Kong, became ever more wary of lending to eurozone banks and member states, fearing that a number would almost certainly default on their loans. EU regulators therefore wasted two years, between 2009 and 2011, trying to convince the world that European banks were safe bets and employing stress tests to support their assertions. These stress tests, however, proved not to have followed the rigorous US model but an ever-changing and generally feeble European approximation.

The 2010 test, for example, suggested that just seven banks had failed and needed to raise €3.5 billion. Five of the banks were Spanish – Diada, Espiga, Banca Civica, Unnim and CajaSur. The other two were Germany's Hypo Real Estate and Greece's ATE. But a study by investment bankers Goldman Sachs found ten banks in danger of failure with a capital shortfall of €37.6 billion. Investors sided with Goldman, not the Committee of European Bank Supervisors. There was a general consensus that write-down on government bonds included in the official results was so modest as to be unbelievable.

Broker Cantor Fitzgerald's chief global equity strategist Stephen Pope memorably and caustically observed: 'I see nothing stressful about this test. It's like sending the banks away for a weekend of R&R.' Richard Cranfield, a lawyer at City firm Allen & Overy, added: 'There is little evidence that the tests have been applied consistently and there is a distinct lack of credibility, making this a wasted opportunity.' To underline the questionable validity of the tests, two banks that passed them – Allied Irish Banks and Bank of Ireland – failed only four months later, as Ireland's banking network imploded, and Dublin received an €85 billion bailout from the EU and the IMF.

In 2011 the EU tried again. By now the Committee of European Bank Supervisors had been replaced by the London-based European Banking Authority (EBA) which promised a tougher approach to the stress-test procedure. This time 90 banks were tested across 21 countries, and eight failed with a shortfall of €2.5 billion. A ninth bank Helaba, in Germany, withheld the results of its test after a row with the EBA over the quality of its capital (it is largely regarded as having failed the test). Of the remaining eight banks five were in Spain – CAM, Paster, Caja3, CatalunyaCaixa and Unnim again. Two were in Greece – EFG Eurobank and ATE again. The final one was Austria's Volksbanken.

But again the tests did not convince investors, the media and the broader financial community. Failure to deal with the sovereign debt held on bank balance sheets proved to be a particularly serious source of concern. The EBA asked banks to assume a 15 per cent loss on any Greek government bonds they held, even though at that stage these bonds were trading in the market at half their face value. When a deal was eventually reached between Greek banks and some of their private-sector creditors in January 2012 the write-downs were indeed 50 per cent.

The EBA's chairman Andrea Enria admitted that it had faced great difficulties in getting national regulators to provide accurate data. The wonderfully official word used by the EBA to describe data gathering was 'constrained'. Nevertheless, Enria said, the fact that the EBA was about to carry out a second round of stress tests had prompted 20 banks to raise a combined €26.8 billion of cash to plug black holes. 'The stress test has been a catalyst for pressure to raise capital,' he argued.

The market was still unimpressed. Analysts at Credit Suisse calculated that 14 banks should have failed with a shortfall of €45 billion. Conservative MEP and member of the Economic and Monetary Affairs committee Syed Kamall noted: 'The exposure of banks to sovereign debt is the giant elephant in the room and ignoring this issue could undermine the credibility of these tests.'

Pedro de Noronha, a managing partner at Noster Capital, simply said: 'This was nothing more than a PR exercise.' As an enforcer, in the teeth of crisis, the EBA failed miserably.

A few months later, in October 2011, the Franco–Belgian lender Dexia, which had passed the stress test, fell into deep trouble and had to secure a bailout of up to €90 billion from France, Belgium and Luxembourg. It was the bank's second bailout in three years. Its problems, however, seem to have escaped the EBA's notice.

By 2011 the markets estimated that Europe's banks collectively needed to raise €300 billion. In addition, analysts at RBS said that European banks needed to shed around €3.2 trillion of assets over the next five years. The money markets continued to withhold funds from European banks and their shares and bonds traded at sharp discounts to their US rivals. Between 2010 and late 2013 US money markets cut their exposure to Europe by 60 per cent.

As the EU floundered with its stress tests it also put out a number of proposals for banking reform. These were met with outright hostility from bankers, but they also drew mixed reactions from politicians and regulators in the UK and the US. One was a suggested financial transaction tax that would levy between 0.1 per cent and 1 per cent (the wide margin is still a point of discussion) from every finance deal carried out in Europe.[2] Another was a cap on banker's bonuses to be set at 100 per cent of basic pay, or 200 per cent if approved by shareholders. Among the critics of this latter move were observers in the UK who, as I explain later, suggested that a cap on bonuses would simply drive up basic pay. (A fear was also expressed that any such cap imposed in London would drive bankers to other financial centres such as New York or Hong Kong.)

---

[2] This form of tax is also known as the Tobin tax, because it was first proposed in 1972 by the Nobel Prize-winning American economist James Tobin.

Some moves, though, did bear fruit. In July 2013, for example, the EU's Alternative Investment Fund Managers Directive took effect in the UK. It seeks to regulate part of the vast shadow banking network by bringing hedge-fund managers under tighter regulation. They now come under formal reporting requirements covering business conduct, transparency and marketing.

In December 2011 and February 2012 the European Central Bank (ECB) loaned more than €1 trillion to 1,300 private euro-zone banks in an effort to increase liquidity in the system and encourage lending into what ECB president Mario Draghi called the 'real economy' of businesses who needed the cash to invest. The ECB itself acknowledged that the mechanism used – the long-term refinancing operation (LTRO)[3] – was a sticking plaster, not a sustainable answer to the deep-rooted problems of sovereign debt and banks short of cash. But the bold move was the largest deal in the ECB's history, and took the pressure off the banks' immediate search for capital and calmed talk about the break-up of the euro.

By now Draghi had effectively taken over the role of enforcer as well as central banker. It was a change that paralleled those in the United States and Britain where the Federal Reserve and the Bank of England found themselves empowered by the banking crisis. The Italian central banker spoke of the need to 'dispel the fog' around European bank balance sheets, arguing that once that had been achieved banks would be in a position to seek additional funds so that they could lend to business and aid growth. Thanks to his 'whatever it takes' pledge to save the euro in 2012, which was backed

---

[3] LTRO finance was provided for up to 36 months at a cost of 1 per cent. Under the scheme banks could swap the debt of peripheral countries in exchange for a cash injection. As part of the price the European Central Bank would impose a 'haircut' – a reduction in the value of the collateral offered – depending on its credit rating.

up by the bank's bond-buying programme, such pronouncements carry weight.

Perhaps Draghi's most important move came in October 2013 when he and the ECB decided to bypass the distinctly under-whelming EBA and take over the task of stress-testing the eurozone banks. These new stress tests cover 128 of the region's biggest banks, or around 85 per cent of the euro banking system. The exercise is deploying 1,000 ECB and national regulators and the aim is to complete their assessments by 2015. As Draghi put it: 'A single comprehensive assessment, uniformly applied to all significant banks, accounting for about 85 per cent of the euro area banking system, is an important step forward for Europe and for the future of the euro area economy. We expect that this assessment will strengthen private sector confidence in the soundness of euro area banks and in the quality of their balance sheets.'

All this is part and parcel of a general move towards full European banking union with the ECB as the central institution and regulator. A further step in this direction came in December 2013 when the EU Council appointed Danièle Nouy as the first chair of a new Supervisory Board of the single supervisory mechanism at the ECB. Nouy was previously secretary general of the French financial regulator and held senior positions at the Bank for International Settlements in Basel. To Mario Draghi, Nouy's appointment was highly significant: 'The appointment of the Supervisory Board Chair marks an important milestone as the ECB establishes a single supervisory mechanism for banks in the euro area. Mrs Nouy brings almost 40 years of experience in banking supervision. Her appointment will allow the Supervisory Board to take up its work soon and put in place all organisational requirements with the aim of assuming our supervisory responsibilities starting on 4 November, 2014.'

The plan is that from that date – 4 November 2014 – the European Central Bank will directly supervise the eurozone's 130 biggest banks and have the power to take over the supervision of any of the smaller banks if needed. The EU has also expressed a wish to create a body with the power to wind down or restructure banks that are no longer viable. Its view is that a banking union in the 18 countries that will share the euro from 2014 will help to increase the flow of credit, boost growth and prevent financial crises in the future.

At the level of individual banks, new rules emerged in April 2014 that were designed to replicate many of the reforms already undertaken in Britain and the United States, At their centre was a new policy designed to put shareholders and bondholders, rather than taxpayers, in the front line in the event of a future bank rescue. Not surprisingly, this was hailed by a *Financial Times* headline as 'the biggest shakeup in 20 years'. It certainly marked a considerable advance in thinking about and tackling risk.

One other element that has to be considered in this mix is the Basel Committee on Banking Supervision. Established in February 1975, it is a collection of central bankers from the world's largest economies, who meet three or four times a year in Switzerland. Their purpose is to improve financial stability through the introduction of common standards. At first they represented only the world's largest ten nations, but in 2009, in the wake of the global financial crisis, that membership was expanded to include 27 jurisdictions. The committee's decisions have no legal force, but because it represents so many of the largest nations any bank of any size has to comply with its rulings.

The Basel Committee is part of the world's oldest international finance organisation, the Bank for International Settlements, which was founded in 1930. For over 80 years central bankers have met in Basel in a bid to preserve a stable financial system, which is why the

Bank for International Settlements is sometimes referred to as the central bankers' central bank.

Over the years the Basel Committee has issued three Accords. The first, in July 1988 (now referred to as Basel I), set out agreed standards for capital buffers. It required banks to maintain a ratio of 8 per cent capital to risk-weighted assets (holdings of gold bullion, cash and government stocks were zero-rated). In other words, the simple principle being enunciated was that the greater the risk of the assets held on the balance sheet the higher the requirement for capital.

Basel I was followed in June 2004 by the publication of a Revised Capital Framework, known as Basel II, which required banks to hold more capital for loans to business, as opposed to mortgages, or loans to other banks or governments. 'The new framework', the body stated, 'was designed to improve the way regulatory capital requirements reflect underlying risk and to better address the financial innovation that had occurred in recent years.' In effect Basel II sought to take account of the rising complexity of the financial markets, with their reliance on securitisation, their increasing use of derivative products and their tendency to opt for ever more complex financing mechanisms. It did so, however, by leaving banks' internal compliance departments to self-certify the quality of the assets held, the risk involved and the capital they needed to hold as a safety cushion. Effectively, therefore, it gave the banks carte blanche to set their own internal rules.

They duly did so. What's more, rather than hold core capital, which earns little or no income, they chose to run it down to very low levels. The dangers of this high-risk strategy were exposed when the whirlwind hit the banking sector in 2007–8 and many banks around the world found that they lacked the shock absorbers that capital provides.

Basel II was too trusting. It encouraged banks to become ever more complex and loaded with debt. It turned a blind eye to high-risk strategies (not least the securitisation of mortgages, traditionally rated as low risk, to produce ever higher returns). It helped create an environment in which banks became ever more divorced from their core function of assessing the creditworthiness of a customer.

In September 2008, the month that Lehman Brothers triggered the Great Panic, the Basel Committee began the process of tightening the Basel II rules to make them more durable. A further update was issued in July 2009. But it was not until September 2010, in response to the demands of the G20 political leaders and the newly installed Financial Stability Board for more robust and strictly enforced standards, that Basel III finally emerged.

Basel III essentially sought to ensure that banks adopt safer capital ratios and stipulated that these should rise threefold from 2 per cent to 7 per cent by 2019. In good times, banks would need to hold sufficient capital in cash to fund themselves for at least 30 days in the event of a 2007-type credit crunch. In bad times, if they breached the capital ratio rule, they would have to restrict the distribution of earnings through dividends to keep levels of capital topped up. Banks would also be subject to a leverage ratio for the first time, requiring them to hold equity equivalent to at least 3 per cent of their total lending. In the UK a target date of 2014 was set for the new 3 per cent leverage ratio.

If eurozone reforms and the creation of Basel III imply that Europe has finally got a grip on its banking sector, that is to under-estimate the size of the problems that still remain. Apart from anything else, thanks to the inadequacy of the stress tests carried out by the European Banking Authority it's still far from clear just what the European profit-and-loss sheet looks like. Many banks were still struggling to survive as late as the spring of 2014; at that time the future of the world's oldest bank, the Banca Monte dei Paschi di Siena, hung in the balance. And a return to banking health was in any case dependent on a general economic recovery that is still some way off. As Michel Barnier, the European commissioner responsible for bank reforms, noted in the spring of 2014: 'We may have managed to avoid the worst – a complete collapse of our financial system the eurozone – but Europe continues to pay the economic and social price for the crisis.'

So just how successful have the global regulators been in the years since the credit crunch? Certainly, if fines are anything to go by, banking authorities have confidently moved from rescue plans to punishment. A study by Professor Roger McCormick at the London School of Economics (LSE) found the costs in fines and other penalties for bad behaviour for ten of the world's largest banks in the period 2005–12 amounted to £148 billion. Topping the league table of offenders was Bank of America, which has run up regulatory bills of £54 billion. Next were JPMorgan Chase and the Swiss bank UBS, each with costs of just under £25 billion. Top sinner in the UK has been Lloyds Banking Group with a bill of £9.24 billion.

On publication of the data in November 2013 McCormick noted: 'The banks here are all household names. The fundamental question is: can we expect these costs to start going down soon if these banks have sound ethical cultures? If not, why not?'

The immediate answer to the costs question is probably not. Since the LSE completed its work the ethical failings and fines have been piling up. Jamie Dimon, the once untouchable hero of JPMorgan Chase, has accepted punishment for all manner of sins from the London Whale gambles in the credit default swaps market to mis-selling of sub-prime mortgages (JPMorgan's fine for mortgage mis-selling by the Department of Justice by October 2013 alone totalled $13 billion). In April 2014 Bank of America coughed up a further $772 million settlement when it admitted to having misled customers over the marketing of credit cards, in a case not dissimilar to PPI mis-selling in the UK.

The enforcers have acted against HSBC and RBS over money-laundering activities. Standard Chartered has been punished for busting sanctions imposed on Iran. UBS of Switzerland has paid a $1.5 billion fine over Libor rigging. Barclays has been fined in the US for poor record keeping. Lloyds has paid fines for using high-pressure sales techniques to sell customers products they don't need and the cost of compensation for payment protection insurance has climbed.

So far as bankers' scalps are concerned, while many have left their jobs (willingly or unwillingly), only in Iceland and Ireland – two of the nations most acutely affected by the banking crisis – have individuals actually been jailed for offences leading up to the 2007–8 financial tsunami. The first were put behind bars in 2010. In December 2013 the Reykjavik district court sentenced Hreidar Mar Sigurdsson, Kaupthing's former chief executive, to five and a half years in prison. Former chairman Sigurdur Einarsson received a five-year term for insider-trading offences related to the crisis.

That said, prosecutors have been at work elsewhere and have made a number of arrests. Across Europe there have been isolated cases of high-level convictions, notably in Germany and the Netherlands. In Germany the entire former board of lender HSH Nordbank will face trial over their conduct in the run-up to the crisis. In Ireland justice caught up with senior executives of the Anglo Irish Bank in 2014. The former chief executive Patrick Whelan and the former finance director William McAteer were convicted by a Dublin court of illegally making €450 million of loans to a group of ten key investors to prop up the share price of the bank in the summer of 2008. So far as the US and UK are concerned, those likeliest to be brought to book are those involved in the alleged rigging of Libor interest rates and foreign-exchange markets. Having said that, no senior executive at the large Wall Street banks has yet been convicted of any criminal charge relating to the financial crisis. In Britain, despite the £66 billion bailouts of the Royal Bank of Scotland and Lloyds Banking Group, no charges have been brought against any directors, although in May 2014 it was revealed that the Serious Fraud Office was ready to question as many as a dozen senior former and current Barclays executives under oath over alleged corrupt arrangements made in Qatar as part of the bank's 2008 emergency fundraising operation. Among those to be interviewed were the bank's former chief executives John Varley and Bob Diamond.

But if past misdemeanours are now being punished, the enforcers nonetheless still have a huge job on their hands. Many banks have yet to confront shortages of capital, let alone build up their reserves to a comfortable level. Many still indulge in the kind of highly complex trades that lay behind so many of the problems of 2007 and 2008. And they still have a tendency to resist regulators, arguing that too much regulation stifles business and could threaten the growth that is beginning to return to Western economies. Full disclosure is still not the order of the day.

And then there's the opaque $60 trillion global shadow banking sector to worry about – a network of payday lenders, hedge funds, peer-to-peer lenders and other relatively unregulated financial groups, many of whom have taken advantage of the vacuum left when lending by traditional banks froze in the aftermath of the financial crisis. Payday lenders, for example, seem ever more ubiquitous, with new players springing up on high streets across

Britain. At a more sophisticated level traditional doorstep lenders have used the internet and mobile-phone networks to create a new generation of wage lenders. Wonga is perhaps the best-known example. Crowd funding – where entrepreneurs use digital networks to access potential finance – has become a financial force. Peer-to-peer lending groups, such as Zopa (founded in 2005), have prospered.

At the more commercial end of the market, hedge funds, private equity firms and other unregulated financial groups have expanded, many of them run by breakaway teams from the large investment banks. What they have in common – from Wall Street, to Continental Europe to Mayfair in London's West End (a particularly fecund centre) – is that they are often willing to take on large risks and that they operate largely away from the regulators' scrutiny. Some 232 hedge funds that offer direct lending, previously the territory of the banks, have been set up since the 2007–8 financial crisis. Hedge-fund research group Preqin estimated in September 2013 that the number of hedge funds lending directly had risen by three and a half times since the crisis. Historically, hedge funds sought to exploit mispricing of assets in equity and debt markets. After the Lehman crisis they found they could exploit the market for commercial lending, raising funds directly from investors. In November 2013 the governor of the Bank of England Mark Carney announced that 'identifying and addressing risks in shadow banking, while supporting diverse and resilient sources of market finance' would be a key priority of the Bank's Financial Policy Committee in 2014 and beyond.

Another separate but challenging area for the enforcers is that of complex financial instruments such as derivatives and options contracts. The size of this market is infinitely larger than that of shadow banking. Almost every commercial transaction now undertaken, from foreign-exchange dealings to the interest rate on business loans, includes a hedge or insurance policy against potential losses. The organisation providing the hedge, through the derivatives[4] market, will also protect itself against future losses through its own derivatives contract. The same also applies to almost all professional dealings on stock markets that are also backed up with futures and options contracts. As a result, the use of derivatives has ballooned: it now amounts to $600 trillion or 12 times the total output of the world economy, a figure that is 20 per cent higher than it was during the pit of the recession in 2009. In the US, the biggest market for derivatives, transactions are now policed by the Commodity Futures Trading Commission; in the UK it is the responsibility of the Financial Conduct Authority and, to a lesser extent, the Bank of England's Financial Policy Committee. These various regulators all have their work cut out.

Enforcers, then, are not only dealing with an ever-expanding financial system but one that continuously mutates. It is a little like cleaning out the Augean stables, and simultaneously having to deal with the arrival of ever more horses.

It's also still a system where the 'too big to fail' conundrum still exists. If one of the really big banks like JPMorgan or HSBC were to get into trouble, it's hard to see how the US or the UK government could avoid stepping in to prop it up, because any banking crash on this scale would wreak havoc with national economies. To that extent, it's more than possible that any future misdeeds, if major enough, will go largely unpunished.

One answer, of course, would be to break up the larger banks. America's Citigroup, RBS and Germany's Deutsche Bank, for

---

[4] Derivatives are essentially virtual products that are built on and track the movement of real assets, such as commodities or shares, or real market instruments, such as interest rates and currencies.

example, all have balance sheets of around $1 trillion. Were each to be cut in half, the new entities would still be significant players, but not omnipotent ones. Yet although the idea of breaking up big banks has been mooted, nothing has yet happened. Erecting an electric fence between retail and investment banking, as required by the Vickers report of the Independent Commission on Banking in Britain, is as far as matters have been taken. It's not surprising, therefore, that Neil Barofsky, author and the first special general inspector of America's Troubled Asset Relief Programme (TARP) should argue that the balance of power still hangs in favour of the banks:

> I think we are safer, but not safe. Rather than deal with the fundamental problem of 'too big to fail' institutions, Dodd–Frank nibbles around the edges of the status quo, which preserves the status of the megabanks.

Many argue that, like Dodd–Frank, Basel III – which underpins so much of global banking – offers reforms of a system that actually requires not so much fixing but a radical reappraisal. Basel III still allows banks to operate by borrowing most of the cash they need and holding only a fraction as capital. That leaves shareholders largely out of the firing line, allowing banks to rely on leverage rather than the issue of shares. That in turn encourages the persistence of a culture that rewards success but does not punish failure, and where high levels of risk-taking can seem attractive. Harald Hau, professor of economics and finance at the University of Geneva, has suggested that a banking system where the leverage ratio was radically curtailed and banks had to hold up to 20 per cent of their capital in equity would be inherently more stable. But there is no sign of that happening as yet.

What has happened, though, is a change in attitudes. When the then governor of the Bank of England, Mervyn King, gave a speech at the Lord Mayor's Banquet at Mansion House in 2007 he was sneered at for suggesting that a bank given the highest rating of 'AAA' often resembled a bottle of champagne that, when opened, turned out to be flat. Six years later, in June 2013, the outgoing governor addressed the City's great and good at the same venue in the following cautionary terms:

> Despite the generous provision of liquidity and funding from the state, lending remains lacklustre, and risk premia high. Although the combined balance sheet of our largest banks has shrunk since the height of the crisis in 2008, it is still 400 per cent of the annual GDP. Leverage ratios have fallen, but all our major banks remain highly leveraged. And of course the two biggest lenders to the domestic economy [RBS and Lloyds Banking Group] remain largely in state ownership. It is difficult to imagine a banking sector like that making a real contribution to any economic recovery.

He went on to say: 'It is not in our interest to have banks that are too big to fail, too big to jail, or simply too big.' This time around, it is worth noting, his words were rather more politely received.

Like King, his successor Mark Carney has recognised that the UK for one cannot continually prop up its banks. 'Fairness demands the end of a system that privatises gains but socialises losses,' he has argued. 'And simple economics dictates that the UK state cannot stand behind a banking system that is already many times the size of the economy.'

It's a delicate balancing act. On the one hand, bankers fear that tight regulation will choke off economic recovery. On the other, all the evidence shows that such regulation as has been in force over the past couple of decades has simply not been up to the job of either forestalling disaster or then punishing the perpetrators. Politicians tend to jump from one side of the fence to the other, arguing for reform when public anger is at its height, and then retreating as the banks make their case. And no one can be ignorant of what has happened in the past when banks have been allowed to fail en masse. In the US between 1929 and 1933, 2,500 banks closed and bank credit contracted by one-third. As a result, the stock market fell 75 per cent from its peak and unemployment rose to over 25 per cent. Luigi Zingales, professor of entrepreneurship and finance at the University of Chicago Booth School of Business, noted in October 2013 when surveying the contemporary world of banking: 'These companies become so important politically to the state or country that it is hard to resist transforming their interests into the policy of the country.'

The strongest weapon in the hands of the politicians and enforcers as they struggle to bring an end to reckless finance and combat the power of Wall Street, the City of London and other financial centres is, arguably, public anger. One might have thought that more than five years after the Great Panic the distrust of banking and finance would have subsided. Yet on the streets of Spanish cities such as Barcelona, in a country struggling with youth unemployment of 57.7 per cent in 2014, it is the financiers who are seen as the guilty party. Similar attitudes exist in the United States, where the recovery from the Great Recession has created far fewer jobs than in past recoveries. In the UK it is the bankers who are still blamed for record levels of national debt – standing at nearly 90 per cent of total output in 2014 – and the slow improvement in living standards. All of this takes place amid new disclosures of wrongdoing ranging from

# 10

# Banking Conundrums:
# Five Key Questions

### Are bankers paid too much?

During a drinking bout F. Scott Fitzgerald, author of *The Great Gatsby*, allegedly turned to fellow American writer Ernest Hemingway and said, 'The rich are different from you and me.' To which Hemingway is supposed to have replied: 'Yes. They have more money.' That has certainly been true of bankers.

It was not always thus. In Britain in the 1950s bankers earned salaries that were comparable with those of other professions, such as lawyers and doctors. In the US, similarly, pay was at one point relatively restrained. To a large extent the reason for this was that merchant banks or investment banks, as they are now called, were traditionally run as partnerships. Partners in the business staked their own cash and in good times took generous sums out of business. In bad times, however, they had to show restraint and might even be asked to inject cash into the company. Many law firms and accountancy practices, vast international concerns, still operate on this model. The Bank of England's executive director for financial stability, Andy Haldane, describes this as ensuring that people 'have skin in the game right up until the death'.

In the late 1970s, however, financial regulation was relaxed in the

US and the old barriers between commercial banks and investment banks, as required by the Depression-era Glass–Steagall Act, fell away. The distinction between commercial or utility banking and investment banking blurred. Commercial banks became more involved in the advisory and trading activities that were traditionally the province of investment banks and the latter became more directly involved in fundraising and corporate lending. The rationale for the breakdown of the traditional barriers was that banks offering universal services would be better able to service multinational clients in a globalised world.

Many of the investment banks chose to jettison partnership status altogether and float on the markets as public companies. This made it easier to raise capital and to spread the risks more widely with outside investors. Others went for high-profile mergers, throwing in their lot with other big commercial banks. The old-established New York house of Salomon Brothers was the first major Wall Street firm to seek a commercial partner and at the same time gain a public quotation when the partners sold it to the publicly listed commodities trader Phibro in 1981.

The zenith of this transformation came in 1999 when Goldman Sachs under the co-chairmanship of future US Senator Jon Corzine and Hank Paulson (US Treasury Secretary from 2006 to 2009) became the last of the major US investment banks to discard the partnership model and float on the New York Stock Exchange. As a partnership Goldman Sachs, the most adventurous and smartest of the investment banks, had been able to shield itself from close public scrutiny. As a publicly quoted enterprise the sources of its income and earnings and the rewards to employees, from receptionists to senior executives, became available for all to see. The sheer scale of the Goldman bonuses and share awards in the good times helped to trigger an arms race in pay, bonuses and benefits.

Change in Britain can be dated back to the Big Bang in October 1986 when Margaret Thatcher's government swept the ancient structures of the City into the sea. The divisions between stockbrokers and jobbers – who set the prices – were abolished, creating a new breed of market makers. The barriers between merchant banking and stockbroking fell away. Ancient practices in the City that gave a privileged position to accepting houses and discount houses which handled bills issued by the Bank of England were eroded. Membership of an exclusive fraternity was opened up and international investors poured through the gates.

Pay and bonuses rose remorselessly. By the second decade of the 20th century, according to research from accountants PricewaterhouseCoopers, a UK banker could command six times what a doctor or lawyer earned. Nor has the financial crisis had much of an impact. Since 2008 pay among bankers has not only remained high but has actually risen (overall payouts at the big four UK high-street banks – Barclays, HSBC, RBS and Lloyds – rose between 2007 and 2012 from £26.5 billion to £27.9 billion). At Barclays Capital between 2002 and 2009 its long-term incentive plan (LTIP) paid out an average of £170 million a year to a changing group of around 60 key bankers. Total staff numbers may have fallen in the crisis years but pay for the upper echelons remained a constant.

City lawyer Anthony Salz, brought in by Barclays to review its ethical failings after the Libor scandal, was among those who believed that the bank had been sucked into the cauldron of high pay without really thinking about the consequences. 'With hindsight it appears that certain of Barclays' LTIPs were overly generous,' he concluded in his April 2013 report. In 2013, the year of Barclays' disgrace over Libor, no fewer than 428 bankers at Barclays received pay packages worth £1 million each and a further five bankers earned more than £5 million.

As one would expect, given London's position in the financial world, Britain leads the European table. A July 2013 survey by the European Banking Authority found that 3,529 bankers earned €1 million or more in 2012, of which 2,714 were based in the UK. Average total pay including fixed salaries and bonuses for the UK's top-earning bankers grew from €1.4 million in 2011 to €2 million in 2012. German high earners on average received bonuses worth just over twice their basic salary. Among other European countries Ireland had 16 in the top bracket, down from 21 a year earlier. Cyprus had three and Greece just one.

Such has been the impact of rises at the top end that overall average pay has shifted markedly, too. At high-paying Barclays, average pay across all parts of the bank (including the investment and retail units) rose from £54,000 to £70,000 over the five years from 2007 to 2012. Incomes rose at more moderate Lloyds from £40,000 to £50,000 over the same period.

All this has had a distorting influence on society as a whole. Leading figures in business, such as Sir John Rose, the former chief executive of Rolls-Royce, argue that such high salaries in banking tend to damage the economy because they encourage good engineers and mathematicians to gravitate to the City rather than to research and manufacturing. They also distort a nation's geography. London, for example, as the magnet for the financial sector and the legal, consulting and other professional services that feed off it, has become a city for affluent financiers and their associates (lawyers and so on), rather as 17th-century Venice was the city of merchants. Data from the Office for National Statistics (ONS) shows that in 2011 disposable income in London (after taxes, national insurance and other deductions) stood at an average of £20,509 a year, as against £16,034 nationally. And if that 25 per cent disparity is not remarkable enough, the ONS numbers for the economic contribution made by different areas of the country shows that whereas the Gross Value Added figure for the North-West (the UK's traditional manufacturing centre) stood at a modest £17,754 per person in 2011, in central and west London it was some £115,519.

London's housing market has swelled in tandem. Great swathes of west London, including Kensington and Chelsea, have been colonised by the global banking community. The strength of banking in London has also made it honeypot for émigré financiers from Russia, Ukraine, Hong Kong, China and all points east. As recovery gained a hold in Britain in 2014 London house prices were forecast to rise 9 per cent for the year with the average London price climbing to £500,000.

Many feel that such distortions are damaging to society as a whole, but the charge more regularly levelled against the scale of remuneration at the top end of banking is that it has caused (and is causing) individual bankers to take unnecessary – and often suicidal – risks. It is the undiscriminating nature of this risk-taking that has led to so many of the problems the world has witnessed since 2007 and what's more, the charge runs, there is no evidence that the rewards are removed when the risk-taking doesn't pay off. As Professor Alexander Pepper of the Department of Management of the London School of Economics argues:

> I have no problem with people being highly rewarded if they take high risks. Successful entrepreneurs earn huge sums of money, but they take huge risks. The problem in people's minds with banking and executive pay is that they believe the relationship between risk and reward has broken down and I would agree with that.

This worry even extends to the world of retail banking. Here, of course, salaries and bonuses are much lower. Branch bankers at the end of the food chain earn relatively modest annual salaries of £20,000 to £25,000 a year. 'Advisers' might command up to £35,000. But a carrot-and-stick approach has been shown to be behind much of the mis-selling of products in recent years. A Lloyds TSB adviser on a mid-level salary of £33,076 not hitting 90 per cent of their sales target over a nine-month period could see their annual base salary drop to £25,927, the Financial Conduct Authority found when a disciplinary investigation into sales practices within the Lloyds banking group was released in 2014. If the sales adviser was demoted by two levels, pay could plummet to just £18,189. If, on the other hand, sales targets were met, workers would be entitled to a 'champagne bonus' that could increase monthly pay by as much as 35 per cent.

At the Halifax and Bank of Scotland (both owned by Lloyds) star advisers had the opportunity to win a one-off cash bonus of £1,000, known a 'grand-in-the-hand'. The slang of the trading floor in investment banking had found its way into the pay manuals of branch banking.

In their defence the banks argue, firstly, that incentives are essential to attract people into high-stress, high-achieving jobs, and secondly that they must pay the going rate for salaries or they will lose key staff to rivals. And money matters to bankers – particularly investment bankers: it's the way they measure personal success. RBS chairman Sir Philip Hampton described in November 2013 a conversation with a £4 million-a-year banker in which the banker expressed 'outrage' at discovering that 'somebody doing a comparable job at another bank' was getting £6 million. In many industries high wage demands from employees are dismissed by employers. In banking, however, the fear that a high-flying banker might leave, taking their key clients with them, is enough to keep pay negotiations going.

When it comes to wage restraint, then, the banks are unlikely to lead the way. Neither, as a rule, are shareholders. The 2011 Barclays annual general meeting where 31.5 per cent of shareholders rejected the pay report, including payments worth £17 million to Bob Diamond, was a rare exception. Particular anger was directed at the chair of the pay committee Alison Carnwath, who was to resign her role at Barclays in 2012 (and who went on to be made a dame in the 2014 New Year Honours list). Nevertheless, the pay awards went ahead.

Carnwath was replaced as remuneration chairman by Sir John Sunderland, the former chief executive of Cadbury. He quickly came under fire too, after approving a 10 per cent rise in the Barclays bonus pot for 2013 to £2.4 billion despite a 32 per cent drop in the bank's profits. In the face of a shareholders' revolt Sunderland stepped down on 15 April 2014.

Kieran Quinn, chairman of the Local Authority Pension Fund Forum, one of the investor groups seeking Sunderland's head, noted: 'This is absolutely the right thing for the Barclays board to have done, it is a shame that it took pressure from investors to get them there.' He added that Barclays should 'reassess' its pay 'so this year's and future bonuses will be in line with legitimate returns to shareholders'.

In 2009 former deputy governor of the Bank of England and City regulator Sir David Walker (paradoxically the chairman of Barclays) recommended that banks should have to disclose, in banded form, the number of those employees, including executive directors, who earn £1 million to £2.5 million, £2.5 million to £5 million and above £5 million. (He rejected proposals that the highest paid – who are not directors – be identified by name as is required by the Securities and Exchange Commission in the United States.) He also proposed that there should be strict rules to defer incentive payments so that rewards would be brought more in line with the economic cycle and could potentially be clawed back more easily on the discovery of wrongdoing. At least half of longer-term incentives, essentially bonuses and options, would be in the shape of options on shares with half the award vesting (turning into cash) after three years and the remainder after five years. Short-term bonus awards should be paid over a three-year period with not more than one-third paid in the first year.

The reality is, however, that even if bonuses are deferred for five years it may not be long enough to prevent bankers being rewarded for misconduct. Some of the payment protection insurance mis-selling dates back almost a decade; Libor manipulation goes back to before the credit crunch and the generation of sub-prime mortgages to the boom years of the early 2000s. The time that elapses between discovery, investigation and final acceptance of a problem by the banks can stretch up to a decade. 'We had roughly a 20-year boom in the run-up to this crisis, so measuring performance only over a three- or five-year window is far too short,' says the Bank of England's Andy Haldane.

There is not much evidence that the Walker recommendations, many of which were subsequently incorporated in the recommendations of the Parliamentary Commission on Banking Standards and adopted by City rule-makers[1], have dramatically changed the behaviour in the financial community. The amount of pay deferred by banks is low and has been falling. Deferred pay as

[1] In Britain recommendations on pay are adopted by the Financial Reporting Council, a City quango responsible for policing corporate governance. It sets the standards but it is up to boards of directors to adhere to them and investors to vote the pay report and the directors down if dissatisfied that best practice is being circumvented.

a proportion of total pay at HSBC fell from 8 per cent in 2010 to 3.6 per cent in 2012. At RBS that figure slipped from 8.4 per cent to 5.2 per cent over the same period. Among the major UK banks only Barclays saw the figure rise, from 16 per cent in 2010 to 17.4 per cent in 2012. Nor has definitive action yet been taken on the June 2013 recommendation of the Parliamentary Commission on Banking Standards that 'a substantial part of remuneration' should be deferred for up to ten years.

Superficially, things seem to have taken a rather different turn in Europe. In 2013 the European Commission in Brussels introduced legislation that limited bankers' bonuses across the region for those earning more than €500,000 a year to 100 per cent of basic pay, or 200 per cent if shareholders approved. The British government challenged this move, worried that it would render the City less attractive to international finance, but the laws nevertheless came into force in March 2014. They have proved so easy to circumvent, however, that one wonders why Brussels should have bothered to expend so much time and ink on them. Faced with a cap on bonuses, all banks have to do is to raise the fixed element of pay. Among the first at the gate was London-based HSBC which revealed in March 2014 that it was introducing a monthly 'allowance' for its top bankers and traders in addition to basic pay and bonuses. The legislation became virtually meaningless as soon as it was enacted.

Bankers' salaries and bonuses tend to get most of the media attention, but they are only part of the equation. Senior bankers are also in line for huge pension entitlements. Former HBOS chief Andy Hornby's pension pot is worth £2.8 million and was accumulated at twice the pace of most final-salary pensions. Northern Rock chief executive Adam Applegarth has a pension worth £2.6 million. And RBS chief executive Fred Goodwin still has a pot worth £12.2 million after eventually bowing to government pressure to cut it by a third. There's no sign that the regulators will be acting to curb bankers' pensions any time soon.

In my various conversations with senior bankers I have found that even those most publicly committed to more ethical banking and to cultural change, such as Barclays' earnest chief executive Antony Jenkins, insist that they have no choice but to be part of the pay arms race or die. It looks, then, as though high levels of pay are here to stay, and with them the systemic tendency to chase profit at the expense of prudence that has caused so many problems in the past.

## Can banks reform themselves?

The changing of the guard at the UK banks, with Antony Jenkins replacing Diamond at Barclays in 2012, Horta-Osorio taking over from Eric Daniels at Lloyds in 2011 and Ross McEwan inheriting Stephen Hester's mantle at RBS in 2013, does suggest transformation. Jenkins at Barclays likes to claim that a rich cocktail of measures, including a corporate code, is evidence that banks are getting to grips with the new environment. On 17 January 2013 he sent a memo to all of the bank's 140,000 staff asking them to sign up to a new ethical code of conduct, or leave.

The demands of the code of conduct were praiseworthy enough, but then Barclays has had some experience of codes of conduct. In 2005 the then chief executive John Varley stated the group's five guiding principles. He wanted the bank to be customer-focused, winning together, best people, pioneering and trusted. It was a rather random collection of the sort of fine-sounding words that are so beloved by the upper echelons of management. For his part, Bob Diamond during his 17-month reign as chief executive launched a One Barclays plan, which aimed to roll out the best culture and practices across all of the group's business units.

Writing a new corporate code is the easiest thing a firm can do – it is sticking to it that counts. The Co-operative Bank wrote one into its articles of association – promising to adhere to ethical values – just weeks before the former chairman and vice-chairman of the whole Co-operative movement was arrested for buying illegal drugs. As for Barclays' new code, the Parliamentary Commission on Banking Standards has pointedly remarked that it is 'remarkably similar' to the code of conduct set out in Enron's 2000 Annual Report the year before the energy-trading firm filed for bankruptcy due to systematic accounting fraud. In early 2014 Jenkins admitted it might take five to ten years to effect cultural change.

Back in the 1970s Gus Levy, senior partner at Goldman Sachs, famously urged the firm to be 'long-term greedy', by which he meant the business should forgo short-term profits if they came at the expense of client relationships. In 2009 the Goldman Sachs code of business conduct and ethics lauded 'integrity and honesty' as being 'at the heart of our business'. The shrewdest business on Wall Street added the caveat that 'from time to time, the firm may waive certain provisions of this Code.' A year later in 2010 Goldman Sachs was fined $550 million by the Securities and Exchange Commission for misleading clients.

All this suggests that fine words and intentions in themselves will achieve little. The problem is that the worst aspects of the banking culture are so deeply embedded that they are astonishingly difficult to shift. City lawyer Anthony Salz caught the atmosphere inside Barclays and the investment-banking community as a whole in his independent review of Barclays' business practices released in April 2013: 'Winning at all costs comes at a price: collateral issues of rivalry, arrogance, selfishness and a lack of humility and generosity.' The report added that employees in the investment-banking unit were proud of their 'cleverness', which showed itself in a 'tendency to take robust positions with regulators, to determine its position by the letter rather than the spirit of the rules, and in the "edgy" way it pushed its own business agenda'. Barclays Capital's flamboyant former co-chief executive, the appropriately named Rich Ricci, has admitted: 'We were a culture that did not like people who admired problems; we liked people who drove solutions. I think that shift may have been too much.'

Indeed, there is even evidence that the fines imposed on banks for mis-selling to customers, cheating on Libor and foreign-exchange markets, and circumventing money-laundering law have now become so much a matter of routine that they are regarded in some quarters simply as an extra tax that has to be paid for bending the rules. Of course, there does come a point when the fines are so huge that they give pause for thought. This certainly was the case for JPMorgan Chase, which agreed in October 2013 to pay the US Justice Department the astonishing sum of $13 billion to settle claims that sub-prime mortgages and products built around them had been poorly sold. Nevertheless, there remains a view in some banks that penalties might be worth paying if the resulting profits and bonuses are generous enough. An internal probe at Barclays Wealth America found the unit had a 'culture of fear' that was 'actively hostile to compliance' and was 'ruled with an iron fist to remove any intervention from those who speak up in opposition'.

One possible way forward, according to the UK's Parliamentary Commission on Banking Standards, is to introduce more female traders on to the macho trading floors of major banks. The French managing director of the International Monetary Fund, Christine Lagarde, has similarly encouraged bigger roles for women in high finance: 'I have joked that a "male" culture of reckless financial risk taking was at the heart of the global crisis. Studies back this up. Men trade more often – some say 45 per cent more often – and risk taking can be mapped to trading room profits and losses. Mixing genders can help. Companies with more women on their boards have higher sales, higher returns on equity, and higher profitability.'

Another key route to creating better run and safer financial institutions is to end the allergy in the boardrooms of banks to holding more equity – share capital. Quite simply, if banks have much more equity, or a greater number of shares, then they will be less likely to become insolvent or fail and governments will be less likely to be forced into a position where they have to choose between bailouts and bank failures. In the post-crisis era, however, the incentives for the banks in the form of deposit insurance (which offers notional guarantees to customers) and tax incentives favour them holding as little capital as possible and bolstering returns accordingly. It's a difficult balancing act between profit and dividends to shareholders on the one hand and lower returns but greater stability on the other. Bankers favour the former; regulators and governments are wary about forcing banks to adopt the latter.

The fact is that banks remain fatally attracted to complex, short-term gambits that might yield quick wins. It's become part of the culture. In this context, it is worth recalling the words of John Reed, who in 1998 was one of the architects of the merger of Citibank of New York with the San Francisco-based financial conglomerate Travelers and the resultant creation of Citigroup. Looking back in 2013 over 30 years of investment banking he noted with regret how bankers had gone from building businesses to focusing purely on increasing returns:

> The amount of money that's handled by professional investors is really astronomical and the result is that there's a whole industry that's trying to create products that are attractive to

investors. That's what the investment banking business has become. They are trying to package things or create synthetic things they might sell an investor to get a better return than in a traditional portfolio.

All that said, recent events suggest that there may be glimmerings of light on the horizon, in the case of one bank at least. In April 2014 the Barclays board suffered a battering from shareholders at a stormy annual general meeting at the Royal Festival Hall on London's South Bank. Institutional and private investors were clearly losing patience with a senior management that was prepared to grant 2013 bonus settlements for top bankers that dwarfed the dividend distribution to shareholders in a financial year when profits fell and a major cash call on investors for new capital was made.

The following month, however, after a long and careful strategic review, Antony Jenkins announced that he was taking an axe to the investment arm of the bank. In part this move reflected a decline in the financial significance of casino banking to Barclays over the previous few years. In 2009 the bank had reported revenues of £17.8 billion, of which fixed interest and currencies made up £13.7 billion. In 2013, however, total revenues had fallen to £10.7 billion of which only £5.5 billion came from fixed income, currencies and commodities trading. In other words, the investment bank was eating capital but no longer producing anything like the income it had achieved before the crisis.

But Jenkins also made it clear that he proposed to tackle the issue of risk-taking. In future, he said, the risk-weighted capital deployed in casino banking would be capped at 30 per cent of the bank's capital against the 60 per cent deployed at its peak and 50 per cent in 2013. The amount of capital exposed to the investment bank would be cut in half and 7,000 casino banking jobs – in New York, London and Asia – were to be lost. Many of the bank's weaker businesses, including commodity trading and the European retail banking operations, were to be hived off into a 'non-core' unit – effectively a 'bad bank' – a term that Jenkins declined to use in a conversation with me about the changes.

At the same time, it was announced that, owing to the inexorable rise of new technology – particularly in online and mobile banking – the retail bank would shrink. Up to 400 branches out of a UK branch network of 1,600 branches would be closed and 12,000 jobs lost at branch level and from processing centres. In this Barclays was following in the steps already taken by other high-street banks such as RBS and Lloyds to cut costs.

'This is a bold simplification of Barclays,' Jenkins declared. 'In the future Barclays will be leaner, stronger, better balanced and well positioned to deliver lower volatility, higher returns and growth.'

The changes Jenkins announced were significant and potentially far-reaching. They acknowledged a new era of tougher regulation (previous efforts by Barclays to persuade the American regulator, the Federal Reserve, to ease capital rules for the investment banking operations – that are largely in New York – at a series of meetings in 2013–14 proved abortive). They accepted that there needed to be an end to over-complex banking. And the removal of 7,000 highly paid investment bankers from their posts, including some of those involved in the most risky and sometimes lucrative activities, inevitably means that the bonus pool (the amount on money set aside for bonuses) will drop sharply. (It should be noted, though, that Jenkins made no commitment to curb the bonuses for those investment bankers who remain in place.)

'These are final decisions,' Jenkins said. 'We don't intend to retrade them.'

## Can stakeholders reform the banks?

In the years before the Big Bang in the 1980s and Gordon Brown's reshaping of City regulation a decade later, one outlet for expressing dissatisfaction with the behaviour of a bank was the governor of the Bank of England's eyebrow. The slightest raising of it was sufficient to send a warning signal to the chairman of a clearing bank. This was a skill neglected in the pre-crisis era and only revived when Mervyn King let it be known to the top echelons at Barclays in 2012 that Bob Diamond should go. So unfamiliar were the politicians with the conventions of the old City that the Treasury Select Committee went so far as to suggest that King had exceeded his authority in suggesting that it was time for Diamond to resign.

The main outlet for dissent, however, is through the shareholders, the ultimate owners of the business. In the pre-Big Bang era a handful of British insurers, often led by the Prudential (which held a 3 per cent stake in most FTSE100 companies) would discreetly whisper any dissatisfaction they might feel into the ear of the chairman or a senior executive. A more direct route was through the annual general meeting. In the late 1970s it was a sustained campaign by dissident investors that eventually persuaded Barclays to disinvest from apartheid-era South Africa.

In the post-crisis era the shareholder channel has changed dramatically in the UK, at least – the biggest owner of RBS and Lloyds now being UK Financial Investments. Theoretically, UKFI is the investor set up to keep the British government at arm's length from the banks, but so closely involved are politicians in the running of the financial sector that this is little more than a fiction. Politicians now operate within banking both at the broad policy level – for example, driving the selling-off of Lloyds Banking Group shares in the hope that this might deliver a profit for the taxpayer – and at a more micro level, George Osborne's involvement in the dismissal of Stephen Hester from RBS in 2013 being a case in point. As banking stakeholders politicians are a mixed blessing. Some have proved thoughtful reformers and advocates for change, but the desire for quick wins and flattering headlines on the part of others is not always conducive to wise decision-making.

The next category of banking investors are the global-fund managers who in many cases now outpace the traditional insurers and pension funds on shareholder registers. Many of the global funds may have offices in the UK but they are largely the creatures of their overseas owners. Their primary concern is to see a return in terms of capital and income. Questions of governance and culture tend to be of secondary importance.

In 1969 just 6.6 per cent of the UK stock market was held by institutions outside Britain. By 2013 this figure had leapt to 53.2 per cent. The enormous change in ownership reflects the globalisation of the world economy and Britain's extraordinary openness to trade. Waves of British firms in key sectors such as energy, water and chemicals, including nuclear-power generator British Energy and the larger utility Thames Water, have been bought by foreign enterprises. Many of Britain's most iconic corporations – Cadbury, BAA, P&O, Harrods and top football clubs such as Manchester United and Chelsea – are in overseas ownership. Full foreign ownership together with majority overseas shareholding in many publicly quoted enterprises has led to a deepening disconnect between companies and their ultimate owners.

In its 2013 report the Parliamentary Commission on Banking Standards pointed out: 'Overseas investors [are] typically more interested in the short-term performance of companies than in generating sustainable returns by promoting their long-term success. Any influence they wield over the management of the company is manifested through selling their stock rather than through voting and engaging with the boards of their investee companies.'

Some investors certainly go the distance. Value funds, such as Invesco Perpetual in Britain and Franklin Templeton in the US, for example, are there for the long term because they are interested in the intrinsic worth of the enterprise with which they are involved. Nevertheless, overall, the turnover on share registers has become more rapid, with entities such as hedge funds tending to hold stocks for much shorter periods than in the past. Andy Haldane of the Bank of England notes that holding periods for bank shares had fallen from three years in 1998 to just three months by 2008.

Reviewing this phenomenon, the Parliamentary Commission commented: 'Investors that hold shares for a short period are less likely to be concerned by the long-term prospects of the company they own, other than to the extent that it affects short-term movements in the share price.' It should be noted, too, that many investors are wary about becoming too embroiled in the minutiae of the banks with which they are involved. Bank balance sheets and accounts have become so complex in recent times that even their own directors, let alone outsiders, can have trouble making sense of them.

Investors did, of course, talk to banks in the boom years. But it tended only to be about one thing. They pressured banks to lend more, take on more risk, in a bid to boost equity returns. Those banks which resisted were criticised. The most cautious of the pre-crisis banks, Lloyds, often came under fire for failing to do all the adventurous things the other high-street banks were doing, from buying up banks overseas to becoming more involved in trading activity. The company's share price suffered accordingly, making it one of the highest yielding (in terms of dividend) stocks quoted in London. All that came to an end when Lloyds went for a shotgun wedding with HBOS.

As was stated in Lloyds' written testimony[2] on corporate governance, included in the Parliamentary Commission on Banking Standards report in June 2013: 'Shareholder behaviour "pre-crunch" focused on a drive for growth with emphasis placed on delivering potentially unsustainable returns, without recognition of the downside risks. This was a factor in creating a culture that arguably led to failure in the sector.'

HSBC faced many of the same pressures, and the result was a series of ill-judged mergers and acquisitions during the tenure of Sir John Bond as chairman. One of Bond's successors, Douglas Flint who took the chair in 2010, told the Treasury Committee in February 2011:

> There was a great deal of pressure coming from shareholders who were looking for enhanced returns and were pointing to business models that have, with hindsight, been shown to be flawed and in particular very leveraged business models and saying, 'You guys are inefficient. You have a lazy balance sheet. There are people out there that are doing much better than you are', and there was tremendous pressure during 2006–2007.

Indeed, until the crisis that nearly wiped them out, it made some sense for shareholders to urge bank executives to be ever more gung-ho about taking risks. Under the old Basel rules shareholders were required to put up fractional amounts of capital. Most of the rest of the resources came from bondholders and depositors. The power of shareholder capital was therefore magnified many times over by other sources of funding and the potential rewards, in terms

---

[2] The submission was originally made to the Kay review on UK equity markets that was released in 2012.

of a rising share price and a generous dividend flow, looked to be unlimited.

For their part, bondholders tend to be more risk averse, opting for steady payments over a long period of time. That said, during the pre-crash years there was a general assumption among those who lent to major banks that if the worst came to the worst, national governments would be on hand to sort everything out. It's not surprising, therefore, that when bondholders were asked to help make good the £1.5 billion black hole at the heart of the Co-operative Bank in 2013, they should have rebelled, forcing the ultimate owners, the Co-op Group, to give them a better deal.

'Fear of . . . losses can incentivise bondholders to limit the risks banks take,' the Parliamentary Commission concluded. 'However, if bondholders regard the risks as small, particularly due to the perception of the existence of the implicit or explicit taxpayer guarantee, these incentives are correspondingly reduced. This may particularly apply to banks that are regarded as too big to fail.'

In the wave of banking failures during the Great Panic few bondholders lost money. And as some banks got bigger as they swallowed struggling rivals, many bondholders must have assumed that the 'too big to fail' mantra still held – that big banks would continue to be backed by big government come what might. In fact bondholders did find themselves in the firing line in one or two cases – as did depositors – but what happened at the Co-operative Bank in 2013 and at Cypriot banks in the same year was exceptional.

The supreme irony is that while shareholders may have helped drive banking excesses, they have not really benefited from their efforts. Sir Mervyn King, a consistent critic of banking misbehaviour, told the Parliamentary Commission in Banking Standards in March 2013: 'It is striking that, looking back at the returns that investment banking has generated, almost all of them have gone to the employees in the industry and not to the shareholders.' The creation of a new class of super-rich bankers has been partly at the expense of investors. They have lost out on dividend income, and have had to look on helplessly as the capital value of many bank shares has plummeted. Ordinary savers and depositors also have suffered as the returns on cash held in deposit accounts have been slashed in an era of ultra-low interest rates.

The problem is that the increasing remoteness of shareholders from the banks and other companies in which they invest has weakened their involvement. Shareholder registers are now dominated by global funds, such as the American firm Black Rock with $4.3 trillion of assets under management in 2014, which invest on the basis of worldwide market trends. Similarly, increasing amounts of equity investment is held in mutual funds, such as unit trusts, and tax-free wrappers such as individual retirement accounts, where the connection between the ultimate owners – the individual investors – and the banks in which they invest is severed.

In some jurisdictions, such as Italy, shareholders were still closely involved before the crisis. Most banks were owned by 'foundations', local business syndicates of the great and the good, that down the centuries and the decades have sought to maintain stability. Even this long-standing link was weakened during the crisis when the foundations could no longer raise sufficient funds to support the capital of failing banks, and had to sell down their stakes in the open market. In Britain there has been a sustained effort to try to hold shareholders' feet to the fire. The Financial Reporting Council, a City enforcer responsible for accounting and governance standards inside publicly quoted enterprises, set up a stewardship code in 2010, strengthened in 2013, designed to improve engagement between companies and their investors. Some investors, notably the Scottish asset manager and insurer Standard

Life, take the code extremely seriously and are willing to go public with their criticisms. Others such as the independent fund manager Henderson, one of the City's longest established investors, prefer to engage behind closed doors.

In the United States the California Public Employees' Retirement System (Calpers) is a notably active investor. In 2013 it joined the rebels at the annual general meeting of JPMorgan Chase in demanding that chairman and chief executive Jamie Dimon split his role. Similar fortitude has been shown in Britain by Pension & Investment Research Consultants (PIRC), representing many local-authority and trade-union pension funds, which is active in seeking better governance and regularly objects and votes against remuneration policy at the banks. That activism can work was seen at Barclays in 2011–13 when two successive chairs of the pay committee, Alison Carnwath and Sir John Sunderland, stood down.

Gradually, then, it seems that shareholders are becoming more responsible and more willing to speak out. But the fact is that as long as executives and boards are delivering the goods, in the shape of greater capital and income returns, shareholders prefer to keep their heads below the parapet. In the conflict between responsibility and delivering returns to investors (and incidentally the bonuses and incentives also paid to fund managers) it is too often short-term thinking that wins out over stewardship.

## Can governments and regulators reform the banks?

Governments have still to decide what they actually want banks to do. Do they want them to be heavily regulated utilities that take in savings and make plain vanilla loans? Or would they prefer them to be lightly regulated businesses out to make the greatest amount of money possible for management, shareholders and the taxpayer (as long as they remain afloat)?

By 2014 governments on both sides of the Atlantic and across the world were groping towards the goals of creating safer and more durable banks and limiting the taxpayer exposure created by the 'too big to fail' problem. Much of the general rule-making has emerged from Mark Carney's Financial Stability Board, set up as a result of the G20 process after the crisis. It has created a consensus that 'too big to fail' must be tackled. Two routes have been taken in resolving this problem.

The first is through the Basel III process that seeks to build the defences of banks by requiring them to hold greater levels of loss-absorbing capital against risk. The second route is through legislation that creates special bankruptcy arrangements for banks, giving regulators and the courts the powers to separate out the healthy arms of banks from the weaker parts and bring them back into operation as quickly as possible, preferably over a weekend. It is a model based on that deployed by the Federal Deposit Insurance Corporation in the United States but – so far – it is untested on a complex global bank. New financial legislation in the US, Britain and most recently the European Union has given the authorities these far-reaching powers.

The legislation is in place but much of the work is only half done. The process of strengthening capital is still under way and regulators are in a constant struggle with the banks over the speed of balance-sheet repair and the size of the equity injections needed. In Britain the ring-fencing of retail from casino banking is still in its infancy. In the US many of the large changes required by the Dodd–Frank financial reform act have still to be implemented. In the European Union the new regulator, the European Central Bank, is still struggling to establish the health of the banks in its charge, many of which are still seriously wounded. In China the biggest worry is the rise of an uncontrolled shadow banking system paralleling that which has grown up in the G7 advanced economies since the 2007–8 crisis.

The conflict between creating safer, more tightly controlled banks while at the same time restoring the banking system to health so that it can support recovering economies is profound. What are banks actually for? Are they there to benefit their owners and employers? Or are they there for the 'common good'? Uncertainty as to the answer here – or, at least, uncertainty as to the balance that should be struck between the two positions – is what lies at the root of government uncertainty and tinkering.

Consequently what we currently have is a nervous half-solution that looks to tweak the 'light-touch' system that prevailed before the crash without running the risk of upsetting the big beasts of the City or tipping the management of financial affairs into the lap of an uncontrolled shadow banking system that seeks to arbitrage gaps in regulation. Certainly, governments and regulators have gathered to themselves powers that allow them to be far more interventionist. New laws in Britain, for instance, that allow prosecutions to be brought against 'reckless' banking re-arm the enforcers. In the United States the timidity of prosecutors in the immediate aftermath of the crisis has been corrected.

Yet the challenge of the authorities to the bonus culture, which was at the root of the 2007–9 crisis, is weak. We have seen the ability of the bankers to run rings around the enforcers by coming up with new devices, such as monthly allowances, that evade rules, regulations and legislation. The animal spirits that drive global finance are still largely untrammelled and bankers still have far too much sway over politicians in the public discourse. Ironically, too, in the post-crash years some of the big banks – JPMorgan, Bank of America, Santander, Barclays and Lloyds among them – far from getting smaller have actually grown bigger as they have swallowed ailing rivals. Unless these mighty entities were to be forcibly split into smaller banks, it's hard to see how the 'too big to fail' conundrum will disappear.

## Will there be further banking scandals?

Trust lies at the heart of successful banking, but it is a quality that has been in short supply in recent years. When it evaporated in 2007 and 2008, the result was a run on the Northern Rock bank, the collapse of Lehman Brothers and the near collapse of RBS and HBOS. When the 2013 Edelman Trust Barometer was published it revealed that faith in the standards of world banking stood at only 50 per cent and that in Britain just 22 per cent of those surveyed retained any confidence in the banks.

The waning of trust doesn't just reflect recent scandals but reveals a general dissatisfaction with the current culture of banking. Former Bank of England deputy governor Paul Tucker has talked about 'an industrialisation of high street banking' in the course of which the big retail banks have 'drifted away from relationship banking'. He noted that 'branch managers are much less empowered than they were 20 or 30 years ago and that is a major problem of culture in its own right – irrespective of what happens to global investment banking.' In testimony before the Parliamentary Commission on Banking Standards in January 2013 Stuart Davies, a union regional officer for Unite, which represents bank branch workers, was disdainful of the new, pushy sales culture of retail banking:

> Our concern sits around a very, very aggressive sales culture that sits in the banks and a very aggressive performance-management culture that exists in the banks, to the extent of e-mail trails that go round and round individual performance on performance targets and whiteboards that contain information

on individual performance. That feeds into increased pressure on staff, which feeds into, perhaps, some dysfunctional selling to customers, because they are concerned for their jobs.

Some of these pressures may have lessened in the wake of the PPI debacle and the adviser sales scandal at Lloyds, as major high-street banks move to abolish crude sales targets for front-line staff and to replace them with a range of assessments which include customer feedback and branch growth. But the pressures are still there. The 2013 Salz review conducted for Barclays, for example, has stated: 'Sales incentives may have gone, but it appears that sales targets still exist at both branch and individual level (either formally or informally). Such contradictions need addressing.' Former Barclays chief executive Martin Taylor, who sits on the Bank of England's Financial Policy Committee, points out: 'You cannot tell people to operate to professional standards on Monday and then, on Tuesday, give them the kind of sales targets that requires them not to operate to such standards.'

It's hard to see seismic change in the commercial arms of banks, either. High levels of risks are still there, scandals are still being unearthed. Governments and regulators scurry around, but as Bob Diamond pointed out in September 2013, they have still not tackled the fundamental problem of modern banking: the 'too big to fail' conundrum that leaves major offenders with a get-out-of-jail-free card. As he says, what is still missing is 'an international plan to wind down an important bank in an orderly fashion'.

The Archbishop of Canterbury Justin Welby, who spent 11 years as an oil executive and sat on the Parliamentary Commission on Banking Standards, reflected on the financial system from the pulpit of St Paul's in the summer of 2013: 'The biggest weakness of all in the analysis of the failure of banks to be good banks has been around understanding about human beings,' he said, adding that 'at the heart of good banks have to be good people'.

Welby had listened to months of testimony from the bankers responsible for Libor rigging, the wrongful selling of PPI and the collapse of HBOS. He had heard nothing to convince him that the bankers were contrite, that the institutions they served had truly changed their nature, or that there had been a revolution in banking practice. On that much there still seems to be widespread agreement among moral leaders, politicians, regulators, investors and the more thoughtful bankers. That there is still so much unfinished business, after the trauma of the worst financial crisis for a century, must be an enormous cause for concern. The era of bad banks is a long way from being fixed.

# Afterword

Despite this near death experience [the crisis of 2007–8] banks continued to engage in sharp practices up until about 2012. The resulting fines, increased compliance costs and loss of reputation has cost customers, banks and their shareholders billions of pounds.

This was the view taken by New City Agenda[1] – a ginger group demanding banking reform – in a report it issued in November 2014. It estimated the total cost of fines levied on UK banks, and the sums paid out to redress customers, at £38.5 billion (the global figure for fines and penalties since the banking crisis of 2007–8 erupted stands at £150 billion). New City Agenda also noted that customer complaints had shot up from 75,000 in 2008–9, in the early years of the crisis, to 400,000 in 2013–14.

Given the continual litany of abuses uncovered, sins confessed and fines levied, that level of complaint is scarcely surprising. In March 2014, for example, Santander UK, the Spanish-owned bank built out of the remnants of Abbey National, Alliance & Leicester and Bradford & Bingley, found itself in the dock for giving unsuitable

[1] New City Agenda: A not-for-profit think tank founded by Lord McFall, the Rt Hon David Davis MP and Lord Sharkey, and supported by Which? Prudential, HSBC, Berenberg UK, The London Stock Exchange Group and City of London Corporation

advice to customers at its branches. It was fined £12.4 million after the Financial Conduct Authority (FCA) found 'serious failings' in the way the bank advised customers. It was a particular blow to Santander's charismatic chief executive Ana Botín[2] who had worked hard to bring the bank's customer service up to scratch.

In May 2014 it emerged that Lloyds' staff were being set 'unachievable' targets for selling products to customers, risking what the FCA called the 'wrong kind of behaviours'. Such practices had, in fact, been uncovered by the FCA back in December 2013, but, as the *Daily Mail* revealed, that didn't seem to have put a stop to them. It was further shown that Lloyds customers were receiving high-pressure sales calls from staff seeking to sell them products such as consumer loans, even when the customers had specifically asked not to be contacted.

In the same month, May 2014, Barclays was fined £26 million for trying to fix the price of gold bullion. Just a month later, the Yorkshire Building Society and Credit Suisse were fined a total of £4 million for selling a complex investment product, known as the Cliquet, which appeared to promise maximum returns that in reality could only be realised if the FTSE100 share index performed particularly well. The product had been sold to unsophisticated customers with little understanding of financial markets. The regulator deemed the accompanying sales literature 'a serious breach of the requirement to be clear, fair and not misleading' and described its use as 'unacceptable' behaviour. What was particularly disturbing was that a building society with a local reputation as a reliable lender and deposit taker should have been involved in such a complex product in the first place.

---

[2] Ana Botín left Santander UK in September 2014 to take control of its Madrid parent, Europe's biggest bank, after the sudden death of her father Emilio Botín.

In September Barclays was again in trouble, this time for putting £16.5 billion of client funds at risk by failing to segregate them properly from other monies held by the bank. The FCA, having established significant control and systems deficiencies, levied a £38 million penalty. One way and another, investment and retail banks were rarely far from news headlines throughout the year – and the stories about them were seldom positive.

In December 2014 I attended a private dinner in the palatial Mayfair offices of one of one of Britain's biggest banks. Festive candles twinkled on the mantelpiece above a grand fireplace, and the table was loaded with fine foods and vintage claret. The chief executive, however, was in combative and sombre mood as he outlined how in the post-financial crisis era, investors and other stakeholders would have to get used to the idea that banks could never be as profitable as they had been before the crash of 2007–8.

Costs were on the rise, he said, because his bank had been required to take on armies of 'compliance' staff to make sure that voluminous new post-crash regulations were not being breached. At the same time, requirements to hold more capital in the form of equity and strict enforcement of leverage ratios (in other words, the balance between core capital and total assets) were crimping the ability of bankers to make super-charged returns.

Just a month or so earlier, on 12 November 2014, this particular chief executive's bank had been one of a consortium of five global lenders, which, after investigation by the FCA over allegations of rigging foreign exchange markets, had agreed to record fines totalling £1.1 billion. The offences had been committed during and – more worryingly – after the disclosure of the Libor interest scandal in the summer of 2012.

At the pre-Christmas dinner, the senior banker expressed his disgust at what had happened. He also reflected, though, on his belief that increased regulation, including the claw-back of bonuses and other income from errant traders, was never going to be enough to curb unscrupulous activity: 'That won't happen until the rogue traders are rounded up, tried and are forced to serve long prison sentences,' he said. 'That would be a really effective deterrent.'

It's a view that I never heard expressed by such a senior banker during the worst of the crisis, but it's one that is now shared by other key figures, and it suggests a certain sea-change in attitude among the most senior people in finance. The ebullient founder and CEO of inter-dealer broker ICAP, Michael Spencer, for example, has said that the full force of the law should be brought to bear on those involved in Libor manipulation, and that the guilty should be jailed and the keys 'thrown away'.

The governor of the Bank of England, Mark Carney, has gone further. For him it's not just a matter of bad apples. In a speech given in Singapore on 17 November 2014, on his way back from the Brisbane G20 summit where new standards for banking stability were established, he pointed at wider systemic failings in the banking system:

> Leaders and senior managers must be personally responsible for setting the cultural norms of their institutions. But in some parts of the financial sector the link between seniority and accountability had become blurred, and in some cases, severed.
>
> The public were rightly angered that so many of the leaders and senior managers who were responsible for sowing the seeds of the crisis and for allowing cultures to develop in which gross misconduct took place have walked away from their actions or inactions.

Not only did he point the finger at poor management within the banks, he suggested that excessive levels of remuneration were also to blame – or, as he put it in his calmer central banker's language, 'compensation schemes [that] overvalued the present and heavily discounted the future, encouraging imprudent risk taking and short-termism'.

It's not only senior figures in British finance who have expressed their concerns with the continuing status quo. In the US, William Dudley – the former Goldman Sachs economist who is president of the Federal Reserve Bank of New York (the operational arm of America's central bank) – has been similarly critical, telling a group of bankers in 2014: 'If those of you here today as stewards of these large financial institutions do not do your part in pushing forcefully for change across the industry, then bad behaviour will undoubtedly persist.' He went on to argue that if change was not forthcoming, then the conclusion would be drawn that 'firms are too big and too complex' and that they will therefore 'need to be dramatically downsized and simplified so they can be managed effectively'.

Yet the wringing of senior hands has not, seemingly, brought an end to adverse headlines. Of course, some of these reflect problems that go back a number of years but that are still working their way through the system. Lloyds, for example, continues to struggle with a seemingly endless series of compensation claims for mis-selling payment protection insurance (PPI) and incentivising staff to sell products to customers that they did not need. When the bank reported its half-year profits in July 2014 it acknowledged that its bill for the PPI scandal had risen by a further £600 million. This brought the total of PPI costs at Lloyds to £10.4 billion out of an industry total of £23 billion (and still climbing). Lloyds also owned up to foreign exchange market manipulation in its admittedly very small investment banking operation, agreeing to pay fines of

£226 million for rigging that took place between 2006 and 2009. The bank's chairman, Lord Blackwell, wrote to Mark Carney to apologise personally for what had happened, even though it preceded his time at the bank. He vowed to look 'at all options' to claw back bonuses paid as a result of the offences.

In November 2014 RBS, along with its offshoots NatWest and Ulster Bank, was fined £56 million for the 2012 breakdown of its computer systems that led cash machines to stop working and denied customers access to their own bank accounts (the bank had already set aside some £125 million to cover compensation claims). It was a problem that stemmed from years of neglect when disgraced former chief executive Fred Goodwin was at the helm. Meanwhile in Italy, the jailing in October 2014 of three senior executives of the world's oldest bank, Monte dei Paschi di Siena, was the culmination of a scandal that stretched back to the early days of the financial crisis (in November 2014, with its coffers empty, the bank put itself up for sale after being found to be the worst performer of 130 banks inspected by the regulator, the European Central Bank).

In some cases, the passage of time has served to shine fresh light on past misdemeanours. In November 2014, for example, RBS chairman Sir Philip Hampton felt compelled to apologise to the Commons Treasury Select Committee for 'incorrect' information given to them during their 2013 investigation into the workings of RBS's Global Restructuring Group (GRG), which had rushed businesses into administration and grabbed back assets when they had failed to keep up repayments (see pp. 240–2). The two executives who had appeared before the select committee in 2013 had claimed that the GRG was 'absolutely not a profit centre'. This, Hampton said, was not in fact the case, though he also claimed that his two executives had been guilty only of an 'honest mistake'. The GRG was wound down in August 2014 and the FCA has announced an inquiry.

But two recent scandals suggest that the banking sector is still capable of creating fresh crises. The first concerns the unregulated foreign exchange rate market – likened by some to the 'Wild West'. Here, every day, an astonishing £3 trillion of overseas currencies – a sum equal to twice Britain's annual output – is bought and sold by banks around the world, 40 per cent of the trades being carried out in the City of London. Obviously this includes currency transactions carried out by people travelling abroad, but a far more significant slice of the business is taken up by big investors, such as pension funds.

What emerged in June 2013 was that the market was being manipulated rather in the same way as had occurred with the Libor interest rate markets. Given the vast scale of currency trading it may seem surprising that exchange rates can be manipulated at all: the displays of rates in banks and bureaux de change give the reassuring impression that they are arrived at scientifically. The fact is, though, that both rates can be artificially moved by a 'cartel' of traders agreeing among themselves to shift the numbers by a tiny increment.

In London's foreign exchange (forex or FX) markets – the world's largest – the prices of currencies are fixed at 4pm each day, the new rates being based on trades conducted in the 30 seconds or so immediately before. And – so it was revealed – it was during this vital half-minute that rigging had been taking place. Traders around the globe using electronic chat rooms to monitor market developments were discussing and sharing with rivals information about the size and volume of trades they intended to place. The names of these chat rooms were revealing: they included 'The Cartel', 'The Bandits Club', 'One Team, One Dream' and 'The Mafia.' It was collusion on a grand scale.

So far some 30 foreign exchange traders, working for banks in London and other major financial markets, have been fired or suspended for alleged corrupt behaviour. They are currently being investigated by fraud authorities on three continents.

The foreign exchange scandal reaches so deeply into the banking system as a whole that it has emerged that, as a result of informal meetings with the traders concerned, even the Bank of England's own foreign exchange department had some knowledge of what was going on. An inquiry into the Bank's role, ordered by the Bank's independent 'Oversight Committee' and conducted by Lord Grabiner QC, was published in November 2014. Its principal finding was that 'there was no evidence that any Bank of England official was involved in any unlawful or improper behaviour in the FX market.' But it also said:

> One Bank official was aware that bank traders were sharing aggregated information about client orders for the purpose of 'matching' – a practice that is not necessarily improper, but can increase the potential for improper conduct – and was uncomfortable with the practice in that it could involve collusive behaviour and lead to market participants being disadvantaged. Notwithstanding those concerns, the Bank official did not escalate the matter to an appropriate person.
>
> This constituted an error in judgment that deserved criticism, but such criticism should be limited in that the individual was not acting in bad faith.

The official concerned, the Bank's top currency trader Martin Mallett, was dismissed on the day of the report's publication for 'serious misconduct', the Bank maintaining that in the course of the foreign exchange probe other matters were uncovered that led to his sacking. The Bank has not commented further – which is surprising for a public institution that is meant to be transparent about its actions – so it is impossible to know why this decision was taken.

The stench from the scandal on the forex markets has been such that the Government has felt compelled to take action. In his showcase speech to the City at the Mansion House in June 2014, the Chancellor announced that he intended to make it a criminal offence to rig rates on the foreign exchanges, in the commodity markets and in the bond markets. This follows new laws, passed in December 2013, which made 'reckless banking' a criminal matter.

Five banks – the US's Citibank, HSBC, JPMorgan Chase, Royal Bank of Scotland and UBS of Switzerland – owned up to forex cheating and in November 2014 agreed to pay a £1.1 billion fine to the FCA. In December 2014 the scandal claimed its most senior victim when Stuart Scott, the London-based head of Europe, Middle East and Africa foreign exchange trading at HSBC, was quietly dismissed.

Another bank that was investigated – Barclays – declined to be part of the global settlement with regulators. When the Libor scandal erupted in 2012 its willingness to step up to the plate and cooperate with investigators had meant that it had drawn a lot of the initial fire and, in the aftermath, had been forced to sacrifice its chief executive Bob Diamond. The bank's chairman Marcus Agius resigned shortly afterwards. This time round, Barclays was not going to take the same chance. The bank decided, therefore, not to join the settlement but to fight its corner.

Barclays has also been involved in the second recent crisis to bedevil the banking sector: the 'dark pools' scandal. Dark pools are, essentially, unregulated private trading systems that allow large-scale transactions to be conducted without triggering a move in the share price. They are thus ideal for those big trading organisations, such as hedge funds or banks, who wish to buy or dump large quantities of shares discretely. Supporters of dark pools claim the system offers a more efficient and lower-cost trading platform. Because buyers and sellers are matched directly by the investment banks running the pool transactions can be completed relatively cheaply and quickly. By contrast, modern electronic stock exchanges, although they too offer facilities for speedy trading in equities, generally attract higher costs and in certain cash markets, including London, a transactions tax known as stamp duty.

Critics argue that the secretive nature of dark pools shatters the fundamental principle that everyone – regardless of status – has precisely the same access to a 'best price' quoted on an open market. They also point out that the arrangement inevitably favours the big players. And they contend that it is a magnet for computer-savvy, high-frequency traders who use their technological know-how – including superfast fibre-optic cables – to buy and sell vast quantities of stocks before the rest of those trading have caught up.

Equality of dealing opportunity doesn't exist in a dark pool: just a nanosecond's advantage (one billionth of a second) can yield huge profits for those involved, and that means that the person with the faster trading system will always win. If, for example, a pension fund sets out to buy a big tranche of shares in a dark pool, it's perfectly feasible that a trader with a faster network could see that order and exploit their technological advantage to buy the shares themselves, before then going on to sell them to the pension fund at a higher price.

Dark pools have become a vast trading system. In the course of 2014 there were many days when the number of shares traded in these private systems exceeded 910 million. And they have been taken up by many leading banks, such as Goldman Sachs. It has been alleged that traders at Barclays routed almost all of the bank's client orders through dark pools instead of passing them through official exchanges, thereby boosting their own commission on the trades, and thus their potential bonus pots. Normally when a large transaction passes through a recognised exchange it has to be handled by a consortium of banks and stockbrokers – because the buyers are not known to the sellers – and the commissions from such deals must be widely shared. This does not have to happen when a dark pool is involved.

In June 2014 Barclays chief executive Antony Jenkins sent a memorandum relating to these allegations to the bank's 140,000 staff. 'These are serious charges that allege a grave failure to live up to our values and to the culture at Barclays we are trying to create,' he said. 'I will not tolerate any circumstances in which our clients are lied to or misled, and any instances I discover will be dealt with severely.'

The angry response by the Barclays chief executive reflected his determination to stamp out any behaviour at the bank that could be deemed ethically suspect. Nevertheless, Barclays was not convinced of the strength of the case brought by the US regulators. In line with American traditions of litigation it chose a robust response.

Barclays challenged the enforcers, filing a motion in July 2014 via its lawyers Sullivan & Cromwell to dismiss a fraud lawsuit brought by New York Attorney General Eric Schneiderman, in which the British bank stands accused of misleading its customers about the prevalence of aggressive high-frequency trading in the dark pool known as 'Barclays LX'. The essence of the Barclays rebuttal is that the literature it gave out to clients about dark pools was not in any way misleading. The bank maintains that the workings of dark pools were clearly explained, and that their potential downside was highlighted, pointing to a chart on the Barclays brochure which identifies nine per cent of those trading in the pools as being aggressive (in other words, using methods such as high-frequency trading).

In the same month that Barclays challenged the regulators, Goldman Sachs was fined $800,000 for failing, in the course of some 395,000 transactions, to protect its clients who lost out because of trades placed through dark pools. Other major banks with dark pool operations, including Credit Suisse, Deutsche Bank and UBS, have also come under scrutiny.

What the forex and dark pools scandals demonstrate is that long after the lessons of the financial crisis have theoretically been learned, bankers and their clients are still seeking to game the system. And what the dark pools controversy in particular reveals is the part that is increasingly being played by highly advanced technology. Savvy operators building faster communications systems than their competitors can make supercharged profits. Moreover, the speed and sophistication of their technology makes monitoring them that much harder. Dark pools have triggered sudden and unexpected changes in the prices of shares and indexes, serving to make equity markets an uncomfortable place for ordinary retail investors and fund managers used to trading on fundamental values rather than complex algorithms.

Returning from the Brisbane summit in the autumn of 2014, Mark Carney claimed a 'landmark' had been reached, in that banks were now better capitalised than before, and that risks were no longer hidden in complex financial arrangements – such as the packages of sub-prime mortgages at the heart of the 2008 crisis. Many commentators would agree: it does seem to be the case that the balance sheets of banks have been de-cluttered, and that they are now less complicated than they once were and so easier to regulate. Carney is also right to say that, now that banks are better capitalised, the risk to the taxpayer has been reduced (though some might argue that the risk has merely been shifted to the pension funds and savings institutions that are responsible for the extra capital that banks are now required to hold in order to make them safer).

For its part, government continues to play a more interventionist approach in banking than has previously been the case. In his 2014 Autumn Statement, for example, the Chancellor of the Exchequer George Osborne announced that he was removing a loophole that had traditionally allowed the banks to write off past losses against current taxes. The move helped assuage a public mood that the banks were still getting off too lightly, as well as yielding the Exchequer an additional £3 billion over the forecast period of five years.

Osborne, in a smart piece of political footwork, also earmarked the Libor and forex fines, the biggest to have been levied, for spending on the armed forces and the National Health Service. Previously, some had been recycled to regulators to reduce the cost to the Exchequer and the charges levied on City institutions, while other sums had been directly applied to the reduction of the nation debt.

Meanwhile in the US, penalties have soared as the federal government has sought to extract redress for wrongdoings committed in earlier years, levying fines of $3.59 billion for crisis related offences in 2014. In the year to September 2014 some 70 chief executives and senior corporate officers were charged with a variety of regulatory offences by the Securities and Exchange Commission (the US market watchdog).

The net has also been closing around banks involved in Libor and forex fixing. The European Union, for example, is probing alleged interest rate fixing in the Euribor market, the equivalent of Libor. In November 2014 the British government announced a Competition & Markets Authority (CMA) probe into retail and small business banking. This was partly in response to suggestions from the opposition Labour Party that the market share of Britain's major banks is too big and should be capped so as to give consumers more choice. It is quite possible that the CMA (the successor to the

Competition Commission) may yet decide that Lloyds' takeover of HBOS in 2008, which gave them almost 30 per cent of the mortgage market and dominance in current accounts, resulted in a bank which needs to slim down or be broken up.

Banks, too, are playing a more active role in putting things right, seeking to shift responsibility to the perpetrators of the mistakes and their line managers by clawing back share awards and bonuses. They are also facing healthy competition from newcomers. 2014 saw the arrival on the stock market of a number of new challenger banks including TSB and Virgin Money.[3]

The worry, though, is that there is something in the culture of banking that refuses to change. The New City Agenda report found that 'cultural change in major banks remains fragile.' It noted that while senior executives have committed to reform, and openly promoted it, there is still widespread concern that 'the message could get lost in the middle of these large institutions and ultimately fail to make a difference on the front line.'

Sir David Walker, who stepped down as chairman of Barclays in 2015, believes that it could take a decade at least to change the way bankers think. One reform that might possibly help the process along is the formation of a new voluntary Banking Standards Review Council. Headed by City and regulatory veteran Dame Colette Bowe it aims to produce a debut report on 'culture, competence and customer outcomes'. It's a venture that all the major UK lenders have signed up to. The concern must be that, like other attempts to improve the moral and ethical underpinnings of the financial sector, the improved standards promised will quickly be forgotten as memories of the 2007–9 crisis fade into the distance.

---

[3] TSB was formed from the 632 Lloyds Bank 'Project Verde' branches hived off as a result of a European Commission ruling. Virgin Money incorporated the Northern Rock 'good bank' bought from the government for £747 million in November 2011.

Just how much still needs to be done was underlined by Minouche Shafik, the deputy governor of the Bank of England for Markets and Banking, in an October 2014 speech at the London School of Economics. The former deputy managing director of the International Monetary Fund expressed her dissatisfaction at the 'truly shocking evidence about the behaviour of some individuals' in foreign exchange and other markets. In particular she cited a conversation between two submitters of interest rates in the Yen Libor market seeking to rig outcomes. One declared 'every little helps...it's like Tescos.' The other trader replied, 'Absolutely, every little helps.' 'As somebody who believes in markets, I find this behaviour outrageous,' Shafik stated.

In fact, it has to be said that the stubbornly unchanging nature of that intangible entity, 'banking culture', still leaves the financial sector vulnerable to crisis, from the eurozone to China, and beyond. Certainly in Britain and the United States the cultural changes hoped for have yet to cascade down to middle managers, traders and the staff in some of the retail banks. The intractability of banking culture – and the difficulty of force-feeding change – can be seen in the way banks have responded to attempts made by the European Union to cap bonuses at twice times salary (with shareholder approval): they've simply created a new type of payment known as 'allowances', which is paid alongside basic salary on a monthly basis. There is some evidence that total pay and bonus payouts have been reduced as a proportion of banks' expenses, but they remain wildly out of kilter with rewards in almost every other field of economic activity.

Some bankers, contemptuous of the new rules and regulations, have left the main theatre and set up small boutique operations and hedge funds that are not directly in the sights of the enforcers. Many believe that this informal financial sector comprising hedge funds, private equity and so-called shadow banking – institutions that provide banking services without the usual licences – will be the next source of grief in international finance. And while many of the traditional banks show a current determination to revert to more traditional (if less profitable) banking, their previous track record suggests that they may revert to more questionable behaviour as and when economies start to expand again and the regulators consequently take a more relaxed approach. The famous 'bezzle' as the late Harvard economist J K Galbraith defined it – the determination to make money by hook or by crook – has a tendency ultimately to triumph.

# Glossary

**'AAA':** top rating set by credit rating agencies such as Moody's and Standard & Poor's

**Asset Protection Scheme:** scheme designed by the UK government in 2009 to insure the damaged assets of UK banks. It was only ever used by the Royal Bank of Scotland (RBS)

**ATM:** automated teller machine, better known as 'hole in the wall' cash-withdrawal machine

**Bank for International Settlements:** Basel-based central bankers' club, established between the First and Second World Wars, that sets banking standards

**Bank of England:** the UK's central bank, founded in 1694, which regained responsibility for prudential regulation of the banking system and an enhanced role in ensuring financial stability after the crisis of 2007–9

**Basel II:** second of the Basel Accords – revised international capital framework published by the Basel Committee on Banking Supervision in June 2004

**Basel III:** third of the Basel Accords – international regulatory framework for banks published by the Basel Committee on Banking Supervision in June 2011 (Capital) and January 2013 (Liquidity). Effective as of 1 January 2014

**BBA:** British Bankers' Association, which was responsible for setting Libor interest rates

**bond yield:** the coupon or interest rate on bonds. It acts like a see-saw, rising when the price of the bond falls and falling when the bond price rises

**budget deficit:** the annual gap between what governments collect in taxes and charges and what they spend

**Calpers:** California Public Employees' Retirement System, Californian state employee pension funds

**capital ratio:** capital expressed as a percentage of a bank's risk-weighted assets

**capital shortfall:** a situation in which a bank's capital requirements exceed its capital resources

**CFTC:** Commodity Futures Trading Commission, the US regulator that polices commodities and derivatives markets

**CIO:** Chief Investment Office, which was responsible for managing the London Whale at JPMorgan Chase

**Competition Commission:** The UK's competition regulator at the time of the Great Panic in 2008. Replaced by the Competition and Markets Authority in October 2013

**Credit-Rating Agencies:** Privately owned financial groups that assess the creditworthiness of commercial organisations and nations

**Dodd–Frank:** the voluminous American financial reform act passed as a response to the Great Panic

**Dow Jones Industrial Average (DJIA):** the index of the top 30 American shares, often used to describe the health of Wall Street

**due diligence:** an investigation to confirm the material facts regarding the sale of a business

**Edelman Trust Barometer:** An annual survey of 26 markets that measures the trust in businesses, sectors and industries

**ERM:** Introduced in 1979 the Exchange Rate System was the precursor to the eurozone. It came apart at the seams in 1992 when Britain and Italy were forced out by heavy speculation

**Euribor:** European Interbank Offered Rate (euro equivalent of Libor reference rate)

**Eurobonds:** sovereign bonds issued by the ECB

**European Banking Authority (EBA):** London-based regulator that was in charge of stress tests on European banks in the wake of the 2008–9 crisis

**European Central Bank (ECB):** Frankfurt-based central bank responsible for setting interest rates for countries that use the euro. In 2013 it was also given responsibility for policing significant banks in the euro area

**European Stability Mechanism (ESM):** European bailout fund (Germany provided 27 per cent of the capital)

**Fannie Mae and Freddie Mac:** the American mortgage intermediaries that refinance home loans and were at the core of the Great Panic

**FDIC:** Federal Deposit Insurance Corporation, an American banking regulator that provides insurance to depositors and supervises America's smaller banks

**Federal Reserve:** American central bank based in Washington, DC

**Financial Conduct Authority (FCA):** regulatory body formed on 1 April 2013 as a successor, along with the Prudential Regulatory Authority (PRA), to the Financial Services Authority (FSA)

**Financial Policy Committee:** the strengthened financial stability committee of the Bank of England established after the crisis. It is chaired by the governor of the Bank and produces a biannual stability report

**Financial Reporting Council (FRC):** independent regulator responsible for corporate governance and financial reporting in the UK

**Financial Services Authority (FSA):** former regulatory body for the UK financial services industry. It was abolished on 1 April 2013, its responsibilities being split between the FCA and the PRA

**foreclosure:** a legal process by which a lender obtains a court order to terminate a borrower's loan

**Foreign Corrupt Practices Act:** the American law that proscribes bribery and corruption in foreign countries

**Glass–Steagall Act:** the 1933 Great Depression-era law in the US that separated investment banks from high-street banks

**Great Panic:** the market turmoil that followed the collapse of Lehman Brothers in the autumn of 2008

**GRG:** the Royal Bank of Scotland's Global Restructuring Group responsible for reorganising the finances of troubled firms

**Gross Domestic Product (GDP):** total output or wealth of an economy, closely watched by the financial markets and policymakers

**Gross Value Added:** a measure used by Britain's Office for National Statistics (ONS) that seeks to assess the wealth added to national output in different regions of the country

**HBMX:** HSBC Mexico

**HBUS:** HSBC Bank USA

**hedge funds:** investor consortia that seek to exploit mispricing in markets

**IBC:** Independent Banking Commission, established by the UK government in 2010, which reported in September 2011

**IMF:** International Monetary Fund, founded in 1944 and based in Washington, DC, which imposes economic remedies and provides loans to countries in difficulty

**Kelly review:** independent review by Sir Christopher Kelly into the failings of the Co-op Bank published on 30 April 2014

**Libor:** London Interbank Offered Rate, the interest rate which is used to set the cost of commercial loans, mortgages and other transactions

**long:** A position taken by investors on the grounds that the asset bought will rise in value over the long haul

**LTIP:** long-term incentive plan, provided to directors. It is often the spigot that never stops paying as the LTIPs build up over the years

**LTRO:** long-term refinancing operation, under which the European Central Bank provides low-interest three-year loans in exchange for sovereign debt

**ML:** money laundering

**Myners review:** independent review of the Co-op Group's governance led by Lord Myners

**NAFTA:** North American Free Trade Agreement, between the US, Canada and Mexico

**national debt:** the accumulated budget deficits of sovereign nations

**OCC:** Office of the Comptroller of the Currency, one of the American financial regulators that was involved in both the JPMorgan Chase London Whale affair and in monitoring money laundering

**Office of Fair Trading (OFT):** British consumer regulator (merged with the Competition Commission in 2013) that investigated payment protection insurance (PPI) claims

**OMT:** Outright Monetary Transactions, a scheme that allows banks in the euro area to swap loans on their books for cash at the European Central Bank

**Parliamentary Commission on Banking Standards:** appointed by George Osborne in 2011 to investigate the Libor scandal, which reported in 2012

**PPI:** payment protection insurance, cover for loan repayments in the event of sickness or unemployment, sold by the banks to consumers

**Protium:** vehicle used by Barclays Bank to park toxic mortgage assets in the Cayman Islands to tidy up its balance sheet

**Prudential Regulation Authority (PRA):** regulatory body formed on 1 April 2013 as a successor, along with the FCA, to the FSA. It operates as a division of the Bank of England

**reserve currency:** foreign exchange held by central banks. The US dollar has been considered the main reserve currency since the Second World War

**rights issue:** an issue of new shares to existing investors. Often takes place at times of stress to strengthen capital

**ring-fencing:** the proposal made by Britain's Independent Banking Commission that investment banking activities be separated from retail banking within the same financial organisation

**risk-weighted assets (RWA):** a measure of a bank's assets adjusted for risk

**Salz review:** independent review into Barclays' business practices published in April 2013

**SCP:** credit default swaps portfolio that was at the core of the 'London Whale' scandal at JPMorgan Chase

**Securities and Exchange Commission (SEC):** the Wall Street regulator that monitors investment banks and market activity

**Senate Permanent Subcommittee on Investigations:** Carl Levin's committee that conducted separate investigations into the sub-prime mortgage crisis and money laundering by HSBC

**SFO:** Serious Fraud Office, responsible for investigating and prosecuting cases of complex fraud and corruption

**short:** A position taken by investors on the ground that they expect the price of the asset to fall. Such positions are often taken using 'borrowed' shares and can become self-fulfilling

**SMEs:** small and medium-sized enterprises

**sovereign wealth funds:** funds used by nations to invest surpluses for the long term

**spread:** the interest-rate spread is the gap between what it costs the bank to fund itself through retail deposits and the money markets and the interest rate that it charges customers for loans

**Stewardship Code:** First published in July 2010 by the Financial Reporting Council (FRC) it is intended to improve the dialogue between public companies and institutional shareholders

**TARP:** Troubled Asset Relief Programme, introduced by the US Treasury in 2008 to pump capital into damaged banks

**Troika:** ECB, European Commission and IMF group dealing with crisis nations in euroland

**TSC:** House of Commons Treasury Select Committee

**VaR:** Value at Risk is the proportion of an investment book that could move into loss on any given day or measured time period.

**Verde:** sometimes known as Project Verde. Retail bank consisting of 632 branches that the European Commission forced Lloyds Banking Group to divest following Lloyds TSB's acquisition of HBOS in 2008 and subsequent state aid

**Walker review:** independent review of corporate governance in the UK banking industry, led by Sir David Walker and published in 2009

# Bibliography

## Autobiographies

Brown, Gordon, *Beyond the Crash: Overcoming the First Crisis of Globalisation* (London: Simon & Schuster, 2010)

Darling, Alistair, *Back From the Brink: 1,000 Days at Number 11* (London: Atlantic Books, 2011)

Greenspan, Alan, *The Age of Turbulence: Adventures in a New World* (London: Allen Lane, 2007)

## Monographs

Admati, Anat, & Hellwig, Martin, *The Bankers' New Clothes: What's Wrong with Banking and What to Do about It* (Woodstock: Princeton University Press, 2013)

Ahamed, Liaquat, *Lords of Finance: 1929, The Great Depression, and the Bankers Who Broke the World* (London: William Heinemann, 2009)

Augar, Philip, *The Greed Merchants: How the Investment Banks Played the Free Market Game* (London: Allen Lane, 2005)

Blustein, Paul, *The Chastening: Inside the Crisis That Rocked the Global Financial System and Humbled the IMF* (New York: PublicAffairs, 2001)

Boyes, Roger, *Meltdown Iceland: How the Global Financial Crisis Bankrupted an Entire Country* (London: Bloomsbury, 2009)

Brummer, Alex, *The Crunch: How Greed and Incompetence Sparked the Credit Crisis* (London: Random House, 2009)

Calomiris, Charles W., & Haber, Stephen H., *Fragile by Design: The Political Origins of Banking Crises & Scarce Credit* (Woodstock: Princeton University Press, 2014)

Collins, Philip & Harrington, Peter, eds, *After the Apocalypse: Lessons from the Global Financial Crisis* (London: Demos, 2008)

Conaghan, Dan, *The Bank: Inside the Bank of England* (London: Biteback, 2012)

Doyle, Larry, *In Bed with Wall Street: The Conspiracy Crippling Our Global Economy* (New York: Palgrave Macmillan, 2014)

Marsh, David, *Europe's Deadlock: How the Euro Crisis Could Be Solved – and Why It Won't Happen* (London: Yale University Press, 2013)

Martin, Ian, *Making It Happen: Fred Goodwin, RBS, and the Men Who Blew Up the British Economy* (London: Simon & Schuster, 2013)

Perman, Ray, *Hubris: How HBOS Wrecked the Best Bank in Britain* (Edinburgh: Birlinn, 2012)

Peston, Robert, & Knight, Laurence, *How Do We Fix This Mess? The Economic Price of Having It All and the Route to Lasting Prosperity* (London: Hodder & Stoughton, 2012)

Roberts, Richard, *Did Anyone Learn Anything from the Equitable Life? Lessons and Learning from Financial Crises* (London: Institute of Contemporary British History, Kings College London, 2012)

Roberts, Richard, *Saving the City: The Great Financial Crisis of 1914* (Oxford: Oxford University Press, 2013)

Rubin, Robert E., & Weisberg, Jacob, *In an Uncertain World: Tough Choices from Wall Street to Washington* (New York: Thomson Texere, 2003)

Sorkin, Andrew Ross, *Too Big to Fail: Inside the Battle to Save Wall Street* (London: Allen Lane, 2009)

**Newspapers and magazines**
*Daily Mail*
*The Economist*
*Financial Times*
*Financial World*
*New York Times*
*Wall Street Journal*

**Published official documents**
Financial Services Authority, *The Turner Review: A regulatory response to the global banking crisis* (London: FSA, March 2009)

Financial Services Authority, *Turner Review Conference Discussion Paper: A regulatory response to the global banking crisis – systemically important banks and assessing the cumulative impact* (London: FSA, October 2009)

Financial Services Authority, *The Failure of the Royal Bank of Scotland* (London: FSA, December 2011)

Financial Services Authority, *Final Notice: The Royal Bank of Scotland* (London: FSA, 6 February 2013)

Financial Services Authority, *Final Notice: Lloyds TSB Bank plc and Bank of Scotland plc* (London: FSA, 10 December 2013)

Financial Services Authority, *Internal Audit Report: A review of the extent of awareness within the FSA of inappropriate LIBOR submissions* (London: FSA, March 2013)

HM Treasury, *RBS and the Case for a Bad Bank: The government's review* (London: HM Treasury, November 2013)

House of Commons Treasury Committee, *The Run on the Rock – Fifth Report of Session 2007–08*, HC 56-1 (London: Stationery Office, 26 January 2008)

House of Commons Treasury Committee, *Banking Crisis: Dealing with the failure of the UK banks – Seventh Report of Session 2008–09*, HC 416 (London: Stationery Office, 1 May 2009)

House of Commons Treasury Committee, *Banking Crisis: Reforming corporate governance and pay in the City – Ninth Report of Session 2008–09*, HC 519 (London: Stationery Office, 15 May 2009)

House of Commons Treasury Committee, *Banking Crisis: Reforming corporate governance and pay in the City: Government, UK Financial Investments Ltd and Financial Services Authority Responses to the Ninth Report from the Committee – Eighth Special Report of Session 2008–09*, HC 462 (London: Stationery Office, 24 July 2009)

House of Commons Treasury Committee, *Banking Crisis: Regulation and supervision – Fourteenth Report of Session 2008–09*, HC 767 (London: Stationery Office, 31 July 2009)

House of Commons Treasury Committee, *The FSA's Report into the Failure of RBS – Fifth Report of Session 2012–13*, HC 640 (London: Stationery Office, 19 October 2012)

Independent Commission on Banking, *Final Report: Recommendations* (London: Dorman Group, September 2011)

Kelly, Christopher, *Failings in Management and Governance: Report of the independent review into the events leading to the Co-operative Bank's capital shortfall*, 30 April 2014

New York State Department of Financial Services, *Consent Order to Standard Chartered Bank, New York Branch: Order Pursuant to Banking Law 39*, 6 August 2012

Parliamentary Commission on Banking Standards, *Written Evidence from the Royal Bank of Scotland Group*, 24 June 2013

Parliamentary Commission on Banking Standards, *Changing Banking for Good, Vol I: Summary, and Conclusions and Recommendations*, HL Paper 27-1, HC 175-1 (London: Stationery Office, June 2013)

# BIBLIOGRAPHY

Parliamentary Commission on Banking Standards, *First Report, Volume I: Report, Minutes* (London: Stationery Office, 21 December 2012)

Plenderleith, Ian, *Review of the Bank of England's Provision of Emergency Liquidity Assistance in 2008–09* (London: Bank of England, October 2012)

Salz, Anthony, *Salz Review: An Independent Review of Barclays' Business Practices* (London: April 2013)

Tomlinson, Lawrence, *Banks' Lending Practices: Treatment of Businesses in Distress* (London: 25 November 2013)

# Index